Arkansas,
1800–1860

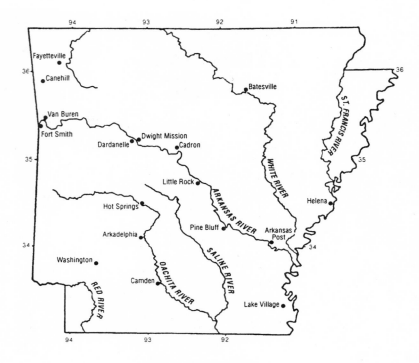

Arkansas, 1800–1860

Histories of Arkansas

Elliott West, general editor

Arkansas, 1800–1860

Remote and Restless

S. Charles Bolton

The University of Arkansas Press
Fayetteville   1998

02   01   00   99   98   5   4   3   2   1

Designed by Liz Lester

⊛   The paper used in this publication meets the minimum
requirements of the American National Standard for
Permanence of Paper for Printed Library Materials Z39.48-
1984.

LIBRARY OF CONGRESS CATALOGING-IN-PUBLICATION DATA

Bolton, S. Charles.
     Arkansas, 1800–1860 : remote and restless /
S. Charles Bolton.
         p.   cm. — (Histories of Arkansas)
     Includes bibliographical references (p.   ) and index.
     ISBN 1-55728-518-7 (cloth : alk. paper). — ISBN
1-55728-519-5 (pbk. : alk. paper)
         1. Arkansas—History—19th century.
     2. Arkansas—Politics and government—To 1950.
     I. Title.   II. Series.
     F411.B72   1998
     976.7'03—dc 21   98-16180
                                                      CIP

For Conevery and Jesse,
who immigrated to Arkansas with me

Acknowledgments

Elliott West, the editor of the Histories of Arkansas series, read the manuscript for this book several times, and his comments and encouragement did much to improve it. An anonymous reader for the University of Arkansas Press also offered helpful suggestions. C. Fred Williams, my colleague, read the entire manuscript and helped me to remove a number of errors. Conevery A. Bolton gave it a careful editing that improved both the style and the substance.

The University of Arkansas at Little Rock provided me in the fall of 1995 with an off-campus duty assignment that allowed me to write the first chapters of this book. Throughout my work, the staff of the Ottenheimer Library on that campus, and particularly the staff of its Archives and Special Collections, have been unfailingly helpful. The same is true of the Arkansas History Commission and the Arkansas Territorial Restoration.

Readers of my *Territorial Ambition: Land and Society in Arkansas, 1800 to 1840* will find some of this material familiar, but all has been rewritten for the larger context of this book. I have benefited from the work of countless other authors, particularly those of the last several decades who have done much to increase our understanding of Arkansas.

All the maps used here were originally drawn by Gerald T. Hanson, although some of them have been substantially altered and given new titles. "Arkansas, 1800–1860" and "Arkansas Territory" originally appeared in Michael B. Dougan, *Arkansas Odessy: The Saga of Arkansas from Prehistoric Times to Present* (Little Rock: Rose Publishing, 1993); "Arkansas Counties on the Census of 1820" and "Indian Lands" first appeared in S. Charles Bolton, *Territorial Ambition: Land and Society in Arkansas, 1800–1840* (Fayetteville: University of Arkansas Press, 1993); and "Highlands and Lowlands," "Arkansas Counties in 1836," and "Arkansas Counties in 1860" are from Gerald T. Hanson and Carl H. Moneyhon, *Historical Atlas of Arkansas* (Norman and London: University of Oklahoma Press, 1989).

Contents

Foreword

Washington Irving, the literary lion of his day and one of our first distinctively American writers, briefly visited Arkansas in 1832. Heading home from a tour of the plains, this gentleman romantic had a fine time churning down the Arkansas River by steamboat. He met a holdover from the French colonial period, a "Grand Seigneur" who entertained him while occasionally tossing half-eaten chicken legs to his huge gape-jawed mastiff. He liked the man's slave, "the politest negro I met," as well as another local with an earring and a merry disposition. Arkansas Post summed up the territory's special appeal. Residents of the dilapidated village showed no interest in improvements, but "if they work but little," Irving wrote, "they dance a great deal, and a fiddle is the joy of their heart." As his boat pulled away, he wistfully hoped that Arkansas would remain forever an island of happy ignorance in a dynamic nation hell-bent on progress and fat profits.

It was an early instance of an enduring impression. For nearly two centuries the image of Arkansans has been that of a people whose slow pace has left them out of step with the world. America of 1832 had embarked on some of the most wrenching changes of its history, yet Irving wrote of a society passing the years in a prolonged snooze. Similar descriptions, many far less charitable, would be written in the generations ahead.

Charles Bolton's fine new history will remind its readers that, image aside, Arkansas always has been a place of deceptive complexities. *Arkansas, 1800–1860: Remote and Restless* is the second volume published in the Histories of Arkansas series. Like Carl Moneyhon's perceptive survey of the late nineteenth and early twentieth centuries (*Arkansas and the New South, 1874–1929* [Fayetteville: University of Arkansas Press, 1997]), Bolton's vision certainly recognizes some of the territory's idiosyncrasies, displayed most colorfully perhaps in the brawl of its politics; but with Moneyhon he also tells a story of a land and people surprisingly reflective of their nation and region.

As Bolton's choice of title indicates, Arkansas during these years was, to be sure, on the far fringe of national life. Its remoteness gave it a special character that seemed most obvious to transient observers like Irving. Yet Arkansas could also be understood not as a backwater but as a confluence of several streams of national development during the first half of the century.

Take, for instance, its human makeup. Bolton shows how northern and southern flows of settlers mingled on this territorial frontier, with many families, white and slave, immigrating to the delta out of Mississippi as others slid southwestward out of the Ohio valley, through Missouri and into the plateaus, mountains, and valleys of the north and northwest. The delta resembled more the culture and economy of the plantation South, while the northern settlements, often resentful of the slave system, would have reminded visitors of the middle South and Midwest. Southern and western portions of the territory had their own look and feel. Unlike many past writers, Bolton gives special attention to the influences of Native Americans who lived and left their marks there, some as remnants of peoples who had worked this land for scores of generations and others as part of the diaspora of peoples displaced from throughout eastern America. Towns and the few infant cities offered still another setting, this one quickening with forces found elsewhere on the urban frontier. This social and cultural array was spread across a landscape with a diversity that still contributes to the state's disarming variety. Except for Louisiana, Arkansas is the smallest state west of the Mississippi, yet is the only one with four formally distinct geographical regions—the delta, the Ozark Highlands, the Ouachita Mountains, and the northernmost extension of the Gulf Coastal Plain.

Bolton takes us on a tour through an Arkansas that was forming a sense of itself as it felt its way through the changes and dislocations of these crucial years. His story begins as a new nation reached to incorporate this disparate country that only recently had been the tussling ground of European empires. It ends as that nation confronted questions and dilemmas, laid out vividly in Arkansas, that soon would take us into our deepest tragedy. He shows us the land and its people through the words of travelers, settlers, and journalists, establishing a long tradition of humor and bombast. We see the continuing dance of Native American and white cultures and the relentless push that would send most Indian peoples across the territory's western boundary. In a superb chapter on African

Americans, Bolton reveals not only the deeply troubling realities of slavery but also, within them, the making of vital communities whose descendants, traditions, and values continue to enrich our state.

The Histories of Arkansas series aspires to give Arkansans, and everyone else, a proper appreciation of this state's remarkable legacy. Charles Bolton's *Arkansas, 1800–1860: Remote and Restless* is a long and vigorous step toward that goal. In a trip immeasurably more careful, probing, and revealing than Washington Irving's, he opens our eyes to a people and a place at once distinctive and reflective of a changing America. His book is both its own portrait and an invitation to follow the fascinating story of Arkansas to the predicaments and achievements of our own day.

Elliott West
University of Arkansas, Fayetteville

Introduction

In the summer of 1820, the Reverend Cephas Washburn, a Vermont-born missionary for the American Board of Commissioners for Foreign Missions, made his way into Arkansas, which he called "a perfect *terra incognita.*" In fact, Arkansas was not unknown. It was home to some fifteen thousand people, including a few French and Native Americans, but most residents were immigrants from the United States. These settlers—some of them with slaves—had come to Arkansas to build a new life for themselves on western land that was both fertile and abundant. Indeed, Arkansas was already a separate territory, and Washburn would soon deliver a sermon in the new capital at Little Rock. If not unknown, however, Arkansas was remote, away from the beaten trails and the navigable rivers that had carried so many Americans to Louisiana and Missouri that the former became a state in 1812 and the latter in 1821.

Arkansas's remoteness had something to do with its geography. It was difficult to get to and hard to travel though. Swamplands along the Mississippi River deterred immigrants, roads were little more than forest paths, and rivers flooded in the spring and ran nearly dry in the summer. About half the state was made up of highlands and was only fit for small farming operations. And isolation led to a degree of primitiveness. Crime and violence were common in Arkansas Territory, and travelers usually went well armed. There were also spectacular events: the territorial secretary shot and killed the territorial delegate in 1827, and the speaker stabbed a delegate to death on the floor of the House of Assembly in 1836. Similar less well-publicized events continued down to the Civil War.

If Arkansas was remote, however, its citizens were hardly inert. In fact they pursued happiness with the same restless energy that was characteristic of Americans elsewhere. The cultivation of cotton in the lowlands of southern and eastern Arkansas began during the territorial period and flourished in the antebellum period. Corn and livestock were produced in prodigious quantities all over Arkansas. The desire for land led

Arkansans to remove Native Americans as quickly as possible, exemplifying the greed and racism that were common to Americans as a whole. Politics was also exciting, with hard-fought elections driven by the ambition of would-be leaders, who fought occasional duels to advance themselves. Even a disastrous attempt to create a banking system for the state was spectacular in its failure. Arkansans also moved restlessly: some left for Texas in search of better land, and others went to California in 1849 in a quest to gain wealth more rapidly.

The society that emerged under these conditions was western in its frontier qualities, but it gradually became more and more southern. The social and political leaders of Arkansas were largely from the small class of cotton planters who flourished in the south and east. Almost everyone else was a yeoman farmer, living more or less independently on his own or government land, and often assisted by a hard-working and fecund woman. Conditions were rude, but economic advancement was common. Like other Americans, Arkansans distributed wealth in an unequal manner: about 70 percent of taxable wealth was owned by the wealthiest 10 percent of taxpayers. By 1860, a full 26 percent of the population were African Americans, whose toil enriched their masters, whose lives were hard and sometimes brutal, but whose pain was somewhat eased by the love and community they shared with one another. Masters and slaves were usually evangelical Christians, but they often worshiped in separate ways and prayed for different things.

Early Arkansans were unique in some ways, but they were much less different from other Americans than they are often portrayed. To illustrate that point, I have placed Arkansas events and developments within their national and southern contexts. I have also dealt with Arkansas history in terms of its major themes. Each of the following chapters follows a single topic over the course of the sixty-year development covered in this work, with the exception of territorial and state politics, which are treated in separate chapters. This approach—longitudinal through time rather than latitudinal across a period of time—allows for a sharp focus on the main elements of Arkansas's history, both as a territory and as an antebellum state.

CHAPTER ONE

American Takeover

The American settlement of Arkansas was part of the restless movement of people in search of economic improvement that had originated in Early Modern Europe, particularly in the British Isles. A useful starting point for our story is the period between 1760 and 1775, when extensive immigration and a high natural increase raised the population of the American colonies from about 1.6 million to about 2.5 million. Within its geographical boundaries, from Maine to Georgia and westward to the Appalachian Mountains, colonial society was becoming crowded. A host of new towns were founded at the extremities of New England's territory, settlers moved up New York's Hudson River and out along the Mohawk River, and rival speculators in New York and New Hampshire fought over the rugged terrain of what would become Vermont. Most important for Arkansas was the mass of new arrivals who entered America at Philadelphia and followed a heavily traveled route that led into southeastern Pennsylvania and then down the Great Wagon Road into the Shenandoah Valley and the western portion of the southern colonies.

This southern backcountry was heavily settled by immigrants from Scotland, Northern Ireland, and the north of England—North Britons, as they have been called—who came in large numbers at different times between 1720 and 1775. Many of them were Scots-Irish Presbyterians whose ancestors had settled in Ulster in the early seventeenth century, and who left it a century later because of religious differences and economic difficulties. The earliest of the North Britons in America settled in the western parts of Maryland and Virginia, and later immigrants moved on to the backcountry of North Carolina and South Carolina. By the 1770s new settlers had to go as far south as the upper Savannah River in Georgia. By that time a distinct backcountry society had emerged, made up of small farmers and artisans who were intensely proud and quick to defend their religious and political convictions.

During the American Revolution, this backcountry society began to move west. In 1775 Daniel Boone guided an initial group of colonists along the Wilderness Road that led from Virginia through the Cumberland Gap into Kentucky. Settlers were also moving into the western parts of colonial North Carolina that would later become Tennessee. These pioneers lived in or near small, fortified settlements to protect themselves from Indians. They hunted game to stay alive, but also cleared land and grew corn as soon as they could. Rudimentary trade developed, with livestock and other domestic products serving as currency, and institutions of local government soon followed. As these first trans-Appalachian settlements were acquiring some degree of permanence, to the north other Americans were leaving Pittsburgh on flatboats and descending the Ohio River to make new homes in the Northwest Territory.

By 1790 there were 74,000 people in Kentucky and another 36,000 in Tennessee. Ten years later the population of Kentucky had risen to 221,000, Tennessee had 106,000 people, and another 9,000 settlers were living farther south in what would become Mississippi Territory. North of the Ohio River, 45,000 Americans had settled in the future state of Ohio, and 6,000 had settled in Indiana. In all, some 7 percent of the American people lived west of the Appalachian Mountains in 1800; by 1820 that figure had increased to 23 percent. Trans-Appalachian states and territories contained 47 percent of the American population by 1860.

Westward expansion received some direction and assistance from the national government. The Land Ordinance of 1785 provided that federal territory would be surveyed before settlement into square-mile townships subdivided into thirty-six sections of 640 acres each, and the Northwest Ordinance of 1787 established a system of government for federal territories that ensured they could one day become states. President George Washington acted to deal with the immediate problems facing western settlers. A federal army under Anthony Wayne defeated the northwest tribes at the Battle of Fallen Timbers in 1794, opening up a large portion of southeastern Ohio for settlement. The following year, Thomas

Pinckney negotiated the Treaty of San Lorenzo by which Spain gave Americans the use of the Mississippi River, thereby ensuring western settlers access to the New Orleans market.

The American government supported westward expansion, but the political parties that arose in the 1790s approached that subject from different perspectives. Alexander Hamilton believed that the United States would best be served by promoting commerce and manufacturing. In general, Hamilton and the Federalist Party were not opposed to westward expansion, providing it took place on their own terms. According to historian Andrew Cayton, Federalists opposed what they believed were the frontier vices of "disorganization, laziness, selfishness, and parochialism." Instead they wanted "progress across space and time into a world of commerce and manufacturing, canals and cities, science and order, blending interests in national harmony."

Thomas Jefferson's Democratic-Republican Party, by contrast, was unambiguous in its support of expansion. On a moral level, Jefferson believed that "those who labour in the earth [were] the chosen people of God." For him, agriculture was an ennobling activity associated with a virtuous people. In political terms, he also felt that small farmers owning their own land would be good republican citizens, possessed of a salutary independence. Jefferson believed that by acquiring copious land, the United States might escape the overpopulation that Thomas Malthus had predicted for Europe. Moreover, there was the economic reality that European demand for American foodstuffs had been growing since the early 1790s. The overseas market offered real trade opportunity to western farmers capable of producing a surplus in wheat or other cereals.

Of course, after he became president, Jefferson did more than think about expansion. Sending Lewis and Clark to the Pacific Ocean, a decision made before the United States owned any land west of the Mississippi River, was an act of audacious initiative. By contrast, the purchase of Louisiana in 1803 was a windfall event that no American president could have turned down. Nonetheless, the consequences of that land deal were enormous. Louisiana was defined as all the land drained by rivers flowing east into the Mississippi; its acquisition doubled the size of the United States and provided a seemingly inexhaustible amount of land for American farmers of the future. Included in that vast expanse was an ill-defined area in the lower Mississippi Valley known as Arkansas.

* * *

As early as the 1780s, American families in small numbers, harbingers of expansion, began to arrive at Arkansas Post, a small village located on the Arkansas River some thirty-six miles from its confluence with the Mississippi River. It was founded in 1686 as part of Sieur de La Salle's effort to explore and develop Louisiana as a French colony. Henri de Tonti, La Salle's lieutenant, left six men at the Quapaw Indian village on the Arkansas River in the hope of creating a fur-trading post. The operation failed within a few years, and the site was vacant of European occupation until 1721, when French settlers associated with John Law's colony located there. From that time forward, Arkansas Post maintained a precarious existence as a small French community of hunters, traders, farmers, and soldiers. It was the northern outpost of a French frontier economy that stretched up the lower Mississippi Valley from its hub in New Orleans, valuable for the pelts, skins, oil, and meat that were brought in by the Quapaws from the abundant forests in the St. Francis and Arkansas River basins. When France ceded Louisiana to Spain as a result of the Seven Years' War, the soldiers and administrators changed at Arkansas Post, but the character of the community and the lives of the inhabitants appear to have remained much the same. A Spanish census of 1798 listed 393 men, women, and children, of whom 56 were slaves.

Arkansas Post came under American control in March of 1804, when Capt. Francisco Caso y Luengo of Spain turned the fort at Arkansas Post over to Lt. James B. Many of the United States. For a time, this change made little difference. When William Treat arrived at Arkansas Post in 1805 to set up a factory or goverment trading post so that the United States could win both the commerce and the friendship of Native Americans, he found a society that was not much different from the one that had existed in the 1790s. There were sixty to seventy families at the village, all of them French except for nine or ten from Virginia, Maryland, and Pennsylvania. Another seven or eight families lived up the Arkansas River, from fifty to one hundred miles from the Arkansas Post. The community also contained some sixty black people, almost all of whom were slaves. The total population probably numbered fewer than five hundred people. Treat claimed that they were all farmers, traders, or hunters and that the Americans were among "the most industrious farmers." He was probably right, for the Americans, unlike their French predecessors, were the vanguard of an agricultural empire.

As the United States took possession of Arkansas, it also made some attempt to explore the new territory. With the support of the U.S.

Congress and under the direction of his friend, President Thomas Jefferson, William Dunbar, a planter and scientist who lived on a plantation near Natchez, led a government-assisted expedition up the Ouachita River in late 1804 and early 1805. Dunbar and his associate, George Hunter of Philadelphia, returned with much information about the plants, animals, and geography of the Ouachita Valley. They were, not surprisingly, much taken with the thermal waters at Hot Springs, which were already being used: "We found at Hot-Springs an open Log Cabin and a few huts of split boards, all calculated for summer encampment, & have been erected by persons resorting to the Springs for the recovery of their health."

Arkansas grew slowly in these early years. The Census of 1810 lists two centers of population. One of them, called "Hope Field and St. Francis," designated the area opposite Memphis and running south to the mouth of the St. Francis River, where 188 persons were enumerated. "Settlements on the Arkansas" contained 874 persons. Eastern Arkansas thus contained 1,062 persons, more or less, in 1810. A count of adult males made by Missouri Territory for apportionment purposes indicated that this population had grown to about 1,600 people by 1814. This was still gradual growth. The westward expansion of the United States had not yet hit Arkansas, or, more accurately, it had not yet hit eastern Arkansas.

By 1810 settlers were beginning to enter Arkansas overland from Missouri, ignoring Arkansas Post and eastern Arkansas altogether. Exclusive of its Arkansas portion, Missouri grew from about 6,000 to about 20,000 people in the first decade of the century as Americans came down the Ohio River and crossed the Mississippi River in search of land in the Louisiana Purchase. By 1820, Missouri had a population of some 68,000 people. As early as 1808, a few settlers made their way out of what is now southeast Missouri and into what is now Arkansas by crossing the Current River and moving in a southwesterly direction along the edge of the highlands. This route, which became known as the Southwest Trail, stretched from Ste. Genevieve on the Mississippi River in Missouri into what would become Texas and intersected all of the southeasterly flowing rivers of Arkansas.

The northern portion of the Southwest Trail ran through the watershed of the White River, crossing the Eleven Point River, the Spring River, the Strawberry River, the White River itself, and finally the Little Red River. Many immigrants settled in the valleys of these rivers, and Poke Bayou on the White River became a center for trade. At least two families lived there by 1810, and Richard C. Luttig was operating a trading post at the site in 1815. He bought tallow and pelts from white hunters and Native Americans and corn and tar from the settlers. The White River quickly acquired a reputation as a fine agricultural area. Samuel Brown's *Western Gazetteer,* published in 1817, claimed that "the country by the waters of the White River, perhaps two hundred and fifty miles square, is one of the finest for settlements in western American." He compared it to an earlier stopping place for the migration of southerners: "The description of Kentucky, at first deemed romance, would be applicable to this country." Timothy Flint, writing a decade later, mentioned that the area was called "New Kentucky, either from its being fertile, rolling and abundant in lime stone springs or from its being more congenial to the staple crops of Kentucky." He tempered his praise for its agricultural potential with the admonition that the river valleys were subject to severe flooding that often inundated "corn and cotton."

The man who wrote most about the upper White River, however, cared little about the farming that was taking place. Henry Rowe Schoolcraft, who later became a well-known ethnologist and student of American Indians, tramped west from Potosi, Missouri, in 1818 looking for lead deposits. Eventually he made his way south and reached the White River in what is now Baxter County, Arkansas. Schoolcraft found hunters living along the river in this remote region and became fascinated with their primitive lifestyle. He later wrote about a family named Wells that lived on the White River where it was joined by the North Fork River. The Wells family cultivated a few acres of land, but their passion was hunting. Their cabin was furnished with homemade furniture, and guns, antlers, and deerskin bags hung from its walls. The children wore buckskins, "abundantly dirty and greasy." While Schoolcraft had positive things to say about the Wells family and the other hunters he met, he emphasized their lack of civilization: "In manners, morals, customs, dress, contempt of labor and hospitality, the state of society is not essentially different from that which exists among the savages . . ."

While descending the White River, Schoolcraft came to Poke Bayou, located where the Southwest Trail crossed the river. He noted that the town contained twelve houses and a store and that "the country wears a look of agriculture, industry and increasing population." These comments, upon which he did not elaborate, were largely lost among his observations about the role of hunting and his theory that the hunters of the White River were "descendants of enlightened Europeans [living] in a savage state or at least in a rapid advance towards it." Schoolcraft was the first of many commentators who would make Arkansas seem more rustic than it was.

In 1811, John C. Benedict and three brothers named Standlee, all born in Kentucky, left their most recent home in Missouri and journeyed beyond the White River to the Devil's Fork of the Little Red River, where they cleared land and built cabins before returning home for other family members. Benedict stayed in Missouri for several years and then brought his family to Arkansas. They crossed the Little Red, had a reunion with their relatives, and left their wagon to push on "over a very mountainous country with nothing but a trail to guide our footsteps." Eventually they reached the Arkansas River at a place called Cadron, about twenty-five miles upriver from the future site of Little Rock. Ten or fifteen families lived within a few miles of Cadron Bluff, and they had built a blockhouse to protect themselves from the Osage Indians. According to Benedict, these families had planted nothing up to this time and lived entirely on wild game. Hunting, however, was a temporary way of life. In 1818, the same year that Benedict arrived, three neighbors built a saw- and gristmill, "the first in this country." It was located on a bayou, "run by water power, having two sash saws and one set of large rocks," and it wrought a great change: "the wilderness began to assume a civilized aspect, for the first time . . . corn meal and lumber could be had in any quantity."

Larger settlements occurred earlier below the Arkansas River. In 1814 a Methodist minister by the name of William Stevenson left his home in Belleview, Missouri, and traveled down the Southwest Trail in order to visit his brother, who was operating a farm on the Ouachita River. The route was "mostly wilderness except on the rivers and rich lands, where we found settlements of industrious people." He camped out some of the time; at other times he found lodging and a meal at someone's cabin and always prayed with the families. "At some place we found good beds and better fare; but all was well, for God was with us." At the Ouachita settlements, Stevenson found a Mister McMahon, who was "greatly backslidden," but the clergyman was able to restore his faith. Stevenson found a "great number of small settlements all through the country from five to twenty miles apart." He preached in Turnwaw (Terre Noir), on Wolf Creek, on the Little Missouri River, and at Mound Prairie. An agent of Missouri Gov. William Clark visited the same area in 1816 and estimated that it contained two hundred families who had arrived as early as 1812 and were raising corn and livestock on what he described as "fine farms."

Meanwhile, settlers were also coming up the Arkansas River. John Billingsley was a young boy traveling with his family and two others—eighteen persons in all—from Middle Tennessee when he reached Arkansas Post in 1814. The party traded its flatboat for a keelboat, and the families made their way up the river to Cadron, where by accident they found an uncle of John's who had come to Arkansas from Kentucky. They moved farther up the river to the mouth of the Big Mulberry River. In 1816, as Billingsley remembered it much later, there were thirty families living in the area, subsisting largely on game and honey until they could raise corn and Irish potatoes. When Fort Smith was established, the Mulberry settlers supplied the garrison with buffalo in return for flour, which was a "great treat" for them. The settlers also did business with French traders, who "came up the River in large canoes," presumably from Arkansas Post, and sold fabric and dishes for which they were paid in "bear skins and deer skins and coon skins and bear oil, some beaver and otter skins and beeswax." As Billingsley remembered these early days much later: "We had all things in common. We had no doctors nor lawyers those happy days."

A larger view of the Arkansas River Valley was presented by Thomas Nuttall, a botanist who explored it in 1819. Nuttall found a number of French settlers living on the river below and above Arkansas Post, growing corn and cotton and raising livestock that they let run free to provide for themselves. Arkansas Post itself seemed to have changed little since its colonial past. Nuttall called it "an insignificant village containing three stores, destitute even of a hatter, a shoe-maker, and a taylor [sic] and containing about 20 houses." He thought Arkansas Post did not "flatter the industry of the French immigrants, whose habits, at least those of the Canadians are generally opposed to improvement and regular industry." Nuttall also disliked the French homes, which were encircled by "open galleries, destitute of glass windows, and perforated with numerous doors." They were fine for the summer, in his opinion, but uncomfortable in the winter. He also noted that a large number of the food products that had been imported could have been grown locally if the inhabitants had cultivated even kitchen gardens. Again, according to Nuttall, it was a evidence of a character flaw of ethnic origin: "These Canadian descendants, so long nurtured amidst savages, have become strangers to civilized comforts and regular industry." In the same Francophobic frame of mind, he noted that the French in Arkansas and in other colonies carried their "love of amusement" to what the plant scientist considered extremes, "particularly gambling, and dancing parties or balls."

Continuing up the river, Nuttall passed isolated homes as well as places where groups of families were living in close proximity. The Curran settlement contained six families that were raising between a thousand and fifteen hundred pounds of cotton per acre and fine crops of corn. Joseph Kirkendale, some miles above the Currans, gave the scientist his first taste of Arkansas milk and butter. He continued on past the homes of a Mr. Morrison, Mr. Dardenne, Mr. Mason, Mr. Embree, and Lewismore Vaugin. Little Rock, which would soon be the capital of Arkansas Territory, was then largely a geographical entity, but Nuttall visited with Edmund Hogan, who had lived there for some years. He also noted a few homes located on "high, healthy, and fertile land."

The Southwest Trail crossed the Arkansas River at Little Rock, and Nuttall learned of another settlement farther south on the Saline River. Upstream at the Cadron settlement, the scientist thought the "hills and rocks" of that site and the absence of good land would prevent it from ever becoming a prosperous community. Nonetheless, proprietors were attempting to sell town lots. Nuttall did think it needed a tavern, since it was on one of the "leading routes through this territory": travelers from St. Louis and from the White River region, as well as those from the hot springs of the Ouachita, passed through Cadron. There was also a "leading path" from Arkansas Post northwest to Cadron that passed through Grand Prairie. Above Cadron, and in the vicinity of Petit Jean Mountain, there was the Pecannerie settlement, which consisted of seven or eight houses clustered along three miles of the river, and some miles farther there was another small settlement at Dardanelle.

Nuttall also visited the Cherokee Indians who lived along the upper Arkansas River. In contrast to his views of the French Canadians of Arkansas Post, he found the Cherokees to be industrious and successful. "In their houses, which are decently furnished, and in their farms, which were well fenced and stocked with cattle, we perceive a happy approach toward civilization." Eventually the scientist reached Fort Smith, located on an elevated spot where the Poteau River empties into the Arkansas. Less than two years old, the fort contained two blockhouses as well as barracks for the seventy soldiers who were stationed there. Nuttall found it well sited: "The view is more commanding and picturesque, than any other spot of equal elevation on the banks of the Arkansas."

Nuttall was critical of what he saw in the Arkansas River Valley, but he also recognized the potential of the region and of the nascent society. His summary of the area could apply as well to Arkansas as a whole: "the privations of an infant settlement are already beginning to disappear, grist and saw-mills, now commenced, only wait for support; and the want of good roads is scarcely felt in a level country meandered by rivers."

The results of this settlement process, both along the Southwest Trail and up the Arkansas River, were shown by the Census of 1820. The 1,062 persons of 1810 had grown to 14,273, and the geography of settlement had altered markedly. There were seven counties in Arkansas by the latter period, and five of them were located inland from the Mississippi River Alluvial Plain. In 1820 the inland counties, settled mostly from the Southwest Trail, contained 69 percent of the population. The weight of the population had shifted away from the Mississippi River and toward the center of the state. In 1821, the territorial legislature moved its capital from Arkansas Post to Little Rock, located where the Southwest Trail crossed the Arkansas River. Poke Bayou, now called Batesville, was becoming a commercial and administrative center for the settlements along the northern portion of the trail, and Washington, a village located near the Red River, was functioning the same way at the territory's southern end.

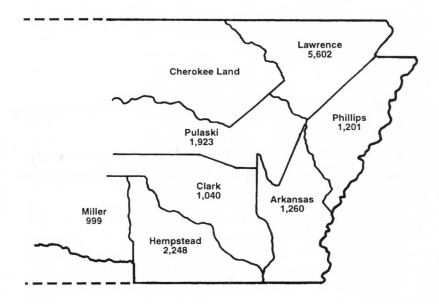

Arkansas Counties on the Census of 1820

As American territory, Arkansas was defined largely by its neighbors. Congress divided the Louisiana Purchase at 33 degrees latitude in 1804. The lower portion was called the Territory of Orleans and had its capital at New Orleans. It became the state of Louisiana in 1812. Arkansas was in the northern portion, which was first known as the District of Louisiana and then the Territory of Louisiana. In 1812 when the Territory of Orleans became the state of Louisiana, the Territory of Louisiana took the name Missouri Territory. Arkansas was the southern portion of Missouri Territory until Missouri applied for statehood and requested a southern boundary at 36 degrees 30 minutes, except for the area between the Mississippi River and the St. Francis River, where the boundary dropped

Arkansas Territory

to 36 degrees in order to accommodate settlers there who wanted to remain in Missouri. The citizens of Arkansas then requested that they become a separate territory bounded by Missouri on the north and Louisiana on the south. In one sense the new territory was a long segment of Mississippi River waterfront property located an inconvenient distance from both New Orleans and St. Louis. At that time, however, Arkansas also ran west across the Louisiana Purchase and shared a boundary with Mexico. The modern western boundary of Arkansas was established as Congress created the Indian Territory that would become Oklahoma. The lower portion was drawn in 1825 as a boundary between

Arkansas and the Choctaw Nation, running from the Red River to Fort Smith. The northern portion developed out of the Cherokee Treaty of 1828 and extended from Forth Smith to the northwest corner of Missouri.

Timothy Flint's *Condensed Geography and History of the Western States*, which was published in 1828, claims that the topography of Arkansas made it "an epitome of the world." He was writing while Arkansas still included much of what is now Oklahoma, but even the foreshortened territory exhibited a remarkable degree of geographical variation that had a profound effect on the location of early settlements.

The river valleys of Arkansas were often attractive to settlers because of their rich, alluvial soil and hardwood forests. The largest waterway was the Arkansas River, which rises in Colorado and flows across Kansas and Oklahoma before entering Arkansas from the west and making its way between the Ouachita and Ozark Mountains and following a southwesterly course through the Delta and emptying into the Mississippi River. The White River rises in northwest Arkansas and then flows north into Missouri before turning south and making its way down eastern Arkansas. It finally empties into the Mississippi River a few miles from the mouth of the Arkansas River. The St. Francis River runs south from Missouri

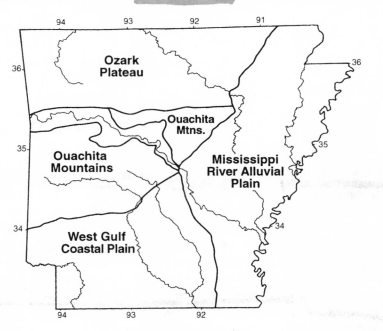

Highlands and Lowlands

down the extreme northeast of Arkansas. The Ouachita River rises in the Ouachita Mountains and flows south into Louisiana. Finally, the Red River comes out of Texas and flows through the extreme southwest corner of Arkansas and also drops into Louisiana.

Arkansas was divided rather evenly into highland and lowland regions along a line that ran from the northeast to the southwest. The eastern portion of the lowland is the Mississippi River Alluvial Plain, which follows the Mississippi River and stretches inland for up to 125 miles. Covered by about two feet of rich soil deposited by the Mississippi River eons in the past, the alluvial plain, or Delta as it came to be known, was excellent farmland. Its value was increased by the fact that most of the area had an average of 220 frost-free days a year, enough to provide an excellent climate for growing cotton. The Delta was covered with bottomland hardwood forest for the most part, although there were a few grassy prairies, the most important of which was Grand Prairie, a 10-mile swathe of grass and flowers that began at Arkansas Post and ran northwest between the Arkansas and White Rivers for nearly 100 miles.

The Arkansas Delta was a land of great agricultural promise, but it was not always easy to get to or to live in. Timothy Flint pointed out that lower portions of both the Arkansas River and the White River were "an extensive, heavily timbered, and deeply inundated swamp." Moreover, the Mississippi River regularly overflowed the central portion of the eastern border of Arkansas, making it into a "continued and monotonous flooded forest." Travelers who attempted to enter Arkansas on foot from the east would find crossing the swampland of eastern Arkansas a very daunting experience. Not the least of its unpleasantness, for residents as well as visitors, was what Flint called "excessive annoyance from its myriads of musquitos [sic]."

The West Gulf Coastal Plain, which covers south Arkansas east of the Delta, is a vestige of the Gulf of Mexico. It had the same warm climate as the Mississippi River Alluvial Plain, but its soil was reddish yellow in color, sandy and silty in composition, and relatively infertile. Except for the river bottoms, the dominant vegetation was pine forest. The highland areas of Arkansas include the Ouachita Mountains in the west and the Ozark Mountains in the north. Both of them have thin soil, although the oaks, hickories, and other deciduous trees of the Ozarks provide valuable organic material to that region that is lacking in the pine-forested Ouachita region.

The earliest possible way for settlers to acquire portions of Arkansas geography in Arkansas was to have a claim originating under the Spanish government of Louisiana. Under the terms of the Louisiana Purchase, the United States agreed to protect the property rights of existing inhabitants. To put this concept into practice, Congress passed a law in 1805 confirming the title of grants that were made and settled by October 1, 1800, when Spain returned Louisiana to France, and all settlements that were made before December 20, 1803, when the U.S. flag was raised over the area. Washington also created a Board of Land Commissioners for Louisiana Territory, which was empowered to take evidence about specific claims and make decisions about their validity. After hearing evidence in Missouri and at Arkansas Post, the board issued a report in 1812 that accepted 1,340 claims, less that one-third of those it had considered. Congress then selected Frederick Bates, one of the three land commissioners, to rehear the rejected claims. His report, issued in 1816, resulted in the approval of another 1,756 claims.

Only 145 of the accepted claims were in Arkansas, an outcome that was reasonable enough given the small number of persons living in the area at the time of the Louisiana Purchase. More than one-third of the surnames on the Arkansas Post census of 1798 show up on the list of successful claimants. Forty-five claims were based on concessions or grants made by the government of Spain, and 100 claims recognized existing settlements. The acreage of the former tended to be small, usually several hundred acres; the claims accepted on the basis of settlement were larger, however, usually about 600 acres. Moreover, many individuals and families received more than a single claim, so that the number of separate claimants was only slightly over one hundred. Many of the grants were for only 200 or 300 acres, but Bates approved seventy-seven grants based on settlement, and most of them were in the neighborhood of 640 acres. Benjamin Fooy of Hopefield received five tracts of land totaling 2,040 acres, and Sylvanus Phillips, for whom Phillips County is named, also received 2,040 acres. In all, the claims process confirmed the ownership of about one hundred square miles of Arkansas.

The most famous unconfirmed grants involved members of the Winter family, Elisha and his two sons, William and Gabriel. According to their supporting documents, Elisha had gone from Kentucky to New Orleans, where he had built a rope walk that was subsequently destroyed by fire. Because of the loss and the friendship between them, Baron de Carondolet, governor of Louisiana, gave Elisha Winter "1,000 arpents square" and his sons 500 each of the same in 1797. An arpent is a French measure of surface area that is equal to about 85 percent of an acre; it was sometimes used, however, as a linear measure equal to one side of a square arpent. The difference is important. If "arpents square" meant simply arpents arranged in a square, than Elisha's claim, for example, would have been for 850 acres. If the term meant an area that was 1,000 linear arpents by 1,000 linear arpents, than Elisha was entitled to 1,000,000 arpents, or 850,000 acres. In the latter case, the boys would each get 425,000 acres. In all, the Winter claim amounted to about 5 percent of the land area of modern Arkansas. Aside from its sheer size, there were technical problems that weakened the Winter claim. In 1834 a congressional committee recommended giving the heirs of Elisha Winter 2,000 acres based on his actual settlement near Arkansas Post in 1797.

In addition to the Spanish Grants, portions of Arkansas were made available as military bounty lands. During the War of 1812, Congress had offered 160 acres of land to individuals who would enlist in the military for five years. To pay off that debt, it set aside 6 million acres of the public domain, 2 million of which was located in Arkansas between the Arkansas and St. Francis Rivers. The land in this area was surveyed beginning in 1816 and distributed two years later. Few veterans came to Arkansas, however. Some apparently sold their claims to speculators. In the fall of 1823, Arkansas Territory began to tax the land and sell it at auction if the taxes were not paid. At tax sales held in 1824, individuals were able to buy bounty lands at a fraction of what they would have paid to the government for public land.

The public land system of the United States began to operate in Arkansas when surveying began in 1815. The Fifth Principal Meridian was established north from the mouth of the Arkansas River and a baseline was surveyed west from the mouth of the St. Francis River. Land sales might have begun in 1818, but the necessary forms had not arrived. By 1822, land officers were functioning in Poke Bayou and in Little Rock. In the first year of sales, Arkansans purchased 22,000 acres of land, most of it under the Preemption Act of April 12, 1814, which gave squatters the right to purchase the land they occupied for the minimum price. During the rest of the 1820s, however, sales were very slow, and less than 60,000 acres had been sold by the end of the decade.

In the 1830s both population and land sales greatly increased. To handle the new business, the General Land Office opened new branches at Fayetteville and Washington in 1832 and at Helena in 1834. In 1836, the peak year of the decade both in Arkansas and for the General Land Office, the Arkansas land offices sold nearly a million acres of land. Many

Arkansas settlers, however, continued to squat on public lands as late as 1840, confident that they could buy the land whenever they wanted to and unwilling to pay taxes until it was necessary. Per capita ownership for each white man, woman, and child had been a little over two acres in 1830, but it was nearly thirty-two acres in 1840.

During the 1840s the newly declared state of Arkansas passed a series of measures that put land on the market under more favorable conditions. First was the Donation Law of 1840, under which land that had been forfeited for nonpayment of taxes would be given free to male heads of families who wanted it. A new owner could receive only 160 acres, he had to live on the land or improve it, and he had to pay his taxes. Later modifications of the law made it even more generous, allowing the head of household to acquire 160 acres of land for each member of his family. Even though the amount of land was limited, the Donation Law created a favorable image of Arkansas among families thinking about moving west. Arkansas also marketed large amounts of land it had received from the federal government. In 1841 it offered to sell 500,000 acres granted for the purpose of financing internal improvements at $1.25 an acre, with a credit provision that allowed the purchaser up to five years to pay for the land at 6 percent annual interest. The U.S. government was also selling land at $1.25 an acre but without credit provisions. Two years later, 930,000 acres that had been set aside for common schools were put up for sale by the state at $2.00 per acre with an option to pay over ten years.

The greatest impact on land sales in Arkansas came from the Swamp Land Act passed by the United States in December 1850. Under its terms and those of related measures, Congress gave twelve states, including Arkansas, "swamp and overflowed lands" within the public domain, with the provision that the states use the profits from selling the acreage to carry out drainage projects and build levees in order to make the land productive. The process of defining the land to which the law applied was imprecise at best, and in practice the decisions were largely left to the states, who had an obvious interest in increasing the amount of land they could acquire free of charge. Down to the Civil War, state officials in Arkansas found more than 10 million acres—29 percent of the state—which they believed fit the definition of the Swamp Land Act, and several million acres were actually confirmed and turned over to the state. Contractors who built levees were paid in scrip that could be used to purchase land, and they often sold it at very low prices. In this and other ways, the land found its way into private hands. The levees were often poorly constructed, however, and the flood-control aspects of the law were largely a failure.

"Our territory is rapidly emerging from the sable gloom which so long shrouded and concealed its merits from the citizens of the states," wrote "A Citizen" in the *Arkansas Gazette* in 1820, when both Arkansas Territory and the newspaper were a year old. The proof of this progress was in immigration, or so he argued: "Men from every quarter of the Union, and of every profession flock to the fertile and salubrious plains of Arkansas." In fact, however, immigration was slow in the 1820s; the fourteen thousand people in the new territory in 1820 grew to only thirty thousand in the Census of 1830. Part of the problem was the Panic of 1819, which slowed the westward movement in general. Arkansas may also have suffered from the fact that the Quapaw, Cherokee, and Choctaw Indians all owned significant portions of Arkansas during the 1820s.

Large-scale immigration to Arkansas began in the 1830s, a decade of unprecedented expansion for the United States as a whole. In May 1830, the *Arkansas Advocate,* Little Rock's second newspaper, exulted in the change, referring to a "vast tide of immigration . . . Not only is every steam-boat crowded with cabin and deck passengers, but the roads also are lined with wagons, conveying families to the Eden of Arkansas." The *Arkansas Gazette* reported later in the year that 1,500 immigrants had crossed the Mississippi River on the Memphis ferry since the spring, most of them from Tennessee, Alabama, North Carolina, South Carolina, and Georgia. These travelers claimed that "the rage for emigration to Arkansas, from those States, is still increasing." A report from Chicot County in the southeast corner of Arkansas referred to the "continually progressing settlements of cotton planters" and bragged that the newcomers were "mostly persons of considerable capitol [*sic*] and means for the planting business." The 30,000 Arkansans of 1830 more than tripled to 98,000 by 1840, a growth rate that allowed the territory to become a state in 1836.

And the population became still larger in the last two decades before the Civil War. In April 1841, the *Arkansas Gazette* reported that 130 settlers had arrived at Little Rock on the steamboat *Odessa,* and in January 1842, the *Gazette* announced that 99 new arrivals were in Batesville. Large numbers of people were reported on the road from Memphis to Little Rock all through the middle of the decade, and the throng actually increased in 1848 and 1849. The 98,000 Arkansans of 1840 more than doubled to 210,000 in 1850. Then, in the 1850s, immigration increased again. In 1852, a Memphis newspaper reported that settlers had discovered that "there are thousands on thousands of acres of as good land as any in the world to be had in Arkansas, at far cheaper rates than the same quality of land can be purchased in Texas." Still more settlers arrived after 1855. In 1858 there were long lines of wagons waiting to cross the Mississippi River on the ferry at Helena. During the 1850s, the 210,000 Arkansans grew to 436,000.

Most of the settlers of Arkansas came west across the South, usually making their way to Arkansas in two or more generations. According to historian Robert Walz, one-third or so of the immigrant families lived in Tennessee before moving to Arkansas, and more than 10 percent each arrived from Missouri, Mississippi, and Alabama. The southern nature of Arkansas society was also reflected in the African American slave population, which reached 20 percent of the total population by 1840 and 26 percent by 1860. Geography also conditioned settlements. Immigrants from the upper South, Tennessee and Missouri, were more likely to settle in the highland areas of Arkansas, while those from the lower South states of Mississippi, Alabama, and Georgia preferred the lowlands, where cotton could be grown. By the 1850s, 80 percent of Arkansas slaves lived in the lowlands.

We know relatively little about the process of settlement, about how people made the decision to move, or about how they organized their trips. It is clear, however, that information played an important role, that prospective settlers tried to find out about the areas that were available for settlement. They learned about Arkansas from guidebooks, including Timothy Flint's *Condensed Geography,* Samuel Brown's *Western Gazetteer,* and R. Baird's *Emigrant's Guide.* Southern planters sometimes visited in person. In 1825, for example, the *Arkansas Gazette* claimed that "respectable and wealthy planters from Alabama, Tennessee, &c" had visited the Quapaw lands south of the Arkansas River and "cast a wishful eye." Five years later, the *Arkansas Advocate* reported that "parties of gentlemen from almost every state south of Maryland were visiting Arkansas."

Settlers also corresponded about moving with family members back home. John Martin, who lived in Cape Girardeau County, Missouri, regularly exchanged letters about agricultural economics with his brothers Jared and Allen, who had moved to Arkansas. In 1826, John reported that it was his "wish to be settled in the Arkansas Country," but he felt he should remain where he was until he had sold his land. By 1829, the prospect of moving was "almost continually on my mind," in part because his mother was living in Arkansas also, and he wanted the family united. As late as 1837, however, he was still trying to sell his land in Missouri. In

1842, John Meek, recently settled in Union County, Arkansas, sent a glowing appraisal of his new home to his son-in-law in South Carolina. After touching on the "Christal Springs . . . the pure clean undulating Country with tall forests shading it, . . . a delightful breeze from the Rocky Mountains," he went on to claim that "the poorest land in our country would beat in Corn, Cotton, Wheat, oats or potatoes, any land in [Laurens or Newberry County in South Carolina]." Encouraging his correspondent to immigrate, Meek claimed that he "would be bettered in every way."

Despite its rapid growth after 1830, Arkansas was an underpopulated state by both national and regional standards. The United States Census Bureau defined a frontier in the nineteenth century as an area with 2 to 6 persons per square mile. Even though it was a state, Arkansas had only 1.9 persons per square mile in 1840; it was presumably a wilderness breaking through to frontier status. The growth of the 1840s and 1850s changed the situation considerably. In 1850, Arkansas was in the frontier category with 4 persons per square mile, and by 1860 the state had exceeded this category by containing 8.3 persons per square mile. This progress, however, still left the state well behind its neighbors. Louisiana had 15.6 persons per square miles in 1860, Mississippi had 17.1, Missouri 17.2, and Tennessee had 26.6.

Historian Edward E. Dale claimed that the problem with Arkansas immigration was the Indian Territory on its western border, which prevented settlers from traveling through the state. Dale argued that much of the localism and backwoods quality of Arkansas could be traced to the fact that settlers and their children tended to stay where they were rather than go around the Indian barrier. In his metaphor, Arkansas resembled a mill pond, a still and even stagnant body of water backed up behind a dam. Dale argued that the mill pond effect made Arkansans cling to traditional values and that it inhibited economic progress. Important though it is, this argument fails to note that travelers did flow though Arkansas on their way to Texas and California.

Despite Dale's emphasis on what lay west, Arkansas probably suffered as much from its own location as from anything else. Placed between Louisiana and Missouri, each of which had stronger natural advantages for immigration, Arkansas was simply off the beaten track. With the city of New Orleans functioning as the international port for trade arising anywhere in the Mississippi River basin, Louisiana was bound to be a center of population. Similarly, Missouri benefited greatly from the fact that St.

Louis was a port on the Mississippi River located near the mouths of both the Missouri and Ohio Rivers. The Ohio was a great watery funnel, bringing settlers from Kentucky and the Old Northwest into Missouri. Arkansas would have received a lot more people if the mouth of the Ohio River were located somewhere in Tennessee.

Topography was also an impediment to population growth. In the 1840s and 1850s, when a more substantial migration was moving across the Gulf Coast, many prospective cotton planters moved across Arkansas and into Texas to take advantage of a warm climate and good land at low prices. One reason they preferred Texas may have been that much of Arkansas was unavailable for the production of cotton. Timothy Flint praised the soil of Arkansas, but he also pointed out that the state "was either very level or very hilly" and that "a very considerable portion of the country is broken land, and unfit for cultivation." Baird's *Emigrant's and Traveller's Guide to the West* made the same point. After pointing out that "there is much land of astonishing fertility" in Arkansas, Baird added a significant caveat, noting that there was also much land that "on account of its swampy or its rocky and hilly surface, cannot be cultivated." The Swamp Land Act was designed both to reduce the amount of wetlands in Arkansas and to put acreage in the hands of potential cultivators at bargain prices. Nothing, however, could turn rocky highlands into attractive farmland.

Effective transportation would have improved immigration, but neither nature nor local legislators were much help. Despite its excellent system of rivers, navigation was a problem in Arkansas. The Arkansas River was subject to extreme fluctuations in flow: it flooded in the spring and dried up in the late summer and fall. Many passengers arrived at the mouth of the White River only to find that they would have to travel overland to Little Rock. The Arkansas River also constantly ate into its banks, changing its course and pulling trees into the water, where they became a hazard to steamboats. The White River and the Ouachita had similar problems, and the Red River was choked by vegetation until well into the 1830s. The road situation was even worse. The swamp conditions along the eastern portion of the state made land travel difficult and were a major obstacle to road building. The *Arkansas Advocate* lamented in March of 1831 that "the large Mississippi Swamp at this season of the year is calculated to fill the mind of the traveler with disappointment and regrets." The U.S. government improved the Memphis to Little Rock road in the middle of the 1830s, but it remained all but impassable in wet weather. Other roads in the state covered less formidable terrain, but none were well built. In 1834 geologist George Featherstonhaugh found that Arkansas roads, or, more properly perhaps, horse paths, meandered around fallen trees that settlers were unwilling to cut and clear. Ferries were primitive and bridges did not exist.

As a poor and underpopulated territory, Arkansas did little with respect to transportation other than to request aid from the federal government. Shortly after achieving statehood, it became involved in a banking disaster that left it in debt and without credit. Transportation improvements might have been beneficial to the overall situation of the state, but they were not made. Arkansas grew and developed in the years before the Civil War, but it remained, in a word, remote.

CHAPTER TWO

Government
and Opportunity

For a decade after becoming part of the United States, Arkansas was relatively free of government, annexed to territorial administrations that were too far away to be greatly concerned with the small and still largely French settlement at Arkansas Post and its vicinity. As more Americans entered the area, however, Arkansas acquired more significance, becoming a separate county within Missouri Territory in 1813 and then a territory itself in 1819. The creation of Arkansas Territory gave Arkansans more convenience in dealing with their affairs and more control over them, but it also created political opportunities that led to intense rivalries and an impressive amount of violence. In addition, politicians demonstrated a marked penchant for using public power for private gain. Both traits, however, seem to have had their origins in the national rather than the local culture.

At the time of the American Revolution, writes historian Gordon Wood, the ideal public servant was the republican officeholder, a man of wealth and social position imbued with classical virtues who served out of disinterested patriotism in the manner of the early Romans. This model, however, gave way in later decades to the democratic officeholder, an ambitious figure who sought political position in order to improve his economic and social standing. By the time Arkansas became a territory, according to

Wood, political office was no longer a reward "for established social wealth and authority," but rather was itself "the source of wealth and authority." Officeholding had less to do with responsibility and more to do with opportunity. With respect to Arkansas, this tendency was heightened by what historian Robert Wiebe has called "the equation between opportunity and space," the fact that Americans in the early nineteenth century usually pursued upward mobility through horizontal mobility. Arkansas Territory represented the possibility of advancement, not only for settlers who wanted fertile and inexpensive land but also for aspiring politicians who wanted offices and the influence that came with them.

* * *

The United States received Louisiana from France on December 20, 1803, and on March 23, 1804, Lt. James B. Many of the U.S. Army took possession of Fort Estevan at Arkansas Post from its Spanish commandant. A small contingent of American troops was stationed there for the next four years. Little change seems to have resulted from the shift of administrations; the American officers in charge even played a role in settling civil disputes, as had their Spanish and French predecessors. Meanwhile, in October 1804, Congress divided the Louisiana Purchase at the 33d parallel, the present southern boundary of Arkansas, and created a Territory of Orleans in the south with its capital at New Orleans and a District of Louisiana in the north, which was placed under the control of the territorial government of Indiana. Since Indiana was still in the first stage of territorial government, it had no elected legislature; the people living in what are now the states of Arkansas and Missouri were subject to laws enacted by the governor and three judges meeting in Vincennes, on the Wabash River in what is now southwest Indiana. The following year the District of Louisiana became the Territory of Louisiana with its capital at St. Louis, and the settlers of Arkansas became part of the New Madrid District, the southernmost jurisdiction of the territory.

The town of New Madrid was some 250 miles by river from Arkansas Post, making it difficult for Arkansans to make use of the courts and other aspects of local government located there. On the other hand, there were no more than one thousand U.S. citizens in Arkansas at the time, and about half of them spoke French and had no understanding of or interest in Anglo-American law. The St. Louis government created an Arkansas District in 1806, making the first official American use of the name that had originated in the seventeenth century, when the French first found

Quapaw Indians living on what they called the "Arkansea river." The district was eliminated in 1807, however, only to be recreated by Gov. Meriwether Lewis in 1808. Lewis also set up local courts at Arkansas Post, but their operation was haphazard, largely owing to a lack of judicial expertise.

Still, Arkansas's status was soon upgraded. In 1812 the Territory of Orleans entered the Union as the state of Louisiana, and the Territory of Louisiana became the Territory of Missouri. The next year, the territorial legislature created a separate Arkansas County with its administrative center at Arkansas Post. In January 1815, Henry Cassidy represented Arkansas County in the territorial legislature. As Arkansas grew in population after the War of 1812, it was divided into new counties. Lawrence County, covering the northern one-third of Arkansas, including the White River region, came into being in 1815. In 1818 the St. Louis government added Clark County in the Ouachita River area of south Arkansas, Hempstead County running west of there to the Red River, and Pulaski County, covering the Arkansas River in the central part of Arkansas.

Despite its growth, however, Arkansas was underpopulated, and it was remote from St. Louis. When the rapidly growing Missouri Territory applied for statehood in 1818, its government asked for a southern boundary at 36 degrees 30 minutes, which excluded Arkansas. Because some settlers in lower New Madrid County wished to remain in Missouri, the boundary request was altered, dropping to 36 degrees east of the St. Francis River, to create the present Missouri "bootheel." The settlers of eastern Arkansas do not appear to have been chagrined at being eliminated from Missouri; they petitioned for territorial status and were supported by the territorial delegate from Missouri and Rep. George Robertson of Kentucky, who offered a resolution to that effect. For a time, Arkansas was held hostage to the Missouri Compromise as Congress debated the question of whether slavery should be allowed in either the prospective state or the prospective territory. The southern location of Arkansas—below the line of 36 degrees and 30 minutes that was coming to be recognized as the future boundary between slave and free states in the Louisiana Purchase—encouraged the legislators to accept it as a slave territory. With that settled, Arkansas Territory came into being in March 1819.

In November 1818, anticipating that Arkansas would soon be made into a separate territory, a group of citizens living in Arkansas County of Missouri Territory sent a petition to President James Monroe asking that Perly Wallis be appointed as a federal judge. Wallis had practiced law for ten years at Arkansas Post, and his supporters claimed that he "hath an Interest In the Country and will undoubted [*sic*] do his Duty Promptly." These qualities were important to them because of their vigorous opposition to the idea of "appointing men over us who have no Interest in the happiness and welfare of its Inhabitants but hold offices Purely for the Sallery [*sic*] they Receive." The present judge, who had been appointed in 1814 and was supposed to reside at Arkansas Post, had not been there in eighteen months, apparently preferring to stay at his home in Cape Girardeau, more than three hundred miles away by water.

Fears that future federal officeholders would be more interested in their salaries than in service to the territory were hardly groundless. President Monroe initially sent three judges to Arkansas: Charles Jouett, a native of Virginia who had served as an Indian agent at Chicago and Detroit; Robert P. Letcher of Kentucky, a brother-in-law of Rep. George Robertson of Kentucky, who had led the movement to create Arkansas Territory; and Andrew Scott of Missouri Territory, whose brother was the delegate to Congress from that territory and had also championed the creation of Arkansas Territory. Jouett, Letcher, and Scott were all in Arkansas Post in late July and early August 1819 when the territorial government was organized, but the former two left after that and never came back. The territorial legislature noted that the two judges had departed after passing a small number of laws, including one provision that paid their own salaries. With some sarcasm, the lawmakers went on to declare that "if none of our own inhabitants are to be honored by becoming Judges . . . [we hope] that those who are thus promoted may be taught to know that this Territory is to be their actual home."

The location of Arkansas did seem to put people off. The *Arkansas Gazette* reported that Jouett had tried returning to the territory in the spring of 1820, when he was driven away by mosquitoes at the mouth of the White River. In his resignation letter, the judge said his wife simply would not stay in Arkansas, an explanation that may be compatible with the newspaper account. Jouett was replaced by John Thompson of Ohio, who hoped the warm climate would help an illness in his chest. Thompson traveled as far as Jackson, Missouri, but then turned back after hearing unspecified negative things about his destination. Judge Letcher also resigned, claiming he had never wanted the job in the first place. Finally, in 1821 two new judges joined Andrew Scott, and the judiciary stabilized.

The territory's executive office, however, also suffered from absenteeism. James Miller, the first governor of Arkansas Territory, was a brigadier general in the U.S. Army with more than a decade of service and had performed gallantly in the War of 1812. In addition to these qualifications, the congressional delegation from Miller's home state of New Hampshire pointed out that "he is poor" and would benefit from "the opportunity of removing into a young and thriving country, with his numerous and increasing family, under the favorable auspices of the government." Miller did indeed bring a retinue of about twenty friends and family members with him, some of whom found places in the territorial government. The governor's lack of enthusiasm for the office, however, was evident from the beginning.

Miller was appointed on March 3, 1819, four months before Arkansas became a territory on July 4. The governor's commission, however, was sent to Arkansas Post rather than to New Hampshire, and a new one did not arrive until May 29. Seeing that he could not travel from New Hampshire to Arkansas in the twenty-nine days remaining before the new government would be set up, Miller decided to postpone his departure until the fall. He was particularly concerned about his health. Since he had a "Constitution . . . impaired by privation and exposure to the inclement seasons of the North during the late war," he wanted to avoid the "warm and unhealthy season of the South." After finally leaving on September 10, he stopped at Washington and then at Pittsburgh to pick up arms and ammunition for the territorial militia. Then he descended the Ohio and Mississippi Rivers, arriving at Arkansas Post on December 26. The territorial assembly accepted Miller's explanation of his delay with grace and seemed happy to have a chief executive of his stature. It named Miller County, in the southwestern part of the territory, for him.

Miller was an honest and capable officeholder, but he simply did not like being in Arkansas. He seems to have stayed out of territorial politics, but he worked reasonably hard at civil matters and on the management of Indian affairs. Shortly after arriving, however, he wrote Secretary of War Calhoun to inquire about the availability of the military position he had just resigned. Miller had also left his wife in New Hampshire, which suggests that he viewed his new career as a kind of military campaign. In his letters to her, he criticized territorial society, particularly the relaxed manners of the French settlers at Arkansas Post and their penchant for dancing and gambling. He was also plagued with illness. For nearly four months in the summer of 1820, the governor was sick with an "ague and fever," known locally as "seasoning," and the experience made him anxious to leave the territory during the following summer. With President Monroe's permission, Miller returned to New Hampshire in April 1821 and returned only in November. He left again in June 1823 and remained away from his post until finally resigning in December 1824. All in all, Miller was actually in Arkansas less than half the time he was governor of the territory.

Having nonresident officeholders was a problem for Arkansans in the first few years of the territory, but a long-term and more significant form of political ambition was the desire on the part of some leaders to control the offices of the new government for the benefit of themselves and their own families. Robert C. Henry, an attorney living in Hopkinsville, Kentucky, who hoped to fill the office vacated by Judge Letcher in 1819, was candid and detailed about his ambition in a letter to his brother. Henry rhapsodized about Arkansas as a place "where government was in its first grade, where offices were not filled[,] in short where all the teeming possibilities of a new country were yet to be unraveled." With an appointment as judge, wrote Henry, "I would have it greatly in my power to serve my friends." The territorial judges would make the laws in the first stage of territorial government, and Henry believed that "we could do almost as we pleased," particularly in locating the capital in some "desirable tract of country" where "all our family & friends could settle, . . . and we should thus acquire standing & consequence in the Country."

The sort of ambition that Robert Henry articulated was evidenced by Robert Crittenden, first secretary of Arkansas Territory. Crittenden was only twenty-two years old when he received his appointment, but he had excellent credentials. Richard M. Johnson, then in the U.S. House of Representatives but later Martin Van Buren's vice-president, wrote a recommendation that was impressive in its brevity, pointing out that Robert was the brother of Sen. John J. Crittenden of Kentucky and was "that Self Same Capt. Crittenden who commanded a Company of volunteers in the Seminole War." The young Kentuckian wasted little time taking command of Arkansas in the summer of 1819 when Governor Miller failed to arrive. As acting governor, Crittenden convened the three judges to make up the first territorial legislature. He then went on to appoint circuit court judges and attorneys, an auditor, a treasurer, and sheriffs, coroners, and clerks for each of the counties. In response to a petition by the people, he declared Arkansas to be in the second grade of territorial government in October 1819 and held elections the following month for a legislature and a delegate to the U.S. Congress. Not until the following July, however, did he get around to reporting these actions to Secretary of State John Quincy Adams.

*Robert Crittenden, secretary
of Arkansas Territory,
1819–29.*

Courtesy of the Arkansas
History Commission,
Little Rock.

Crittenden remained the dominant political figure in Arkansas politics for the next five years. Governor Miller's absences and illnesses and his lack of interest in political matters made things easier for the secretary, but Crittenden was an intelligent and forceful leader who developed a personal following among political insiders in the territory. One of them was James Woodson Bates, whose brother was the territorial secretary of Missouri Territory. Bates was elected as delegate to Congress from Arkansas in 1819 and again in 1821. After supporting Bates in the first two elections, Crittenden became disenchanted with him and swung his support to Henry W. Conway in 1823. A first lieutenant in the War of 1812, Conway was a member of a prominent family in Greene County, Tennessee, and his uncle, William Rector, was the surveyor general of Illinois, Missouri, and Arkansas. With Henry W. Conway in Arkansas were his younger brother James Sevier Conway, who would eventually become the first governor of the state of Arkansas, his cousin Ambrose Hundley Sevier, who would be one of its first two U.S. senators, and several Rector cousins. Conway was an able delegate who pleased his constituents by, among other things, helping to remove the Quapaw Indians from Arkansas.

Crittenden's fall was connected with his pride. When Governor Miller resigned, the secretary hoped to be appointed territorial governor, but the outgoing President Monroe chose George Izard, a member of a prominent South Carolina family who had been a major general in the War of 1812. Piqued at the outcome, Crittenden arranged to be away from Little Rock when Izard arrived. The new governor was bothered both by the secretary's absence and by the sloppy way in which he had kept records. More politically astute than Governor Miller, Izard not only reported Crittenden's shortcomings to Washington but also began to cultivate Delegate Conway and other men of political prominence, such as Ambrose Sevier and Chester Ashley.

The election for delegate in 1827 brought major political changes to Arkansas Territory. Conway ran again, but he was no longer in alliance with Crittenden. His opponent, a talented but erratic attorney named Robert C. Oden, was the Crittenden candidate, and during the campaign Oden revealed that Conway had spent six hundred dollars out of seven thousand dollars in U.S. government money that he had been entrusted to bring to Little Rock; this information had to have come from Secretary Crittenden. Charges and countercharges, most of them involving Crittenden rather than Oden, filled the pages of the *Arkansas Gazette,* whose editor, William Woodruff, was publicly impartial but privately a leader of the Conway faction. Conway defended himself by saying that Crittenden had approved his use of the funds and went on to call the secretary a liar in print. The popular Conway easily won re-election, but Crittenden challenged him to a duel, and the two officeholders exchanged shots on the eastern bank of the Mississippi River at the end of October. Conway's ball damaged Crittenden's clothing, but the secretary's shot entered the delegate's side and broke a rib. The wound was not at first considered mortal, but Conway died less than two weeks later.

Ambrose Sevier won a special election called to fill Conway's position as territorial delegate, and soon he showed political skills equal to or better than those of his deceased cousin. He was re-elected four times before the territory became a state. Crittenden, meanwhile, went into eclipse. When Governor Izard died of natural causes in 1828, the secretary once again hoped to gain the gubernatorial appointment. Sevier openly opposed him, admitting to Secretary of State Henry Clay that the delegate had "an unconquerable hatred for Mr. Crittenden, and the same aversion exists with two thirds of our citizens." Sevier called for the appointment of someone from outside of the territory. Eventually it was

President Andrew Jackson rather than President Adams who made the appointment, and Jackson chose John Pope, a Kentucky politician who was a Jackson supporter. The following year, Jackson replaced Crittenden as secretary with William Savin Fulton of Alabama, who had fought with the president in Florida. Crittenden ran against Sevier in 1833 for the delegate position and was soundly trounced. By 1834 he was reduced to writing his brother in the U.S. Senate, complaining about political defeats and financial reverses and asking that the senator and Richard Mentor Johnson use their influence on his behalf. Johnson's support was a long shot for Crittenden, since the senator's brother, Benjamin Johnson, was Sevier's father-in-law.

Governor Pope was a former U.S. senator from Kentucky. He was John Quincy Adams' brother-in-law, but he had worked hard for Andrew Jackson in the election of 1828. Like Governor Miller and Governor Izard, Pope came to Arkansas with some reluctance, having hoped to be named attorney general instead. He was a genial man in his late fifties and comfortable with the style of politics that was practiced in the West. He was sometimes too relaxed, once creating a stir by stating in public that his role in Arkansas was like that of an overseer on a plantation. Pope got into greater difficulty in 1831, when Crittenden's supporters won control of the legislature.

Arkansas had received ten sections of land from the United States in order to finance the construction of a new statehouse. After considering alternative proposals, including one by Chester Ashley, the legislature decided to trade the sixty-four hundred acres to Crittenden in return for the brick home he owned and the block on which it was located. William Woodruff, who had just been deprived of his office as public printer by Crittenden's friends, argued that Crittenden's home was overvalued and unsuitable. He called upon the governor to veto the measure. Several days later, Pope did reject the bill, supporting his action with a well-reasoned statement that emphasized the value of the ten sections, which could be located anywhere in the territory. The governor managed the sale of the land and began the construction of the statehouse itself, earning much more money for the territory than it would have gotten from Crittenden's home. Moreover, he oversaw the building of an even more valuable architectural monument in Little Rock. Known as the Old State House, it still stands.

Meanwhile, Pope became the center of political controversy in the territory. The *Arkansas Advocate* relentlessly attacked his veto of the Ten Section Act and his performance in general. Indeed, when Crittenden ran against Sevier in 1833, he spent much of his time criticizing the governor.

Pope also offended members of his own party. William Fulton, who had replaced Crittenden as secretary, became angry when the governor placed Chester Ashley in charge of the statehouse project during Pope's absence. Fulton told the general assembly that the governor had exceeded his authority in spending money for the statehouse without legislative approval. Pope also quarreled with William Woodruff. The governor apparently wanted the *Arkansas Gazette* to defend him more vigorously, particularly when the *Advocate* charged that Pope had overpaid Woodruff for public business. Woodruff, in turn, became angry when Pope apparently helped a third printer, William Steele, to settle in Little Rock and then provided him with a "good fat job" printing a digest of territorial laws. Governor Pope's increasingly difficult tenure came to an end early in 1835, when President Jackson replaced him with William Fulton. In assessing his problems during his last months in office, Pope blamed the ambitions of his enemies: "This appetite for spoil and plunder is the main spring of the machinery that is working against me." But it was not as if he had not tried to play the game himself: "I have given all the offices and jobs to the friends of Col. Sevier ever since we have been identified in the party struggles of the country." He was hostile toward William Woodruff, "a little toad of an editor," but he professed friendship for Sevier, whom he called upon to disavow Woodruff's behavior.

By this time, the Conway faction that had become the Sevier faction was becoming the Arkansas wing of the Jacksonian Democratic Party and was reveling in the spoils of office. In April 1836 Sevier wrote the president and reminded him that Sevier's cousin, James Sevier Conway, did not wish for the position of surveyor general any more, since he was going to run for governor after Arkansas became a state that summer. Earlier, Sevier had asked that the surveyor general position go to Whorton Rector, who was a cousin of Conway's and a relative of Sevier's as well, but now he was recommending Judge Cross, to whom he was not related. Since Sevier himself was running for the Senate and Conway was running for governor, Sevier worried that "the people of Arkansas will consider that there is too much monopoly in the offices by my relatives and intimate friends—And this may injure the cause in Arkansas." He had cause to worry: Whorton Rector was already an Indian agent, his brother William was a federal marshal, and Sevier's father-in-law, Benjamin Johnson, was a federal judge. In summing up, Sevier asked only that Johnson be put on the federal bench, Elias Rector be appointed federal marshal, and Cross be made surveyor general.

William E. Woodruff, owner and editor of the Arkansas Gazette.

Courtesy of the Arkansas History Commission, Little Rock.

Political factions and politics in general in Arkansas Territory were associated with a pattern of violence of which the Crittenden-Conway duel was only an egregious example. After Crittenden's challenge to Conway but before the duel, Sevier challenged a young Crittenden supporter named Thomas Newton. They met on Cherokee land in western Arkansas and fired at each other once. Neither shot took effect, and their seconds persuaded the two men to give up the fight. The violence continued, however. William Montgomery, who owned a house at the mouth of the White River where Conway had died, quarreled on the streets of Little Rock with Thomas Wyatt Johnston of Kentucky, who was a friend of Crittenden's. The two men attacked each other with pistols, canes, and knives until onlookers stopped the fight. Johnston was badly cut up and missing an eye. In January 1828, William Woodruff and Chester Ashley were in the editor's office when a friend of Crittenden's named John T. Garrett entered and fired at Ashley. Woodruff grabbed Garrett, making the shot go wild, and Ashley fired back, accidentally wounding Woodruff slightly. Garrett then ran out mortally wounded, although exactly how he was injured is not clear. Woodruff, whose gun was not fired, suggested that the attacker had had a second pistol in his pocket that went off by accident. Whatever the case, Sevier was not exaggerating when he explained to Secretary of State Henry Clay: "Party spirit among us has run high—and not infrequently have these political disputes ended in bloodshed."

Nor was it simply the Conway-Crittenden feud that generated violence. Robert Oden had killed a territorial legislator in a duel at Arkansas Post in 1820. At the same place in 1824, Judge Andrew Scott killed Judge Joseph Selden in a duel involving a personal slight. Writing to his wife before the event, Scott exhibited the southern ideal of honor, declaring that he had endured "a host of injuries and insult" and preferred "death itself, to life in disgrace." A young admirer would later call him "the most chivalrous and purest-minded man I think I ever knew." Four years later at Little Rock, Scott quarreled over politics with Edmund Hogan, who had defeated him for a seat on the legislative council. Hogan, a large man, pushed the diminutive Scott down, whereupon Scott drew a spear from his cane and stabbed Hogan four times, killing him in what was ruled as self-defense.

Territorial politics produced another death in 1831, when William Fontaine Pope challenged Charles Fenton Mercer Noland over a newspaper piece Noland had written that was critical of Pope's uncle, the governor. Friends of the two young men attempted to dissuade them, but each was jealous of his honor, and Pope refused the offer of mediation, citing his "deep sense of injury and insult." They fought their duel across the Red River in Texas, and Pope received a wound from which he eventually died.

To explain the violent nature of politics in Arkansas Territory, we may look first at aspects of migration. Dueling, after all, was an American phenomenon, but one that was most widely cherished and practiced in the South. The formal duels in Arkansas may have benefited from an even greater enthusiasm for the activity on the western side of the Mississippi, but they were an expression of the culture that the settlers brought with them. Moreover, while dueling was a gentleman's activity, set off from other forms of violence by its emphasis on honor and its rules of encounter, it was also part of a pattern of southern violence that allowed the plain folk to kill and maim one another with similar, if not greater, abandon. And the difference between the social classes was not all that great. Witness Judge Scott, equally at home killing with his pistol after a challenge or his sword cane after a shove. Secondly, it is important to note that the politicians who came to Arkansas were men of large ambition, determined to make their way in a new country. Writing about the St.

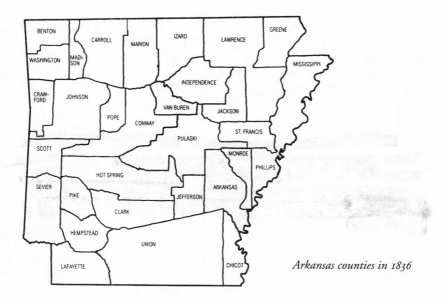

Arkansas counties in 1836

Louis area in the early 1820s, Timothy Flint argued that dueling was largely the result of a single group of people: "the ambitious, fiery, and ungovernable spirits [who] emigrate to obtain consequence and make their fortune . . . [and] have not as yet had their place or their standing assigned them in public opinion." This analysis fits Arkansas Territory equally well.

It is also worth noting that youth probably played a role in both ambition and violence. In Arkansas in 1840, 47 percent of adult males were in their twenties, as compared to 40 percent in the nation as a whole. Nearly three out of four eligible voters in the state that year were younger than 40. In this youthful society, popular leaders were also young. In the fateful year of 1827, Crittenden was 30, Conway was 34, Oden was 29, and Sevier was only 26. William Woodruff was 32 in 1827, while Chester Ashley, James Woodson Bates, and Judge Scott were all 39. By contrast, Governor Izard was 51 in 1827, and Governor Miller, then in Massachusetts, was 51. A few years later, in 1831, Charles Fenton Mercer Noland, who was 21 years old, killed William Fontaine Pope, who was 23, in a duel involving the integrity of Gov. John Pope, who was 61.

The same ambition that led to dueling encouraged the politicians of territorial Arkansas to award themselves a small degree of immortality. The territorial legislature created Miller County in 1820; Izard, Crittenden,

Conway, and Sevier Counties were formed in 1825 and Pope County in 1829; Johnson County was created in 1833, named for Judge Benjamin Johnson, Sevier's uncle; that same year, Scott County immortalized Judge Andrew Scott; and in 1835, Searcy County was named for Sevier's opponent in 1829. In 1838 Desha County was named after another of Sevier's opponents; Fulton County was created in 1842, Ashley County in 1848, and Woodruff County in 1868.

The advantages associated with political office and with territorial government in general in Arkansas often involved land, which was the territory's greatest resource. The removal of the capital from Arkansas Post to Little Rock in 1821 and a fraudulent land scheme known as the Bowie Claims that began in 1827 illustrate how territorial politicians used influence for profit. But if the politicians believed in getting everything they could, particularly from the federal government, so too did the people. Citizens of Arkansas Territory seem to have had few scruples about using illegal means to get government land, and they were tireless in asking for federal assistance with respect to the acquisition of land.

Moving the capital from Arkansas Post was eminently reasonable in the sense that the flow of population from Missouri that had settled the interior portions of the territory made it important to have a centrally located capital rather than one situated to serve the needs of the old colonial society in the east. The decision was not made, however, until a large number of important officeholders were guaranteed financial rewards from the change.

As the territorial legislature discussed leaving Arkansas Post, two rival claims to Little Rock were asserted. One was held by James Bryan and William O'Hara, both of St. Louis, and their agent, Amos Wheeler, and consisted of four New Madrid certificates. These were issued to compensate victims of the massive earthquakes of 1811–12 that devastated the landscape of a small portion of southeast Missouri and northeast Arkansas. The law provided that individuals who had lost at least one acre of land because of the earthquake could claim 160 acres of public land anywhere in the United States. They could also sell their land rights to someone else. The New Madrid claims, many of which were fraudulently obtained, were very useful to speculators, who purchased them for modest amounts and then used them to acquire choice land in Arkansas Territory. In December 1819, Wheeler arrived at Little Rock to make surveys and prepare a proposal for the territorial legislature. The other claimant was William Russell, a surveyor and speculator with great experience in

Arkansas. He claimed to own a preemption right that had originated with William Lewis, a hunter who had lived near Little Rock for a time in 1812. Russell had purchased the preemption from Martha White, an heir of Elisha White, who had bought the claim to "Little Rock Bluff" from Lewis for ten dollars in 1814. Apparently uncertain of his position, however, Russell offered to join with the New Madrid group if they would pay him twenty-five thousand dollars. They not only rejected this offer but also threw Russell off what they were claiming as their land. Undaunted, Russell brought suit for wrongful trespass.

The territorial legislature met in February 1820 and discussed a proposal by the New Madrid group to provide the territory with land and buildings if the capital were moved to Little Rock. Nothing is known of the discussions that ensued, but the house narrowly passed a motion to move to Cadron, a small community on the Arkansas River about twenty miles above Little Rock, and, when the council favored Little Rock, the issue was postponed. At its next session, in October, the house voted in favor of the Little Rock proposal six to three. By that point, the ownership of the Little Rock site had widened to include a number of important politicians.

On March 15, 1820, William O'Hara sold Gov. James Miller and Nathaniel Philbrook one-twelfth of the New Madrid claim for eight hundred dollars. Meanwhile, William Russell had learned that Elisha White had sold his claim to Little Rock before he died so that Martha White had never owned it. In fact, a legal preemption had been filed at Batesville by a man named Benjamin Murphy, and shares in it were owned by William Trimble, an attorney whose brother was also the receiver of public monies of the Batesville Land Office, and Townsend Dickinson, a member of the legislative council. In October Russell paid two thousand dollars to Benjamin Murphy, William Trimble, and Townsend Dickinson for half of William Lewis's preemption claim. Murphy apparently sold out at that point, and Trimble and Dickinson went on to divide their share of the preemption rights with Robert Crittenden, Henry W. Conway, then receiver of public monies, Joseph Hardin, speaker of the house, and Robert C. Oden, a young attorney.

In June 1821, the territorial government began to function at Little Rock, and one of its first actions was a decision by the superior court on Russell's suit against the New Madrid group. The court ruled that Russell's preemption did establish a valid claim to a portion of land located near the rocky point for which the town was named. Angered by this development, the New Madrid party and its henchmen fortified themselves with whiskey, put on thin disguises, and removed or destroyed the buildings that they had constructed on what was now Russell's land. A passing traveler recorded the bizarre events: "First we saw a large wood and stone building in flames and then about 100 men, painted, masked and disguised in almost every conceivable manner, engaged in removing the town. These men, with ropes and chains, would march off a frame house on wheels and logs, place it about 300–400 yards from its former site and then return and move off another."

Finally in November there came what Russell termed a "compromise." The preemptioners turned over seventeen lots to Chester Ashley, then a young attorney acting for the New Madrid party, and Russell purchased them back, in effect combining the interests. Ashley and Russell also bound themselves to support each other's legal rights to the real estate.

When the preemptioners and the New Madrid group effected their settlement, Little Rock was a tiny community with a dozen homes, a store, and several taverns and boarding houses. The legislature met in a two-room log cabin. Land in the capital city was certainly of potential value, however, and it is important to recognize that while land speculators and politicians fought among themselves, they eventually also divided the spoils among themselves. The public was excluded from a process that benefited skilled operatives and those with influence to sell, the latter including the governor, the secretary, and a number of other officeholders.

A more outrageous—and indeed criminal—example of the way in which political influence was used to obtain land is the episode known as the Bowie Claims. In 1824, Congress gave the Superior Court of Arkansas jurisdiction over any new cases arising from Spanish claims. Over the next two years, the court confirmed about ten thousand acres of land that supposedly had been granted by the Spanish government. Then, in the space of a few days in December of 1827, it confirmed 117 claims and left another 7 cases for its next meeting. These 124 cases were soon known as the Bowie Claims. They were put forward together and shared the same documentation; collectively, they involved about fifty thousand acres of land.

George Graham, commissioner of the General Land Office in Washington, first learned of the Bowie Claims from the Little Rock land office, which feared that the claims would flood the market with land, making it impossible for the government to sell its own acreage. As the new claims were processed, doubts arose about their legitimacy, and Graham finally decided to hire a special investigator to look into the situation. Isaac T. Preston, a New Orleans land expert, visited Little Rock and filed a report in October 1829. He pointed out that all of the 124 claims were supported by the testimony of three men, and that the depositions were "substantially, and in general literally" the same. Preston also stated that the signatures of Spanish governors Miro and Gayoso were obvious forgeries. In addition, certain Spanish words were uniformly misspelled throughout the Spanish documents, which were supposedly written by a variety of Spanish officials. Finally, the claims that were ostensibly the work of 124 different people seemed to involve only two different handwritings.

Preston also pointed out that the beneficiaries of these claims could locate on any unoccupied land in Arkansas and thus could "pick the territory" for choice acreage. To him, the issue was whether the United States "can be successfully plundered by the most unparalleled forgery, perjury, and subornation," or, putting it another way, whether "great actors may roll in wealth, whilst an honest man and woman may labor their life-time in these woods to acquire a quarter section of land for their children."

With Preston's report in hand, Commissioner Graham was able to bring the government into action. Congress instructed the Arkansas Superior Court to review the Bowie Claims, and U.S. Attorney Sam Roane, at the direction of the attorney general, prepared evidence and filed motions against the claims. The superior court accepted Roane's motions in May and June of 1830, thereby invalidating the Bowie Claims, but some had already been purchased. Joseph Stewart then sued to obtain a claim that he had bought from John J. Bowie, whose own title was based on the confirmed Spanish claim of Bernardo Sampeyreac. Despite the fact that it had confirmed the claim earlier, the superior court now ruled that Sampeyreac was a fictitious person and that no legitimate title had ever existed. Stewart appealed to the United States Supreme Court, but it upheld the Arkansas decision. The remaining claims were invalidated by the superior court without further litigation, in each instance on the grounds that the original claimant was not a real person. Eventually the United States government awarded preemption rights to third-party purchasers for the land they thought they had bought.

John J. Bowie was the brother of Jim Bowie, whose famous knife was crafted in Washington, Arkansas. John had lived in the New Orleans area, had business involvements in Chicot County, Arkansas, and he later resided in Helena. He played a major role in the fictitious Spanish grants that bear his name and was probably responsible for their production. In

January 1830 the *Arkansas Gazette* published a letter from Ambrose Sevier in which the territorial delegate indicated that Congress would force a review of the claims despite his opposition. Sevier argued that the claims should have stayed in Louisiana because "they have, although unjustly, injured the character of our Courts, our District Attorney, and our citizens generally." A month later William Woodruff editorialized that "if there has been fraud committed, . . . it is not chargeable upon Arkansas, but upon the Bowies of Louisiana . . . Arkansas has no agency in it." But U.S. Attorney Roane knew better. Defending himself, Roane argued: "There is in Arkansas a powerful interest in favor of those claims. The property in them is widely diffused through every part of the country . . . Even before the confirmation, the persons who were the main actors had sold and ramified the interest in them so extensively, that the community were urged by self interest to see them confirmed."

The "main actors" were Bowie, Chester Ashley, and Robert Crittenden; the latter two were the attorneys who brought the claims into court. William S. Fulton, the territorial secretary, wrote President Jackson that these three held all the claims, and he was probably right. A list of sixty-five purchasers of Bowie Claims who were granted preemption relief indicates twenty-five were first assigned to John J. Bowie, twenty-two to Chester Ashley, and nine to Robert Crittenden. The involvement of Ashley and Crittenden also makes it easier to understand what happened. Ashley was a major figure in the political faction headed by Ambrose Sevier, and Crittenden was the leader of the opposition; together they were in a position to insure that the claims were well received by Arkansas officials. Not only did the superior court approve the cases and do so quickly, but also it allowed the paperwork to be withdrawn before it became evidence in a criminal investigation. U.S. Attorney Roane did not seriously question the claims until he was pushed to do so, and the only name to whom he referred was that of John J. Bowie. Sevier and Woodruff, who publicly proclaimed the innocence of Arkansas, were Ashley's allies and friends.

A different kind of land opportunity arose out of the Cherokee Treaty of 1828, which moved the Cherokees west of a line from Fort Smith to the southwest corner of Missouri. Arkansas gained the Cherokee land east of the line, but lost a large part of Lovely County, which extended well to the west of the new boundary and was home to some three hundred families. To compensate for their loss, Congress provided each family a "donation" of 320 acres to be located anywhere on the public domain of the territory. To qualify, a recipient had to be at least twenty-one years old, a head of

Chester Ashley, attorney, land speculator, and U.S. senator, 1844–48.
Courtesy of the Arkansas History Commission, Little Rock.

family, a settler of the area now belonging to the Cherokees on May 6, 1828, when the law was passed, and have moved from the Cherokee land since that time. Commissioner Graham of the General Land Office worried that these so-called donation claims were susceptible to abuse. He warned the land offices at Little Rock and Batesville that "with the limited knowledge which you possess in relation to their number and character of the settlers on the ceded lands, it will be exceedingly difficult to guard against fraud and imposition."

And he turned out to be right. Boys put pieces of paper in their shoes with "21" written on them so that witnesses could swear that they were "over 21"; white men who lived with the Cherokees came back to Arkansas Territory long enough to file for a claim of 320 acres and then returned to the Cherokee land; and boatmen who had traveled up the Arkansas River beyond Fort Smith claimed that they were residents of Lovely County. The *Arkansas Gazette* announced happily that somewhere between four hundred and six hundred claims of 320 acres each were established on the land where only three hundred families had lived. Woodruff pointed out that this would mean two thousand dollars in new tax monies collected annually, and it was acquired without the normal payment of about two hundred thousand dollars to the federal government, which would have served to "diminish the active capital of the Territory."

The donation concept was popular with the legislature as well. Indeed, three years before the donations to families displaced by the Cherokees were granted, the Arkansas legislature had petitioned for "some provision either in money or lands" for what it believed were three thousand Americans living west of the line drawn by the Choctaw Treaty of 1825. The Cherokee donation law prompted a new set of requests for donations. After noting that the settlers of Miller County and Crawford County had arrived earlier and had stayed longer than those in Lovely County, the assembly asked that the 320-acre donation be extended to the settlers south of Fort Smith who were displaced by the Choctaw Treaty. It also asked that donation claims be made available to settlers who had lost their homes because of the first Cherokee Treaty back in 1817. This request was repeated over a number of years, and the alleged victims of the treaty eventually were depicted as pioneers "driven again into the forest, without food, and almost without raiment, the loss of their homes, and their stock, reduc[ing] them to a chilling poverty." A still bolder territorial assembly request in 1829 asked Congress to grant 160 acres to each settler who would take up residence within twenty-four miles of the frontier. This proposal was made on the grounds that the federal government had an interest in securing the land against Native Americans, because "the bold and fearless savage knows no law, but that of force."

The territorial assembly also asked for other improvements in the land system, particularly the extension of preemption privileges. The right to use government land and then purchase one's improvements was viewed in Arkansas as an essential element of economic security on the frontier, as a protection against speculators, and as a reward for pioneers who had suffered hardships extending the dominion of the United States. Even when Congress did pass a general preemption law in 1830, the legislature asked for an extension of the requirement that settlers file claims within one year. In 1833, it asked that the price of land be reduced, claiming that the current policy created resentment on the part of the west toward the east. The legislature also made various requests for grants of land in order to finance the creation of public buildings and institutions—a statehouse, a university, a penitentiary, county courthouses, and county jails.

The need for transportation improvements also gave rise to petitions. The major public works project of the 1820s was the so-called Military

Road, which ran from Memphis to Little Rock through the swampy eastern section of the state. The road was completed in 1831, but portions of it continued to wash out in high water; Congress appropriated more funds, however, and a few years later the overland trip from Memphis to Little Rock was much improved. Between 1829 and 1835, the territorial assembly petitioned for a network of roads that would have linked all of the population centers in the territory. It also requested improvements in water transportation, supporting the continuing federal effort to remove the Red River Raft, asking for the removal of the snags and sawyers that obstructed navigation on the Arkansas River and other waterways of the territory, and even calling for the construction of a canal that would connect Bayou Bartholomew with the Mississippi River.

To the legislators in Little Rock, these requests seemed reasonable in view of what Arkansas brought to the nation: "To Arkansas the general government have indeed been extremely liberal, but from Arkansas the general government may hereafter reasonably expect more than millions for remuneration. Her minds [sic], her navigable streams, her rich and fertile regions and her mild and temperate climate all bespeak her future importance to the government and proclaim the grand stand she must eventually take as a member of the union." Washington seems to have agreed, at least to some degree, since Congress did pass a great deal of legislation to benefit the territory. With respect to transportation alone, territorial Arkansas received $666,000, including $267,000 spent on the Memphis to Little Rock Road and $216,000 on the removal of the Red River Raft.

While it distributed less largess, the hand of territorial government lay lightly on the people. The general assembly devoted much of its time to creating new counties and petitioning Congress. Remarkably little substantive legislation was passed beyond essential elements, such as creating a structure of taxation and a body of law dealing with slavery. Transportation, probably the most pressing need of the territory, was left up to the national government. Local government was largely in the hands of county courts, who were empowered to deal with matters of probate and the administration of estates, the assessment and collection of taxes, the granting of licenses to merchants, tavern keepers, and others, and the building and repair of roads and bridges. Exactly how much activity resulted from all this is not clear, but the condition of territorial roads reflected little effort.

Justice was dispensed at the county level by circuit courts presided over by individual judges of the superior court. Friedrich Gerstäcker attended a court session at Perryville, near the Fourche LaFave River. The town contained only one store, and the court was held in the home of the postmaster, who was also a ferryman. The judge, a prosecuting attorney, and at least one other lawyer had ridden out from Little Rock to conduct the legal proceedings. They sat around two tables pushed together for the occasion, and the jury of local landowners occupied a bench along one wall. After hearing the evidence and arguments in an assault case, the twelve men retired to deliberate in a stable. Normally they would have gone outside, but it was raining. A second case, involving a man accused of shooting and eating someone else's cow, was dealt with in a similar manner. These primitive but legal proceedings were sometimes dispensed with entirely. On another occasion, for example, Gerstäcker watched a group of men tie a horse thief to a tree and beat him nearly senseless. Only the pleas of spectators prevented the vigilantes from adding hanging to the victim's punishment.

The question of statehood for Arkansas was raised in August 1830 by the *Arkansas Advocate,* which supported the Crittenden party. Editor Charles Bertrand noted that the Census of 1830 would show that the territory had grown substantially and was ready to end what he called its "Territorial vassalage." Statehood, he argued, was the "only means of sundering our shackles and giving us the rights and rank to which we are entitled." "Aristides" wrote a letter supporting the paper's position, claiming that statehood would give Arkansas "independence" and would lead to a dramatic increase in population. News that the Chickasaw Indians were to be moved west led the *Advocate* to worry that they might be put in Arkansas unless the territory protected itself by becoming a state.

"Henry," a correspondent in the *Arkansas Gazette,* offered a practical response to the *Advocate*'s enthusiasm. He pointed out that the federal government paid $20,000 in salaries for the territorial governor, secretary, judges, and legislators of the territory. In addition to paying these salaries itself if it became a state, Arkansas would need to pay $15,000 for a constitutional convention, $10,000 to redeem territorial scrip, and $26,000 for public buildings. New taxes would be required, and he was not "willing to see the last cow and calf or the last bed and blanket sold from the poor settlers of the country" to satisfy the ambitions of those who wanted statehood. "Henry" ridiculed the "fanciful" views of "Aristides" about the benefits of statehood and called for patience: "Let us first procure a comfortable living for our families and prepare to take upon ourselves a state sovereignty."

These views of "Henry" reflected those of the Sevier party. Woodruff, the *Arkansas Gazette*'s editor, responded to the *Advocate*'s Bertrand by noting that the Chickasaws could not legally be located in an existing territory and by asserting that it was foolish to talk about statehood until Arkansas had the necessary population. Ambrose Sevier also addressed the "excitable question" in April 1831, as he announced his candidacy for re-election as territorial delegate. Claiming the Congress would want a population of fifty thousand, Sevier said Arkansas had no immediate opportunity to apply for statehood. His position on the matter was similar to that of "Henry." "Taxed high and deeply in debt, I believe we are pursuing our true interest by remaining as we are . . . In the absence of your instructions," he would be "disposed to oppose" statehood until Arkansas was out of debt and had both the necessary population and "the means to support a State Government."

Three years later, however, Sevier ignored his earlier position and requested that the U.S. House Committee on Territories look into the possibility of making Arkansas a state. He explained the circumstances in a long letter to his constituents. Since the Missouri Compromise, Congress had always balanced new slave states with new free states. Michigan was now applying for admission, and if Arkansas did not act, Florida might become the slave state to balance Michigan, leaving Arkansas to wait perhaps twenty-five years for Wisconsin to be ready to apply for statehood. Moreover, the delegate believed "this not an unfavorable opportunity for our admission." Arkansas should be able to escape "trammels upon the subject of slavery," strike a good bargain with respect to its natural resources, and have Congress finish up the most important "works of internal improvements." Still, Sevier was quite concerned about the population of Arkansas and its "embarrassed condition," apparently a reference to the poor state of territorial finances. Were it not for Michigan, in his opinion, "it would be the wiser policy to defer our application for a few years yet to come."

The *Arkansas Gazette* quickly reversed itself and backed Sevier. William Woodruff excused the delegate for going against his pledge not to act without consulting the people: he had acted in the interest of Arkansas, had not bound Arkansans, and the argument for statehood was "strong and cogent." The editor called for debate on the issue, but what he got, and probably expected, was a chorus of approval that sounded much like the earlier position of the *Advocate*. "Seventy-Six" claimed that "there is something humiliating and revolting to the pride and spirit of freemen to be ruled by officers sent from a distance. It is too much like the condition of the old British colonies." "Hickory" asserted that statehood would move Arkansas from "weakness to strength—from poverty to wealth—as she increases in population so will she increase in riches."

The citizens of Arkansas began to unite in favor of statehood, but problems remained. The national Whig Party began to worry that the proposed new states would vote Democratic in 1836. Congress, therefore, authorized Arkansas and Michigan to count their residents to determine if they were eligible for statehood but not to draw up state constitutions. Eventually Michigan decided to write a constitution anyway and simply request statehood, and Arkansas adopted the same strategy, except that Governor Fulton refused to go along until he had the support of President Jackson. A major barrier was surmounted when a census conducted in 1835 gave Arkansas a population of 52,240, well over the 40,000 necessary for statehood.

In the fall, as Arkansas prepared its constitution, sectionalism became an important issue within the state. On one side were the lowlands of the south and east, characterized by the ownership of slaves, the production of cotton, and an incipient planter class; on the other were the highlands, where farms were smaller, slaves were fewer, and the white population more numerous than in the lowlands. These differences became significant in November 1835, when David Walker, a Whig leader from Fayetteville and the territorial legislator from Washington County, wrote a circular letter to his constituents claiming that lowland politicians were attempting to grab more than their share of representation at the constitutional convention. Some legislators from the "east and south," which had a smaller white population, had argued that because their section had more wealth than the north and west, it should receive "additional representation equal to three-fifths of their slave population." In the ensuing debate, the lowland representatives called for representation by "districts" that would be "independent of population," while most of the legislators from the north and west claimed that "the only true basis of representation was the freemen of the country." A week after Walker's letter, another was published in the *Gazette* by a writer calling himself "Senex," who accused the Washington County writer of attempting "to excite discord and sectional jealousies," but confirmed the existence of sectionalism. "Senex" claimed that the apportionment problem had been solved when "the grand divisions" of the country had been given equal representation, and he defined the sections as Walker had. The lowland legislators had gotten what they wanted.

The representation of geographic sections was also an issue in the constitutional convention. This time the state senate was apportioned by districts positioned in relationship to what the *Gazette* called "the imaginary line which some demagogues have attempted to draw through the Territory (or State that shortly is to be)." Eight senators would come from the northern and western side of the line, eight from the southern and eastern side, and one from a center district that included Pulaski County, with the capital city of Little Rock, and its neighbors Saline and White Counties. The lowland south and east in this division had only three-fourths as many white people as did the highland north and west, but it had twice as many slaves. It also produced twelve times as much cotton per capita, and its taxpayers, on average, were almost three times as wealthy. The center district would be dominated by Pulaski County, which was much more populous than its neighbors and very politically sophisticated. Pulaski County did not grow a lot of cotton, but it had a very significant slave population and a good deal of wealth, and it was tied into the economic and political system of the south and east. The Arkansas senate, apportioned on the basis of carefully structured districts, was designed to protect the wealth of the most economically successful group in the territory.

After a long struggle, the Jacksonian Democrats in Washington succeeded in bringing Arkansas into the Union in June 1836. The change may have been premature. Delegate Sevier's reservations about statehood were cogent, and the need to pair with Michigan did not make them less so. Arkansas was still new and sparsely settled. During the territorial period, it had relied heavily on the national government. Statehood was an achievement, but it was also a challenge.

CHAPTER THREE

Agricultural Success
and Banking Failure

Charles Grier Sellers' influential study, *The Market Revolution*, argues that dual economies existed in early America. Settlers along the Atlantic Seaboard were imbued with the commercial capitalism of the eighteenth century and traded in a market that stretched throughout the Atlantic Ocean. Backcountry Americans, however, were involved in subsistence agriculture, feeding themselves by applying the labor of large families to the abundant land and by exchanging services and homemade goods with their neighbors. According to Sellers, subsistence was the goal of the pioneers who moved west in the early years of the American republic. After the War of 1812, however, the market moved inland. The national government assisted in the process, enacting a tariff to aid fledgling factories and making halting attempts to provide a system of transportation that would reduce the cost of moving goods and commodities. Because the Democratic-Republican Party remained tied to Jefferson's parsimonious view of constitutional power, however, the states and the free market wrought most of the necessary changes.

Robert Fulton's first steamboat proved itself on the Hudson River in 1807, and others like it were operating in the Mississippi River basin within a decade. As a result, cotton and other commodities could be carried downriver faster than before, and the wares of New Orleans could be transported against the current to the towns and plantations of the

Mississippi and its tributaries. New York State built the Erie Canal between 1818 and 1825, making it possible for settlers in the Great Lakes' region of the Northwest to ship flour and beef to New York City and receive the latest manufactured goods in return. Other canals and new roads continued the process of linking Americans together, and by the 1850s the railroad was also playing a substantial role in the same unifying process. Increasingly, it would make more sense for farmers in the Mississippi basin to produce specialized cash crops, sell them, and use the money to buy merchandise from a store, rather than making do with domestic or neighborhood production.

Subsistence agriculture kept Arkansans eating throughout the territorial and statehood periods. Corn and livestock were also produced for the market, but cotton slowly emerged as the cash crop of the state. Agricultural production led to economic success, but Arkansans did little to nurture more growth. The territorial legislature successfully solicited transportation improvements from the federal government, and Arkansas benefited from national programs to improve the navigation of rivers, one of which led to the removal in the 1830s of the Red River Raft, a hundred miles of fallen trees and vegetation that clogged the river below Shreveport. After achieving statehood, Arkansas attempted to create a system of banks, which might have spurred economic growth, but the effort was a failure that left only large debts and a suspicion about future financial projects. Transportation, the sinew of the market economy, languished.

* * *

The national market made its presence known in Arkansas on March 31, 1820, when the steamboat *Comet* docked at Arkansas Post. Agriculture in the new territory was in its infancy. Many households lived primarily on hunting, but the settlers typically tended a small cornfield and raised a few pigs to vary their diet. Flatboats and keelboats connected these early Arkansans with the commerce of the Mississippi River, carrying animal skins and agricultural commodities downstream and hauling small amounts of supplies and manufactured goods back up. The steamboats that came to Arkansas Post—and soon to Batesville and Little Rock—made commercial agriculture a much more attractive possibility. Cotton began to flourish on the bottomland along the Mississippi River, the Arkansas River, the White River, and the Red River. By 1840, Arkansas was heavily involved in market activities, even as the sparsely settled state remained a paradise for hunters.

Friedrich Gerstäcker described the subsistence economy of the backwoods. While visiting a fellow German named Hilger on the Little Red River early in 1838, Gerstacker ended up staying the night with a Polish settler named Turoski. The accommodations were crude but utilitarian: "The Pole's dwelling was nothing but a simple rough log-house, without any window . . . Two beds, a table, a couple of chairs, one of them with arms, some iron saucepans, three plates, two tin pots, one saucer, several knives, and a coffee-mill, formed the whole of his furniture and kitchen utensils." Next to his house, Turoski had a storehouse for meat. A cultivated field of four or five acres was nearby and another was located near the river a quarter of a mile away. His livestock included "several good horses, a great many pigs, quantities of fowls, and several milch cows."

Turoski was a bachelor, but Hilger had a family that was important to his role as a subsistence farmer. On another visit the following year, Gerstäcker noted that Hilger "had made vast improvements in his condition." He had been a squatter but now had bought his land. He owned "a pair of horses, several head of cattle and pigs." Most important, he "lived happy and independent in the circle of his family," which had increased with the birth of another child. Hilger's older sons, aged thirteen and fifteen, "worked hard with their father to make their way in the world happily and honestly."

The Hilger boys probably spent much of their summer in the cornfield, helping with the crop that was the basis of their subsistence. Hunting families raised corn in small clearings, family farmers like the Hilgers grew corn extensively, and it was cultivated by slaves on plantations. Southerners ate corn at almost every meal, in a variety of ways, and they also fed it to their animals. Economic historian Sam Hillard estimates that every adult in the South ate about 13 bushels of corn annually, each horse was fed 7.5 bushels, and hogs devoured 4 bushels a piece. Corn was grown all over Arkansas, although it was a more important crop in the highlands than in the lowlands. In addition to being the basis of subsistence, it was a cash crop that could be sold to immigrants or to the army. By the time of the 1840 Census, Arkansas was producing nearly 50 bushels of corn per person, as compared to Missouri, which raised 45 bushels, and Tennessee, which grew 54. The Arkansas crop provided a surplus of about 1.9 million bushels over the state's needs, enough to feed 148,000 adults. Small amounts of potatoes were also grown throughout the state. Other minor crops were produced mostly in the highlands. Wheat was grown along the Missouri border, but not enough to prevent the importation of flour from Missouri. Washington County raised a significant amount of oats, and Searcy and Izard Counties produced tobacco. Fruits and vegetables were also raised for home consumption all over the state.

Livestock was also an important part of southern subsistence. Throughout the South, full-time herdsmen grazed cattle and hogs on the open range, an activity that was connected with the Celtic or North Briton heritage of many southerners. There probably were such herdsmen in Arkansas. Some owners of large cattle herds owned neither land nor slaves and may not have farmed at all. In most cases, however, livestock seems to have been connected with other agricultural activity. Households with larger herds of cattle usually owned larger holdings of land and often more slaves as well. The larger herds of cattle were also more likely to be found in the lowland, cotton-growing region of Arkansas, rather than in the small-farming, highland region. However the livestock industry was organized, it was very large. Arkansas had more horses, cattle, and swine per capita than any of its surrounding states. By 1840 there were two head of cattle for each person in the state, and three-quarters of the people who owned any taxable wealth at all had at least one cow. Cattle were not very valuable, however. The average assessed value of Arkansas cattle in 1840 was only twelve dollars, while that of horses was sixty-three dollars. Part of the reason was that Arkansans usually followed an open-range policy, providing little food for the animals, giving them no shelter, and making no effort to improve them by selective breeding. The results were that the cattle were small and the cows gave little milk.

Southerners ate about four times as much pork as they did beef, and swine were raised all over Arkansas, though they were somewhat more numerous in the highlands, in the same pattern as corn. The 1840 Census indicated that there were four hogs in the state for every human. Hillard estimates that southerners consumed 150 pounds of pork per year, that the average swine would provide 140 pounds of meat, and that half of the hogs could be butchered annually. Given these numbers, after Arkansans ate their full, they could feed another 110,000 adults for a year. Hogs could also be sold, usually at about $3.50 a piece.

While some Arkansans were involved in a subsistence economy, others were growing the great cash crop of the South and were very attuned to the market and its values. Even as early as 1822, the *Arkansas Gazette* could remark on "the general disposition which prevails among our citizens to cultivate . . . large crops of cotton." The following year Thomas Eskridge, a superior court judge and Hempstead County planter, wrote a letter to the same paper extolling the advantages of Arkansas with respect to "climate, soil, and navigation." Eskridge described the whole state and its agricultural potential, but his emphasis was on cotton. With more than a little exaggeration, he claimed that the existing settlers of the territory "were people from the slave-holding states, . . . correct in their morals, kind and liberal among one another, and hospitable to strangers." Hoping to attract more of the southern gentlemen he described, Eskridge praised the benefits of his own Red River region, where the soil was capable of producing fifteen hundred pounds of cotton to the acre and earning a planter three hundred dollars in annual profit from each able-bodied slave. By 1825, the *Gazette* was referring to cotton as the "staple production of our Territory." In December of that year, a correspondent from Arkansas Post described the bustle in that town as steamboats loaded the cotton produced along the lower Arkansas River. Frederick Notrebe, a wealthy merchant, was paying cash for bales of cotton that he would ship to New Orleans on his own account.

In 1840 Arkansas produced about 62 pounds of cotton per capita, a significant amount, but much smaller than the 433 pounds per capita produced in Louisiana or the 514 pounds per capita in Mississippi. Most of the staple came from a rather small number of counties located along navigable rivers in the lowlands: Chicot and Phillips Counties on the Mississippi River, Arkansas and Jefferson Counties on the Arkansas River, Union and Clark Counties on the Ouachita, and Lafayette, Sevier, and Hempstead Counties along the Red. Two counties, Chicot in the southeast and Lafayette in the southwest, produced 40 percent of Arkansas's cotton.

By this time, four years after statehood, Arkansas had an agricultural economy with distinctive characteristics. Almost all the state's taxpayers were farmers. About one-third of them owned their own land, while the rest squatted on the abundant land owned by the government with the assurance that they could buy it at some time in the future. Horses and cattle were ubiquitous, with the average taxpayer owning two of the former and five of the latter. Regional differences were apparent. The farmers of the highlands owned only 43 percent as many acres as their lowland counterparts and only 30 percent as many slaves. Their taxable wealth, consisting mostly of the assessed value of land, slaves, horses, and cattle, was only 36 percent of the wealth of those who lived in the lowlands. Two somewhat different societies were emerging. The highlands area was becoming a society of small farmers, many of them subsistence farmers, while the lowlands region was gradually developing a small class of market-oriented planters.

The commercial development associated with agricultural progress is less well documented. George W. Featherstonhaugh claimed that there were five or six hundred people in Little Rock in the mid-1830s and that the gainfully employed among them were mechanics, "lawyers and doctors without number," and numerous "tradesmen going by the name of merchants." Featherstonhaugh was often unkind in describing Arkansas society, but he was probably right about the businessmen of Little Rock. The capital city exerted a profound political influence over Arkansas, but it did not exercise commercial domination. Indeed, Pulaski County, in which Little Rock was located, ranked only third according to the Census of 1840 in terms of capital invested in merchandise.

At the top of the list was Crawford County, to the west, where the community of Fort Smith had grown up to serve the needs of the army and of the Native Americans, who were being resettled just across the Arkansas border in Indian Territory. In the same county, on the other side of the Arkansas River and six miles downstream, was the town of Van Buren, whose merchants served an agricultural hinterland that stretched north to Fayetteville. Steamboats landing at Van Buren brought goods from New Orleans and Cincinnati and provided Arkansas farmers with a means of getting their crops into the expanding market. In the extreme northwest, Washington County, whose seat was Fayetteville, was the third-largest commercial center. Ideal agricultural conditions had brought a rush of settlers into northwest Arkansas in the 1830s, putting nearly one-tenth of the state's population within the orbit of Fayetteville's wholesale and retail merchants.

The records of a Van Buren company, Henry and Cunningham, provide some insight into the commerce of Arkansas in the early 1840s. Because Van Buren was on the Arkansas River, Henry and Cunningham acted as a wholesale agent for small business firms in northwest Arkansas. In July 1843, for example, H. J. Wilson, who had a store in Benton County, received a shipment that included "copperas" (an ingredient in ink), pepper, salt, brimstone, alum, saleratus (a leavening agent), ginger, and oil of vitriol. At the same time, the firm received goods destined for three different retailers in the community of Cane Hill, located some twenty miles southwest of Fayetteville. J. B. Russell had ordered four barrels of sugar, four sacks of coffee, ten sacks of salt, and one keg of powder. M. Wright, who must have had a different sort of shop, was getting dry goods, hats, "domestics" (probably textiles), and a barrel of "palm hats." W. B. Sutton had ordered domestics also and a large quantity of sugar and a small amount of "pepper sauce." The following year Russell sent Henry and Cunningham 1,624 pounds of "superfine" flour that was "neatly sacked up," for which he wanted credit at the rate of $2.50 per 100 pounds. He also included $30 in specie and "a little Bacon," for which he also wanted credit. Russell asked Henry and Cunningham to send him, by wagon presumably, some "tin Plate" that he had ordered and 100 pounds of iron in bars.

While there were centers of business activity, the river system of Arkansas created a decentralized market. In west Arkansas, for example, Clarksville, which had become the county seat of Johnson County in 1836, was a small business center located on the Arkansas River between the larger markets of Little Rock and Van Buren. Helena, in Phillips County on the Mississippi River, served one of the more important cotton-growing areas in the state. From 1837 a designated river front in Helena was available for steamboats, which could take up to three days to load and unload, and a nearby area was also provided for flatboats and keelboats. Batesville was the political and cultural capital of northeast Arkansas during the territorial period, but it was located inconveniently high on the White River. Jacksonport, which grew up in the 1830s downstream from Batesville where the White River was joined by the Black River, was accessible to steamboats for a larger portion of the year, and it eventually siphoned off a significant amount of trade that had previously gone to Batesville. Washington, the county seat of Hempstead County in southwest Arkansas, was located on the Southwest Trail, not far from the Red River. Abraham Block's store was the largest in town, but there were other shops and services.

Some Arkansas trade may have bypassed all these local centers. In 1842 John Meek wrote a letter explaining how much he liked living in Union County, Arkansas, including the fact that "New Orleans is as it were at our Door." And indeed it was, at least when there was enough water in the Ouachita. A few years later, Meek's son wrote about a harrowing journey during which one steamboat burned on the Alabama River and another gave him an unpleasant ride in heavy seas across the coast to the New Orleans. From the Crescent City to Union County, however, the trip went quickly and well, and he left the Ouachita River within five miles of his father's home.

In 1836, during its first session after statehood, the legislature of Arkansas created two banks, a Real Estate Bank and a Bank of Arkansas, or the State Bank as it was called. The recently adopted constitution had expressly provided for both institutions, a testament to the depth of sentiment on their behalf. Arkansans were concerned that specie, particularly the large sums spent on federal lands, was leaving their state to be deposited in the banks of Tennessee, Mississippi, and Louisiana. They were also anxious to provide capital for the development of the local economy. Despite these laudable aims, both banks soon failed, with serious and long-term consequences. Much of the problem lay with the institutions themselves and with the manner in which they were administered. Banking enthusiasts in Arkansans, like those in many states, were in a hurry to make money and were not very sensitive to the risks they were taking. Moreover, in the case of Arkansas banking, the risks were usually absorbed by the state, while the profit often belonged to the individual. It is also true that Arkansas launched its banks during the Panic of 1837, a major downturn felt throughout the American economy that devastated commodity prices and land values, ruined many banks and businesses, and brought wide unemployment among eastern workers.

The Real Estate Bank was designed to provide the benefits of banking to Arkansas planters. Shares in the institution could be purchased with land, crops, and improvements, which would then become the collateral for bonds that were issued and backed by the state but sold and redeemed by the bank. The bank would use the proceeds from the sale of bonds to make loans, and each stockholder could borrow up to one-half the value of his shares in the institution. Thus the capital of the bank was agricultural real estate and commodities, forms of wealth that were subject to the vagaries of weather and demand.

In order to turn its agricultural assets into money, the Real Estate Bank depended on the state to guarantee the bonds, thereby attracting investors who might otherwise have been reluctant to invest in cotton and cotton land. Moreover, the reputation of the state was tied to an institution over which it had very little control. The Real Estate Bank consisted of a central board, which sold the bonds and oversaw the general operation of the institution, and local branches, which were relatively autonomous. The governor of the state appointed two of nine directors for each branch, and the stockholders elected the rest. The directors of each branch than chose two of their members, one of them an appointed director, to sit on the central board. The law required that the president of the central board, who was chosen by its members, report to the legislature at its request and provide information when asked. There was no other oversight.

The constitution of 1836 had referred to the need for a bank to "promote the great agricultural interests of the country," but the Real Estate Bank had little interest in the abundant corn and livestock of Arkansas. Cotton was its focus. The principal office of the bank was to be at Little Rock, while it had branches at Washington in Hempstead County, Columbia in Chicot County, and Helena in Phillips County, all in the southern and eastern lowlands of Arkansas where cotton was grown in large amounts. By November 1837, the Real Estate Bank had accepted mortgages on 127,500 acres of land valued at $2,600,000, all of it in thirteen lowland counties. In return for these assets, the bank had issued 22,500 shares of stock in certificates of $100 each. Citizens of Chicot County, rich in slaves and cotton, received 28 percent of the stock, and other counties along the Mississippi River and along the Red River also received large amounts. Already, however, dissatisfaction was growing among legislators from the northern and western parts of the state. In addition to their belief that the bank was benefiting only the lowlands, there was a concern that it was being improperly managed. The average value for the mortgaged land was about $20 per acre, which seemed an inflated assessment. Cotton land was valuable, but less than 12 percent of the acres used to acquire bank stock were actually in cultivation.

During the summer of 1838, U.S. Sen. Ambrose Sevier and the new speaker of the Arkansas house, Thomas T. Williamson of Lafayette County, sold $500,000 worth of bonds to the U.S. Treasury and $1,500,000 to the North American Trust and Banking Company. The Real Estate Bank opened its doors for business that December and immediately began to make loans, first to stockholders and then to the general public. Early in 1839, the stock of the bank was trading at a premium, and a new branch opened in Washington in southwest Arkansas. Later in 1839, however, economic conditions worsened throughout the nation, and the impact began to be felt in Arkansas. In November, the Helena branch of the Real Estate Bank suspended specie payment on its notes. As late as May 1841, however, the central board remained positive about the outlook for the bank. It had withdrawn $300,000 in notes and ordered that unissued notes be destroyed. Meanwhile, however, a new problem emerged.

During 1840, the central board of the Real Estate Bank had sent commissioners to eastern bankers in order to secure a loan so that the bank could pay interest due in January 1841. Five hundred $1,000 bonds were sent as collateral. The Arkansas commissioners borrowed $250,000 from the North American Trust and Banking Company, receiving $121,000 immediately and the rest in credit, and turned over the bonds, giving North American Trust and Banking the power to sell them, but apparently only if the Real Estate Bank defaulted on the loan. Using bonds as security for a loan—a process known as hypothecation—was not uncommon in financial circles, but in most cases the collateral was not physically transferred to the lender. Doing so proved to be a significant error for Arkansas. An official at North American Trust and Banking took the bonds to London and sold them for $350,000 to J. Holford and Company, an investment banking firm. In the summer of 1841, Arkansas commissioners again went to New York, this time to pay $125,000 on the bank's debt and to redeem 250 of the bonds. After learning that the bonds were not available and that the financial condition of North American Trust and Banking had deteriorated to the point that it could not provide the remaining credit, the Arkansans went home without making the payment.

In October, the Real Estate Bank claimed that it was not responsible for paying off the five hundred "Holford Bonds," as they were now called. James Holford, the English owner of the securities, appealed to Gov. Archibald Yell, claiming that the good faith of the state of Arkansas was involved. Yell pointed out, however, that the charter of the Real Estate Bank had authorized the sale of bonds but not their hypothecation. By giving up the bonds without selling them, the bank appeared to have violated its own charter. If this were so, suggested the governor, the state should not be obligated to pay a debt arising from what was in effect an illegal contract. Yell also emphasized the fact that the bank had only received $121,000 in return for the $500,000 in bonds. He would not commit the state to any specific action: "Arkansas is free to act, as she shall deem fit and correct." Eventually the Arkansas Supreme Court ruled that the acceptance by the Real Estate Bank of the $121,000 meant that Arkansas was liable for the bonds, regardless of the impropriety of the transaction. Still, the state did nothing to pay off the loan, the interest on the loan, or the bonds until 1868, and provisions that were made in that year were repudiated in 1885.

The situation of the State Bank was not much better. This institution was an agency of the state, whose directors were to be elected by the legislature. It was to secure capital by selling state bonds, but it would also be a repository for state funds. The bank's loans and notes would be based on specie, and its obligations could not exceed three times its capital. Notes of the State Bank could be used to pay debts owed to the state. Unlike the Real Estate Bank, the services of the State Bank were available to the entire state. Between one-quarter and one-half of the loans made by the bank were to be apportioned among Arkansas counties in the same ratio as their representation in the legislature. Its headquarters were in Little Rock, but two of its four branches were in highland communities, Fayetteville in the northwest and Batesville in the northeast, while the other two were in the lowland towns of Arkansas Post and Washington.

The State Bank began operation in an atmosphere of enthusiasm. A senate report in the fall of 1837 talked about the potential of "foreign capital" to mobilize "the elements of wealth that lie scattered in profusion around us" and the duty of government to assist in starting up "the springs of enterprise." Noting that the bank had not obligated more than half its specie, the legislature called upon it to issue $200,000 in notes between the beginning of December and the April 1, 1838. William Field was elected as the new president and re-elected the following year. In 1839 a new branch of the State Bank was created at Washington, Arkansas.

Once again, however, problems developed with the sale of bonds. Arkansas senators Sevier and William S. Fulton were asked to sell 200 bonds in Washington, D.C. Of these, 170 were returned unsold, but 30 were disposed of on credit to Richard Mentor Johnson, the vice-president of the United States, who was also an uncle of Sevier's wife. Johnson had given a mortgage on forty slaves and some land, but the mortgage had not been recorded and was therefore void. Sevier argued that he had been appointed commissioner without his knowledge, that he had made nothing on the sale, and that Johnson had asked for additional time to make the payment, but heard nothing from Little Rock. Fulton claimed that sickness had prevented him from bringing the deed to be recorded, that he was unaware that the recording had to take place within three months, and that he intended to get another mortgage from Johnson.

Soon the slowly spreading ripples of the national depression began to inundate Arkansas banking. Early in 1840 the notes of both Arkansas banks were being discounted in New Orleans by up to 30 percent. Debtors within the state began to fall behind in their payments, and creditors began to institute law suits. Governor Yell's inaugural address pledged to "bring your depreciated State paper to a sound specie standard; or lay the axe at the root of the evil." He also pointed out that the salaries of bank officials had been increased to offset the declining value of bank notes and called for an investigation of the banks. The legislature established a committee to look into the operation of both banks. Its report claimed that the State Bank had no responsibility for a recent suspension of specie payments, which was related to national economic problems. It did say that the Little Rock branch had loaned too much money in Pulaski County and too much to the directors of the bank. The committee believed, however, that both the State Bank and the Real Estate Bank were in a sound position. What was needed was more public confidence. The legislature directed the State Bank to lower the salaries of its officials, limit the loans it made to directors, and resume specie payments whenever that was done by the banks in neighboring states.

In May 1841, public confidence was further shaken. The books of the Fayetteville branch had been stolen, and when they were recovered the cash transactions had been ripped out. The bank now had about twenty-two thousand dollars less than when specie payments had been suspended. Cashier William Mck Ball claimed that he had overreported the specie with the approval of the directors, but they denied it. These mysterious events became clearer in the late summer, when Mck Ball fled to Texas.

Meanwhile, Arkansans began to seek protection under the federal bankruptcy act of 1841 and to use other measures to protect themselves. "Chicot John Smith," writing in the *Arkansas Gazette* of March 30, argued that the bank should redeem its currency first and pay bondholders later, thus helping people living within the state. On May 20 men barricaded themselves in the Phillips County Court House in Helena to prevent the circuit court from bringing action against debtors. Rather than face the angry public, the sheriff and coroner resigned, and the judge left town. By December, however, the court was operating again and judgments against debtors were being executed.

In 1842, the legislature began the process of closing down the State Bank, denying it the power to make new loans and selecting receivers to carry out a liquidation. Assets of the banks were to be used first to retire currency and then to pay interest on state bonds. As late as 1845, the Batesville branch was instituting some suits against its debtors, but it got little relief from the courts. Some of the banks' debtors did manage to pay their loans; others simply went to Texas to start over. Eventually the Batesville bank liquidated its assets at very low values. Its building, constructed at a cost of $15,000, was sold for $100.

In his first message to the legislature in 1846, Gov. Thomas Drew discussed the banking problems of Arkansas with a longer perspective. He claimed that the Real Estate Bank owed $1,622,000 in principal and $517,000 in interest, a sum that was increasing at the rate of $97,000 per year. When the bank was liquidated in April 1842, it had assets of

$2,400,000, but their value in 1846 was closer to $2,000,000. The State Bank owed $1,477,940, with accrued interest of $331,000 and annual interest of $67,000. It had other liabilities of $490,000. Its assets were estimated at $1,753,000, but these assets included $1,200,00 in Real Estate Bank notes. Drew believed that the state was liable for only $395,000 of State Bank debts and a smaller but unspecified amount for the Real Estate Bank. The situation had not improved much when Gov. John Selden Roane addressed the legislature in 1860, and he gave little hope to holders of Arkansas bonds: "We acknowledge the justness of the liability, and frankly say we are unable to pay."

Following Governor Drew's message in 1846, the Arkansas legislature had adopted a constitutional amendment to prohibit the future "incorporation or establishment" of banks within the state. The short and unhappy history of banking in Arkansas must have seemed ample justification for the action. On the other hand, unless Arkansans were willing to turn their backs on the market, financial institutions of some sort were necessary. Without its own banks, Arkansas would be at the mercy of those in other states.

Despite the banking fiasco, Arkansas enjoyed a great deal of economic development during the two decades from 1840 to 1860. The most important aspects of this growth were the emergence of lowland Arkansas as a center of cotton production and the maturation of the plantation society that had been only incipient during the territorial period. Population growth tells part of the story. In 1860 Arkansas had four and a half times its 1840 population, a total of 435,000 persons. The slave population numbered 111,000, 26 percent of the whole, rather than the 20 percent it had been in 1840. The lowland counties had 52 percent of the total population in 1840 but 59 percent in 1860. They also were home to an impressive 87 percent of the slaves.

Some evidence for economic growth and its sectional differences comes from the changing structure of landownership. In 1840 nearly two-thirds of Arkansas taxpayers did not own any land at all. Most of them were squatters, farming acreage that belonged to the government, but which they had a preemption right to purchase in the future. By 1860, the landless taxpayers had dropped to 42 percent for the state as a whole, but that average reflected a figure of 49 percent in the highlands and 38 percent in the lowlands. There was much less squatting in Arkansas on the eve of the Civil War, particularly in the cotton-producing areas, where land was more valuable. The median amount of land owned by Arkansans in 1860 was 165 acres, reflecting the continued significance of subsistence farming throughout the state. Landholdings were larger in the lowlands, however, where 15 percent of taxpayers owned at least 600 acres as compared with only 5 percent of those in the highlands.

The increasingly market-oriented specialization of Arkansas is illustrated by the changing patterns of commodity production and the ownership of agricultural property. In 1840, Arkansas produced fifteen bales of cotton for each one hundred persons in the state; by 1860, it produced eighty-four bales for each one hundred persons, a per capita increase of more than five times. This growth was related to the larger number of slaves in Arkansas and their concentration in the hands of cotton planters. Nineteen percent of Arkansas taxpayers owned slaves in 1840, and the same was true in 1860; by the latter date, however, this privileged group held many more slaves than it had twenty years earlier. In 1860, there were 1,358 slave owners who owned more than twenty slaves, enough to think of themselves as planters. This group made up nearly 12 percent of all slaveholders, up from 9 percent in 1850, the earliest year for which data is available. As Arkansas came more and more to be characterized by cotton and slavery, subsistence crops became less important in overall production. Corn production per capita dropped 17 percent between 1840 and 1860; the ownership of horses fell 15 percent; and cattle and swine were one-third less numerous in the more commercial economy than they had been in the more subsistence economy of 1840.

Historian Carl Moneyhon argues that specialization can be measured in terms of the corn-to-cotton ratio, that is, the number of bushels of corn produced by a county for each bale of cotton. A smaller amount of corn in the ratio indicates less attention to subsistence and an increasing amount of specialization in the staple crop. In 1850 only Chicot County had a ratio of fewer than twenty-five bushels to a single bale, but by 1860 Desha, Phillips, Arkansas, and Jefferson Counties were also in that category. This center of cotton growing in the southeast part of the state was augmented by counties to the north (Crittenden, St. Francis, Monroe, Prairie, and Pulaski) and to the west (Bradley, Calhoun, Union, Dallas, Ouachita, Columbia, Hempstead, Lafayette, and Sevier), where the bushels per bale ranged from twenty-six to fifty.

Moneyhon also illustrates the domination of the planting class over the lowlands region by 1860. Defining plantations as agricultural units with twenty slaves or more, he finds that Chicot County had 83 plantations with an average of eighty-one slaves each. The average size of the Chicot County

Arkansas Counties in 1860

plantations was 2,251 acres, and collectively they included 70 percent of all the taxable land in the county. Land and slaves were a little less concentrated in Phillips County, where there were 113 plantations with an average of forty-one slaves and 1,315 acres, taking up only 47 percent of the land in the county. Union County, drained by the Ouachita River and located on the Gulf Coastal Plain, was less developed than Chicot or Phillips County. Its forty-two planters owned an average of thirty-eight slaves and 2,019 acres. Their land was only 23 percent of all taxable acres. The planters made up 39 percent of all taxpayers in Chicot County, 16 percent in Phillips County, and 5 percent in Union County.

On occasion Arkansas planters could demonstrate impressive economic initiative. After a devastating flood in 1840, the large cotton producers of Chicot County decided that they needed levees to keep the Mississippi River from ruining their crops. That same year they pushed through a state law that empowered the county court to hire a levee commissioner to plan and construct a flood-protection system, to require labor and taxes from local residents for the work, and to enclose bayous and land set aside for schools. Beginning in 1841, the county court, led by Dr. Albert Webb of Columbia, began the work, which was planned and directed by the levee commissioner, Franklin Stuart.

The northern point of Chicot County's Mississippi River border was only thirty-nine miles above the southern border, but the meandering river and its local tributaries required 110 miles of levee. Stuart's plan called for an earthen structure, most of which would be either two and one-half feet high with a ten-foot base or three feet high with a twelve-foot base. The flat crown of the levee was as wide as the levee was high. Planters who lived along the river used the labor of their slaves to construct private levees according to Stuart's specifications. Tax assessments paid the contractors who built public levees to contain the bayous and enclose the school lands. Inland residents paid less, however, than those on the riverfront, who received the primary benefits of flood protection.

The Chicot County levee system was finished in two years, and it helped the county to achieve an economic success unparalleled in antebellum Arkansas. After 1850 the Swamp Land Act passed by the U.S. government encouraged other flood-protection works in Arkansas, but none of them were as successful as the efforts of the Chicot County planters.

The agricultural success of Arkansas was visible by 1860. The state's cotton crop brought an estimated $16 million. After feeding all the people in the state, there were probably enough bushels of corn left to earn more that $4 million. The value of butchered livestock was nearly $4 million, and the wheat crop added more than $1 million. A total of $25 million divided among the 435,450 people in Arkansas meant a per capita income of $57. Distributed among an estimated 64,838 white households, the total meant that each of them would have received $386. Of course, the wealth was not equally distributed; the cotton money went almost entirely to the lowlands, and the planters there received most of it.

Not everyone was happy or prosperous. Certainly there was more opportunity to obtain wealth in the lowlands, but even there problems abounded. Then there was the weather: too much rain seemed to alternate with inadequate rain. Arkansas rivers often flooded in the spring, wreaking havoc on farm improvements, destroying crops in low-lying fields, and even flooding homesteads on occasion. Roads were also a problem. The route to Memphis was still held hostage by the swampland in eastern Arkansas. In addition, many farmers and planters were plagued with debt. Setting oneself up as a planter could cost between $15,000 and

$36,000 for the necessary six hundred acres and between $20,000 and $40,000 for twenty slaves. Smaller farmers needed less money to get started, but their debts were just as difficult to repay. Confounding the credit problems was that fact that all financing came from outside the state, as did the small amount of money that was in circulation. Arkansas paid a price for its failure to develop an adequate banking system. Arkansas planters believed that they were at the mercy of commission merchants in New Orleans, and, indeed, the state as a whole was dependent on outside sources for many of the products and services that it used.

For better or worse, the economy of Arkansas remained almost entirely agricultural, but there were a few attempts at industrial development. The most successful venture was undertaken by Henry Merrell, who learned about factories in his native New York and went on to manage and own industrial enterprises in Georgia. In 1856, at the age of thirty-nine, Merrill moved to Arkansas and purchased land in Pike County. He intended to create a small manufacturing village whose machines would be powered by the Little Missouri River. The aspiring industrialist found some evidence of local business activity: John Matlock, a merchant in Camden, was successful enough to invest fifteen thousand dollars in Merrill's enterprise.

In the hills of southwest Arkansas, Merrell found subsistence farmers of the rudest sort. Pike County, according to the aspiring industrialist, was "well-nigh shoeless, hatless, and in rags." The people lived in "houses of logs, & very rude logs at that, scarcely higher than a man could stand up in, with stick & mud chimneys not a great deal taller than the man himself." They farmed small plots of land, and the failure of one crop left them destitute. Commerce consisted of the "exchange of deer skins and venison hams for a little powder and lead and Tobacco, and a very little 'seed tick' coffee." Several years earlier, many residents had attempted to grow cotton and had borrowed on future crops that did not materialize. After this disastrous experiment with the market, tattered trade goods were seen throughout the county: "The Northern brogan with several toes out making tracks in the mud, the silk hat rimless and crownless, and red tags of broad-cloth and calico here and there upon [the people]." The settlers were uneducated, but Merrell was impressed with their skill and ingenuity in using axes.

Despite formidable obstacles, Merrell created his industrial center. He purchased spinning and carding machinery from New Jersey and shipped it to Arkansas; he dammed the Little Missouri with a wood-frame, wedge-shaped structure that raised the water some ten feet. He proudly recalled the sequence in which the complex was constructed: "First, a store building & a house to live in, next a saw mill, then a grist mill, and flouring mill of three runs of burr stones. After that wool Carding machinery capable of carding into rolls 700 to 800 Pounds of Wool in twenty-four hours, and finally the Cotton-spinning factory, with dwellings, gardens, outhouses, & wells for the operatives; a black-smith ship and a shop for wood workmen." The work force was drawn from the farmers and hunters of Pike County and paid in supplies from the store. Within a year, Merrill's production was providing the area with sawn lumber, flour, wool, and cotton yarn. Early in 1858, a flood damaged his dam, and a fire the same year destroyed his home. Merrill persisted, however, until the Civil War came. Local hostility toward his Yankee origins, combined with jealousy at his success, forced him to sell out to his partner.

During the half century before the Civil War, the Arkansas economy developed in an impressive manner. As settlers entered first the territory and then the state, hunters and part-time farmers gave way to full-time subsistence farmers and then to commercial farmers and planters. Arkansans produced corn in impressive amounts and livestock in large numbers. The steamboat brought ready access to the market cities of the Mississippi River basin. Slowly but inexorably, cotton grew into a major crop that produced significant wealth for the lowland areas of the state. According to wealth statistics collected by the Census of 1860, Arkansas ranked sixteenth among the thirty-four states in terms of real estate and personal wealth per capita.

Despite this success, there were major problems. The transportation infrastructure of the state was poor, and its banking facilities were nonexistent. Another important economic problem was the reliance on cotton and the plantation system with its slave labor. With the clear vision afforded by hindsight, we can see that in 1860 too many of the state's economic eggs were in that highly vulnerable basket.

CHAPTER FOUR

Indian Frontier

The exuberance of Anglo-American expansion had its counterpoint in the pathos of Indian removal, and Arkansas played its role in the latter as it had in the former. When it became part of the United States in 1803, Arkansas contained relatively few Native Americans. The Quapaws, or "Arkansea," who had greeted Father Marquette and Louis Joliet on their arrival in 1673, still lived in their villages near the mouth of the Arkansas River, but they were pitifully few in number. European disease, European alcohol, and warfare undertaken on behalf of European allies had reduced the Quapaws from perhaps six thousand people who met the French explorers to about six hundred who greeted the American settlers.

Much more numerous were the Osages, who had lived on the Osage and Missouri Rivers in the eighteenth century. Males of the tribe were fierce hunters and warriors who hunted and stole horses in the Arkansas and Red River valleys, often attacking Quapaw and European hunting parties. Osage violence was small in scale but deadly. Often it was the result of a mourning war, in which Osage warriors attempted to avenge a dead comrade and provide company for his soul by killing the first non-Osage that they found. The Osages had a greater impact on Arkansas early in the nineteenth century, when a large element of the tribe moved south to the Three Forks area, where the Verdigris River and the Grand River flow into the Arkansas River in what is now Oklahoma. The Arkansas River then became the avenue from which they received trade goods supplied by a couple of important trading companies, Auguste Chouteau of St. Louis and Bright and Company operating out of Arkansas Post. Shortly after the Louisiana Purchase, as Americans began to settle in the St. Louis area, the U.S. government decided to ensure that the Osages stayed in the West. In 1808 the army built a fort near the Osage villages in the vicinity of modern Kansas City, and the government negotiated a treaty by which the Indians agreed to give up all claims to land east of a line running due south from their home to the Arkansas River. The line passed through Arkansas near the modern city of Springdale, and it intersected the Arkansas River at Frog's Bayou, which is near present-day Van Buren.

In the eighteenth century, the Caddo Indians were a large and successful confederacy occupying land in what is now western Louisiana and eastern Texas. One group, the Kadohadachos, lived along the big bend of the Red River and extended their influence into what is now the southwestern portion of Arkansas. The Caddos lived in permanent villages, practiced intensive and sophisticated agriculture, and produced some of the finest pottery in North America. They had extensive contacts with both the Spanish in Texas and the French in Louisiana and became heavily dependent on European goods even as their numbers dropped as a result of European diseases. In 1800, partly because of attacks by the Osages, the Kadohadachos moved some sixty miles south to Caddo Lake on Cypress Creek in what is now Texas, minimizing their involvement with Arkansas.

In its largely depopulated condition, Arkansas presented President Thomas Jefferson and later makers of American Indian policy with an ideal location for eastern Indian tribes that wanted to move west of the Mississippi River. Jefferson encouraged the Cherokees to relocate in Arkansas, and in 1817 the U.S. government gave them a large expanse of land between the Arkansas and White Rivers. Eventually there were some five thousand Cherokees in Arkansas Territory. They were resented by the white settlers of the territory, who wanted the land for themselves, and they existed in a nearly constant state of warfare with the Osages to the west. John C. Calhoun, secretary of war in the Monroe administration, granted a large portion of southwest Arkansas to the Choctaw Indians in 1820, including lands on which thousands of Arkansas settlers were already living. Few Chocktaws migrated to this area, however, and eventually the political power of the white settlers proved greater than that of the Native Americans. The United States pushed both the Choctaw boundary and the Cherokee boundary farther west, defining the western boundary of Arkansas in the process.

The native Quapaws were also removed; they were pushed out because of their extensive and fertile land, which was much sought after by white settlers. Then there was the high tide of Indian removal during the 1830s, known as the Trail of Tears. Arkansas played no part in the process of uprooting the Five Civilized Tribes and sending them west, but the state was a significant part of the itinerary for most of the migrating groups heading for the new Indian Territory in what is now Oklahoma. The forced migration of Indians—on foot, on horseback, and on steamboat—was a common and often sad sight in Arkansas during the entire decade.

Fort Smith, located at the junction of the Poteau River with the Arkansas River, was the center of much federal government activity with respect to the Indians. In the early days of fighting between Cherokees and Osages, the fort played a critical role in minimizing the bloodshed. In 1824, however, the U.S. Army relocated to Fort Gibson, forty miles to the west. The need to police the Choctaw and Cherokee lines, especially against the ubiquitous and nefarious trade in whiskey, gave Fort Smith a new, albeit tenuous, life. A third and more permanent role for the fort came in 1838, when the United States decided to build a chain of forts that would protect the western border of the United States, and sustained lobbying by Arkansans convinced the army to locate a facility at Fort Smith.

* * *

In 1805, there were 575 Quapaws, or Downstream People as they called themselves, living in three villages within a few miles of Arkansas Post. They earned money by selling corn grown by the women and horses raised by the men. They still hunted, but their small numbers meant that the number of deerskins they brought to the traders at the post was insignificant compared with those that came from the Osages. For the same reason, the Quapaws had little military significance as far as the United States was concerned. What they did have was land. The traditional claims of the Quapaw tribe covered a vast area stretching west across the Louisiana Purchase between the Arkansas River and the Canadian River to the north and the Red River to the south. This princely domain would soon be taken by the United States, first to provide a homeland for more numerous eastern tribes, and then to become part of the public domain available to migrating southern planters and farmers.

Dispossession began with deceptive friendliness. In 1816 Gov. William Clark warned citizens of Missouri Territory to vacate lands that belonged to Indians, and he sent messengers to deliver the message personally to the settlers who had recently come down the Southwest Trail to establish homes south of the Arkansas River between the Ouachita and Red Rivers. At the same time Clark invited the Quapaw chiefs to discuss the situation with him in St. Louis. At this meeting, in November 1816, the Quapaws indicated a willingness to give up half their land in return for gifts and other reimbursement from the United States, but Clark was not authorized to make a deal. In March 1818, again in St. Louis, Governor Clark and Auguste Chouteau negotiated a treaty with the Quapaws, who were led by their principal chief, Heckaton. The Quapaws surrendered their vague rights to land north of the Arkansas River and most of the territory south of the Arkansas and Canadian Rivers, to which they had a well-established claim. They retained only about two million acres, lying between the Arkansas, Ouachita, and Saline rivers and bounded by a line running from Arkansas Post to the Ouachita River and from Little Rock to the Saline River. Governor Clark assured them that they could still hunt on the ceded land and that they would receive four thousand dollars in manufactured goods and a one-thousand-dollar annuity to be paid in merchandise.

The Quapaw Treaty of 1818 was a limited success. It seems to have satisfied the Indians, who had lost only land that they could not use and who now saw themselves as allies of the United States. A year later Heckaton proudly showed his copy of the treaty and a military uniform he had been given to naturalist Thomas Nuttall. The agreement also pleased Secretary of War John C. Calhoun, who had authorized the negotiations and had given a large section of the ceded Quapaw land to the Choctaws in 1820 to entice them to move across the Mississippi River. The treaty did not please the white settlers of Arkansas, however, and that would be the undoing of the Downstream People.

The territorial legislature of Arkansas expressed its simmering resentment of the Quapaws in a petition to the president of the United States sent in February 1820. Arguing that the tribe included only three or four hundred people and that it had been allowed to keep eight thousand square miles, the legislators claimed that the Quapaws were left with "at least 20 sqr miles each Indian." The petition suggested that a total grant of twelve square miles for each Native American would be more suitable. Moreover, they complained that the Quapaw land included "the best soil in the Territory," a point elaborated on by Robert Crittenden, secretary of Arkansas Territory, in a letter to Secretary of War Calhoun in 1823. Crittenden claimed that the north side of the Arkansas River overflowed

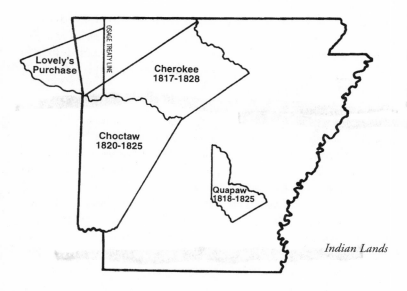

Indian Lands

when the river was high, but that "the south side," owned by the Quapaws, was "high[,] rich and immensely valuable." Cotton would grow there "as well as in any part of the unsettled States." In addition, that portion of the Arkansas River could be navigated nine months of the year. The *Arkansas Gazette* emphasized the fact that the settlement of Arkansas Territory would be retarded if such a large and choice tract of land were allowed to remain in the hands of the Indians. Meanwhile, the Quapaw grant was diminished almost immediately. Its western boundary was surveyed due south from Little Rock to the Saline River rather than southwest as was called for in the treaty, an alteration that deprived the Quapaws of a substantial body of land.

In October 1821, the territorial assembly sent a petition to Congress indicating that acquiring the Quapaw lands was "of the highest importance" to Arkansans. Further, the petition declared that the Indians themselves were willing to vacate the tract so that they could live with some other tribe. Henry Conway, soon to be elected delegate to Congress from Arkansas, elaborated on that theme in June 1822, claiming that "the Quapaws were desirous of selling their lands to the United States and were anxious to join and amalgamate with the Caddo Tribe," which had expressed an interest in having them. Secretary Crittenden advanced the same view with more force when he wrote Calhoun in September 1823. The Quapaws, in his view, were "a poor, indolent, miserable, remnant, of a nation, insignificant and inconsiderable," and he made it clear that he knew how to deal with them: "I have them now in training for a Treaty." In June 1824, the secretary of war sent the secretary of Arkansas Territory seven thousand dollars in expense money to be used "toward the extinguishment of the right of the Quapaws to lands in the Territory of Arkansas."

The Quapaw Treaty of 1824 gave the citizens of Arkansas Territory everything they wanted and more. In preliminary negotiations, Crittenden had agreed to allow the Indians to keep a ten-mile tract between the Arkansas and Ouachita Rivers, but Calhoun's instructions called for a total removal, and the secretary informed the Quapaws they would have to go. Despite claims that the Quapaws were anxious to move, they were disconsolate at leaving Arkansas. In Heckaton's words: "The land we now live on belonged to our forefathers . . . The lands you wish us to go to belong to strangers. Have mercy—send us not there." Crittenden remained adamant. The Quapaws agreed to join the Caddos on the Red River, where they would own no land as a tribe. They were granted four thousand dollars in merchandise, six months' subsistence in their new home, an eleven-year annuity of one thousand dollars, and a small number of individuals received payments of money and land.

The Red River phase of Quapaw history proved to be short and disastrous. The tribe left Arkansas Post in January 1826, led by Antoine Barraque, an immigrant from France who was familiar with the Quapaws and married to a woman related to them. After a month and a half on the trail, the Quapaws reached the Red River in the vicinity of what is now Shreveport, only to learn that the Caddos were not at all happy to have to absorb them. The Kadohadachos had not been consulted about the move, at least not recently, and they were bothered by the fact that the Quapaws were almost as numerous as they were. After a period of negotiations, the Quapaws crossed the river, settled into three villages, and began to plant corn. The Red River flooded their crops in May and again in June, however, and soon the Quapaws were near starvation. In midsummer a quarter of the tribe, led by a chief named Sarasin, returned to Arkansas, where, for the first time, they received some pity. Governor Izard provided corn to tide Sarasin's people over, and Delegate Conway convinced Congress to appropriate two thousand dollars for the distressed tribe. The territorial government allowed Sarasin's Quapaws to remain in Arkansas, and the war department provided them with one-quarter of the tribe's annuity. They lived on the margin of territorial society, however, occupying pieces of land that white settlers did not want.

Another flood struck the Quapaw cornfields on the Red River in 1828, and over the next two years the remainder of the tribe straggled back to Arkansas; Heckaton was among the last of them. The aged chief visited Washington in December 1830 in the company of the new territorial delegate, Ambrose Sevier, to plead the cause of his people and ask that an Indian agent be appointed for them. Heckaton wanted the job to go to Antoine Barraque, on whom the Indians had come to rely, but the government chose Wharton Rector, a relative and political crony of Sevier's. Another difficulty was the fact that Heckaton's people could no longer collect their share of the annuity, since living on the Red River was a condition for payment. Governor Pope of Arkansas Territory wrote to the secretary of war on behalf of the Quapaws in 1832, calling them "a harmless, inoffensive & honest people [who have been] much defrauded and wronged in relation to their annuities."

Their final fate, however, was determined by the Stokes Commission, which had been sent west to arrange the affairs of tribes migrating from the east. A new Quapaw subagent, Richard Hannum, traveled to Fort Gibson where the commission was assembling in May 1833 and persuaded it to address the problems of the Quapaws. One commission member, Rev. J. F. Schermerhorn, came down the Arkansas River and met with the Quapaws near Pine Bluff. Despite Heckaton's desire to remain in Arkansas, Schermerhorn worked out an arrangement by which the Quapaws would receive 150 sections of land for themselves in Indian Territory just west of Missouri. As embodied in a third Quapaw Treaty ratified by the United States in 1834, the agreement provided for transportation and subsistence expenses, livestock and farm equipment, an allotment of one thousand dollars per year for education, and an annuity of two thousand dollars. In September of that year, 161 Quapaws arrived at what they thought was their new home. As it turned out, they were placed in the wrong location and had to make one more short move. The remaining members of the tribe chose to follow Sarasin back to the Red River, where they were able to collect the old annuity. Eventually most of them drifted away to the south, and Sarasin returned to Pine Bluff.

Cherokee Indians began to enter Arkansas in the 1780s, pressured by the American advance to the east and encouraged by the numerical weakness of the Quapaws. Chief Bowles led some Cherokees to the St. Francis River region in 1794 after they had participated in the killing of a group of white people at Mussel Shoals on the Tennessee River. President Jefferson told the eastern Cherokees in 1808 that they could exchange their land in Tennessee for a new home between the Arkansas and White Rivers. The U.S. government made a treaty with the tribe in 1817 that included a provision that any land the Cherokees gave up east of the Mississippi River would be compensated with an equal amount of land located west of a line running from Chataunga Mountain, on the White River near modern Batesville, to Point Remove, near modern Morrilton on the Arkansas River. In encouraging the Cherokees to move to the new location, President James Monroe promised, as the Cherokees put it, "that we should have no limits to the west, that we should have good mill seats and plenty of game and not be surrounded by white people." Under these terms, they did migrate. By 1820, there were at least three thousand Cherokees in Arkansas, most of them living along the Arkansas River from Point Remove west to the Mulberry River, many on the south side of the river, where the land belonged to the Choctaws.

Thomas Nuttall visited the Arkansas Cherokees in 1819 and was impressed by their "decently furnished" homes and their farms, "well fenced and stocked with cattle." He perceived a "happy approach to civilization" in all of this, but also noted that economic success had made the Cherokees materialistic. There were great differences in wealth among the members of the tribe. Nuttall visited Walter Webber, a mixed-blood Cherokee chief who owned a fine farm and several African American slaves, functioned as a trader, and spoke and read English. At Webber's home, the Englishman met John Jolly, the brother of Tahlonteskee, who had led the Arkansas Cherokees until his recent death. Jolly, only recently arrived in Arkansas, was now his brother's successor. He was "half Indian, and dressed as a white man," so that only "his language" made him seem Cherokee. Nuttall found him "very plain, prudent, and unassuming, . . . a [Benjamin] Franklin among his countrymen," who called him "'beloved' father."

In fact, the Cherokees of Arkansas may have manifested white civilization better than the settlers. In 1828, the *Arkansas Gazette* made light of the Cherokee concern about an opening to the West. William Woodruff claimed that the Indians only wanted a western corridor so that they could avoid becoming civilized by contact with the whites. Some months later, the editor, to his credit, printed a reply from a Cherokee named No-Killer, who offered to compare the farms, crops, livestock, and homes of his people with those of the white settlers. No-Killer also claimed that the only meeting house in the territory had been built by the Cherokees, that they had two schools, and that their children were more literate than those of the whites. Finally, he pointed out that more people died violent deaths on the streets of Little Rock than in the villages of the Cherokees.

Woodruff was not, of course, the only white who discounted Cherokee achievements. In the summer of 1820, the Rev. Cephas Washburn made his way up the Arkansas River and founded a mission to the Cherokees about four miles up the Illinois Bayou, near present-day Russellville. After Washburn and his missionary family had cleared and planted land and constructed four log dwellings, a schoolhouse, and other facilities, Dwight Mission, as they called their settlement, was ready to open on the first day of 1822. Believing that it was God's wish that the Gospel have "the glory of taming and humanizing every nation and tribe of barbarians," Washburn planned a comprehensive assault on the traditional culture of the Cherokees. The Indian students would live with the missionaries, gaining both religious and secular education and learning also to practice Christian values and to dress and behave as white people. John Jolly and other leaders accepted the mission, but the Arkansas Cherokees in general were not completely receptive. The school soon had fifty students, but it did not achieve the religious success hoped for by its founder. As Washburn put it, "we were not permitted to enjoy what is usually denominated a revival of religion."

Meanwhile, the bane of the Arkansas Cherokees was the Osage Nation. As the Arkansas Cherokees went hunting to the west, they came into contact with Osage hunting parties from the Three Forks area, and violence became common. William Lovely, an Indian agent who joined the Arkansas Cherokees in 1813, chronicled a series of small-scale aggressions on both sides and added that renegade whites played an important role in the escalating violence. The Osages were more routinely lawless and violent, but the Cherokees were better armed and organized and capable of a more thorough ferocity. They demonstrated these qualities in 1817 at what is euphemistically called the Battle of Claremore Mound. A war party of nearly six hundred Cherokees led by Tick-e-Toke and including Tahlonteskee and other chiefs, attacked an Osage village on the Verdigris River. The Osage warriors were away on their fall buffalo hunt, so the fighting involved Cherokee warriors armed with cannons against Osage old men, women, and children. The Cherokees killed sixty-nine and rode off with one hundred prisoners.

Despite the Cherokee attack, the cause of peace between the two tribes was advanced by the arrival of Maj. William Bradford and a company of rifle regiment soldiers at Belle Point, the confluence of the Poteau

River and the Arkansas River, on Christmas Day 1817. Bradford's force immediately began the construction of Fort Smith, in the process making an impressive statement about the future role of the United States on the southwestern frontier. Moreover, John Jolly, the Cherokee leader, arrived in Arkansas about this time and began to look for ways to end the fighting. He visited Bradford at the fort and enlisted his help in creating a truce with the Osages. The end result of these efforts was a meeting in St. Louis in the summer of 1818, during which Missouri governor William Clark, superintendent of Indian affairs in the territory, negotiated a peace agreement between the two tribes. As part of the deal, the Osages sold the United States a large triangular tract of land lying north of the Arkansas River between the Osage treaty line of 1808 and the Verdigris River. Known as Lovely's Purchase, for the former Cherokee agent who had first tried to buy it in 1816, the tract was designed to separate the Cherokees and the Osages and allow the former an outlet to the hunting grounds in the West.

The agreement of 1818 failed to end hostilities. In February 1820, a band of Osages attacked a Cherokee hunting party in Lovely's Purchase and killed three of them. Shortly after, the Cherokees informed Major Bradford that the Osages must turn over three of the warriors who had participated in the raid, or the Cherokees would launch a full-scale war against them. Meanwhile, James Miller had become governor of Arkansas Territory and superintendent of its Indian affairs. Miller visited both the Cherokees and the Osages in 1820 in hopes of bringing about a settlement. He obtained a promise from the Osages that they would cease trying to get back hostages held by the Cherokees if the Cherokee would give up their demand for the warriors. When the Cherokees refused to accept this idea, the exasperated Miller told them that he would "leave it to yourselves to make the peace in your own way, or get such satisfaction as you pleased."

The following April, a party of four hundred Osages showed up across the river from Fort Smith. They were painted for war and looking for gunpowder to use against the Cherokee villages. Bradford was away, but his undermanned garrison loaded its cannons and refused to ferry the Indians across the river. The Osages frightened some white families on the north shore and killed three Quapaws whom they had captured, but left without their ammunition. Later they carried out some small-scale raids and robberies and eventually returned home. A Cherokee war party entered Osage country in June and killed an Indian trader named Joseph

Revoir. A larger body of Cherokees arrived in September, and one element split off from the main group and attacked a group of Osage women who were gathering food, killing twenty-nine and capturing thirty. The main Cherokee force trailed an Osage hunting party, but they were discovered and driven off.

The Osages suffered more from these hostilities than the Cherokees, and they had fewer resources with which to sustain themselves. Their newly appointed subagent, Nathaniel Philbrook, found them "in real distress, poor & wretched, no meat to eat, nor no ammunition to kill any with." With Philbrook's support, Clermont, the leading chief of the Verdigris Osages, and Tally, his second in command, finally decided that it was time to end the warfare. In a message to Miller, written down and delivered by Philbrook, they stated their terms: "we are willing to make peace with the Cherokees, let us have our women and Children back and we will foreget everything else." Philbrook then visited the Cherokees and got them to agree to a cessation of hostilities. In August 1822, at a council in Fort Smith, the two tribes finally agreed to live in peace. Hostages were returned and agreements were made so that each tribe could hunt in Lovely's Purchase and occasionally cross into the lands of the other. Governor Miller signed the final document, as did Col. Matthew Arbuckle, who had succeeded Major Bradford as the commandant of Fort Smith.

After 1822 the Osages were involved in less conflict with the Cherokees, but the Verdigris Indians did not give up their violent ways. In December 1823, Antoine Barraque led a party of about twelve Quapaws and mixed-blood hunters up the Red River to the Blue River, where they were joined by another group of about eight white hunters led by Maj. Curtis Wilborn. One day while most of the group was out of camp, a large body of Osages attacked those left behind, killing seven, four of them white men. The attackers spared a Quapaw prisoner, apparently because he was a Native American, and they told him that they were from Clermont's band. Barraque and the other survivors made their separate ways 175 miles north to Fort Smith. Colonel Arbuckle believed at first that the attack was a prelude to war, but when the Osages disavowed hostile intentions, he demanded only that they give up those responsible for the attack so that they could be tried in a U.S. court. Subagent Philbrook was shot and killed by an unknown person while carrying that message to the Osages. In the spring of 1824, the army abandoned Fort Smith and moved to Cantonment Gibson, which was located near the mouth of the Grand River, less than fifty miles from Clermont's camp. In June, Clermont and his people visited the new fort, and eventually six of them surrendered themselves to U.S. justice. One escaped soon after, but the remaining five were taken to Little Rock in shackles to stand trail for murder.

The trial of the five Osages took place in the Superior Court of Arkansas Territory in October 1824. Only two, Mad Buffalo and Little Eagle, were found guilty, but they were sentenced to hang. The *Arkansas Gazette* was much taken with Mad Buffalo, who was elderly but still "large and well-proportioned, of fine and commanding mien, and [apparently possessed of] a superior mind and great intelligence, for one of his race." He heard the sentence of death with "the greatest composure and without betraying the slightest emotion of fear." Mad Buffalo may not have feared death, but he was not willing to die with a rope around his neck. He secured a penknife and stabbed his chest a number of times, but the blade was too short to enter his heart. Eventually President John Quincy Adams pardoned both Indians in an "act of Compassion" for his "Red Children."

To the citizens of Arkansas Territory, the land claims of the Cherokees were a bigger threat than the episodic violence between Cherokees and Osages or the occasional Osage attacks on western hunters. The Cherokees had political influence in Washington, particularly with the Monroe administration, which was anxious to please the Arkansas Cherokees so that they would be willing to accept eastern Cherokees. On the other hand, the territorial interest was represented by an elected delegate to Congress, a governor appointed by the president, and a newspaper that both informed and inflamed public opinion. These two forces waged political war over four issues in the decade after the creation of Arkansas Territory in 1819. One involved the creation of a western boundary for the land granted to the Cherokees in 1817. Related to that was the removal of the Cherokees from the area south of the Arkansas River that was given to and then taken from the Choctaws. Most explosive among the four was the question of Lovely's Purchase, which was a highly desirable area that both Indians and whites were anxious to own. Finally, when the first three issues were settled by moving the Cherokees west of Arkansas Territory, there was still the question of where to draw the boundary, another issue that involved the ownership of Lovely's Purchase.

The upper boundary of Cherokee holdings in Arkansas was not surveyed in 1817, because the Indians had been promised an "acre for acre" replacement for the land that the tribe had given up in the East. Governor Miller agreed to do a survey in 1822, but he ordered one that was highly prejudicial against the Cherokees. The lower boundary ran in a north-easterly manner, but the proposed upper boundary was due south from the White River. The Cherokees got their acres, but most of them were in the mountains and along the White River. The southern portion along the Arkansas River was foreshortened. The Cherokees claimed that their land "was a mountainous, broken-barren country fit for nothing" and asked for more acreage on the fertile bottomland along the Arkansas River. They also claimed that the total amount of land was insufficient because certain of their cessions in the East had not been counted. When they were pressed about their settlements south of the Arkansas River, they argued that the land there belonged to the Choctaws, and the United States had no business pushing them off it. Always attracted to the West, they also suggested that their lands should extend east from the western boundary of Arkansas.

Taking all this under consideration, Secretary of War Calhoun fashioned a compromise. After claiming that Miller had made a mistake, he ordered that a new survey be conducted and that it proceed from east to west, but in a manner that made the miles of river fronting on the Arkansas equal to those on the White River. Calhoun reiterated that the Cherokees would have to leave the south side of the Arkansas River, but he said they could stay where they were until the new survey was done. Early in 1825, the *Arkansas Gazette* declared that the new line would intersect the Arkansas River three or four miles west of Fort Smith, giving the Cherokees a portion of Lovely's Purchase. "Arkansans," stated editor Woodruff, "will be disappointed, but can do nothing about it." As it turned out, he underestimated the resourcefulness of local politicians.

In October 1827, the territorial assembly passed a measure that created Lovely County, which was to include all the land in Arkansas Territory that was north of the Arkansas and Canadian Rivers and west of the Cherokee boundary. Immediately settlers flowed into the portion of Lovely's Purchase that was not part of the Cherokee domain. Early in 1828 a Cherokee delegation left Arkansas for Washington. The Cherokees argued that President Monroe had promised them an outlet to the West and that the settlement of Lovely County would mean that they would be surrounded by whites. Eventually Secretary of War James Barbour negotiated a new treaty with the Cherokees that involved moving them west of an Arkansas border that ran from Fort Smith to the southwest corner of Missouri. According to Thomas McKenny, who suggested it, this settlement would "cost but little, and at the same time free the

Citizens of Arkansas, except for a few squatters, from the evils of which they so loudly complain." On the other hand, Ambrose Sevier, recently elected as territorial delegate, complained bitterly to Barbour that five thousand Arkansans living in Lovely County were being sacrificed. Many of the Cherokees were also unhappy at the agreement that their delegation had accepted. In the end, both Cherokees and Arkansans probably gained. The white settlers got rid of the Indians in their midst, the Indians avoided encirclement by the whites, and each side got a portion of Lovely's Purchase.

While John C. Calhoun, secretary of war during the Monroe administration, was overseeing the Quapaw Treaty of 1818, he was also attempting to convince the Choctaw Nation to leave the state of Mississippi and migrate to the West. The Choctaws were one of the Five Civilized Tribes who farmed and raised livestock, much as the white settlers did. They had fought with the Americans in the War of 1812 and hoped to be left undisturbed on their extensive landholdings in southwest Mississippi. White Mississippians, however, wanted to evict the Indians and take the land for themselves, an attitude that was common throughout the South, where the Cherokees, Creeks, Chickasaws, and Seminoles still controlled large and valuable areas of land. The removal of the Choctaws was related to a larger federal policy that emphasized making the Indians more civilized, limiting their lands in accordance with a farming economy rather than a hunting lifestyle, and moving them as far west as possible—out of the way of white settlement.

Negotiations with the Choctaws reached a climax with the Treaty of Doak's Stand, which was signed on October 18, 1820. Andrew Jackson and Gen. Thomas Hinds of Mississippi represented the United States. The indomitable Jackson countered Choctaw reluctance with a thinly disguised threat that the Indians would suffer dire consequences if they elected to stay in Mississippi. The Choctaws were led by Pushmataha, who had also led them in the War of 1812 and had launched a successful attack in support of Jackson at New Orleans. Faced with Jackson's threats, which were backed up by the military strength of the United States, the Choctaws gave up five million acres in Mississippi in return for a much larger area between the Arkansas and Red Rivers in Arkansas Territory. Calhoun had originally intended that the removed Indians be settled west of a line from the mouth of the Poteau River on the Arkansas River to the mouth of the Kiamichi River on the Red River—a line that would have slanted in a southwest direction into Oklahoma from the modern city of Fort Smith. He allowed Jackson to define what portion of the Quapaw Cession would go to the Choctaws, however, and the general drew a line roughly one hundred miles east of the one suggested earlier by the secretary. Jackson's Choctaw boundary began at Point Remove on the Arkansas River, near the modern city of Morrilton, and ran southeast to a point three miles east of where the Little River enters the Red River. Between Jackson's line and Calhoun's was a great deal of land that Arkansas Territory considered its own and upon which large numbers of its citizens were living.

The people of Arkansas Territory were shocked and angered by the Treaty of Doak's Stand. Even while negotiations were taking place, editor William Woodruff of the *Arkansas Gazette* attacked the idea of eastern states getting rid of their Indians by sending "those poor deluded wretches into the weakest and most remote Territories." He emphasized, indeed exaggerated, the dangers for Arkansas Territory in having to deal with "the aggressions of a fierce and savage enemy, whose resentment has already been raised to the highest pitch . . . and calculates on glutting his vengeance on a weak and defenseless people." Woodruff concluded by claiming that Arkansas Territory "is now nearly over-run by marauding savages" and therefore no more should be sent. When the terms of the treaty were known, and it was clear that Arkansas would lose parts of four or five populous and productive counties, the *Arkansas Gazette* became still more bitter. Woodruff stated that if the government was going to treat Arkansas as a "Botany Bay," a penal colony for Indians, then it would be best to abolish the territorial government and discourage the future settlement of whites.

Political officials assessed the situation with similar anger and alarm. Governor Miller wrote Calhoun that one-third of the population of the territory lived in the portion given to the Cherokees and that "all the inhabitants I have seen wear the strong features of distress . . . They have exhausted their little all in moving here, and now they are to be turned pennyless upon the world in search of another habitation." The governor's ironic wish was that the whites be put "on an equal footing with the Savages." If the treaty line were to be carried out, "the Territory is destroyed forever." James Woodson Bates, the territorial delegate to Congress, protested to the secretary of war on behalf of the citizens of Arkansas that the treaty "prostrates their rights, outrages their feelings & treats them as Subjects & vassals."

Leaving aside the hyperbole, it was clear that the Treaty of Doak's

Stand had done a disservice to the citizens of Arkansas Territory by giving the Choctaws land that was already occupied by white settlers. After reconsidering the situation in March 1823, Congress suggested a Choctaw boundary that ran south from the southwest corner of Missouri and crossed the Arkansas River about ten miles west of Fort Smith. This would become the western boundary of Arkansas, but only if the Choctaw Nation accepted the change. Meanwhile, in the next election for territorial delegate, Henry W. Conway ran against Bates and called for a boundary between Arkansas and the Choctaw Nation that would run north and south from the mouth of the Canadian River on the Arkansas River, a line that was about thirty miles west of Fort Smith. Conway won the election and went to Congress where, with the help of Thomas Hart Benton of Missouri, he was able to effect the passage of a new law in 1824 that would run the boundary line south from a point forty miles west of the Missouri Line, about fifty miles west of Fort Smith. Again, however, Congress required the consent of the Choctaws before the new boundary line would go into effect.

A Choctaw delegation went to Washington in the fall of 1824 to negotiate a number of outstanding issues, including the eastern boundary of their western lands. Despite Calhoun's best efforts, the Choctaws refused to agree to the line that Congress had just approved. Eventually a compromise was worked out that included a line that began one hundred paces east of Fort Smith and ran due south to the Red River. Arkansans believed this boundary, embodied in the Choctaw Treaty of 1825, was nearly as bad as the one included in the Treaty of Doak's Stand. An early estimate suggested that three thousand settlers lived west of the new Choctaw Line. In fact, most of the Arkansas settlers lived east of the Fort Smith line. The situation of the white settlers was also improved by James S. Conway, brother of delegate Henry W. Conway and himself the first governor of the state of Arkansas, who surveyed the new line and gave it a slant to the west. Conway's line intersected the Red River about four miles upstream from where it should have. After many attempts to correct the inequity, the Choctaw Nation was finally compensated by the U.S. Supreme Court in 1886 for the land which Conway had taken from them. Meanwhile, as late as 1836, when they prepared a constitution to support their move toward statehood, Arkansas politicians were still hoping to get the western boundary Congress had approved in 1824, the one that began forty miles west of the southwest corner of Missouri.

As boundaries were created and Indians—and sometimes settlers—

were moved, Fort Smith brought some degree of stability to the Arkansas frontier. In 1817, Maj. Stephen H. Long of the U.S. Army Topographical Engineers located the installation at Belle Point, on the east side of the mouth of the Poteau River, and he designed a square fort 132 feet on each side with a 10-foot-high stockade and two 20-foot-square blockhouses at opposite corners. Maj. William Bradford constructed the installation using the labor of a company of troopers from the rifle regiment, specialists in scouting and patrol duty who were skilled marksmen and wore specially designed gray uniforms. The fort was named for Gen. Thomas A. Smith, who commanded the Ninth Military Department of which it was a part. Under Major Bradford and then Colonel Arbuckle, Fort Smith did play an important role in moderating Indian violence in western Arkansas. In 1824, however, the garrison of Fort Smith moved forty miles west and Fort Gibson was built three miles up the east bank of the Grand River. The locus of Indian problems had moved beyond Fort Smith, and Arkansas anticipated that its western boundary would soon move west as well. Fort Smith continued to be the property of the U.S. Army, but it no longer had a staff.

Colonel Arbuckle left the fort in the hands of two civilians, Col. John Nicks and Capt. John Rogers. The former was a sutler for the old garrison, and the latter was a military storekeeper. Several years later, William McClellan, an agent for the Choctaws, visited the fort with the intention of making it a storehouse and way station for the migrating Choctaws. McClellan found it a "perfect Rack [sic]," with windows, doors, and even floors removed by the soldiers. Nicks and Rogers were occupying one blockhouse in which they had installed a cotton gin. They also operated a store, where McClellan believed they were selling whiskey to the Indians. A quarrel broke out between the two entrepreneurs and McClellan over the operation of the army ferry across the Arkansas River. Nicks and Rogers claimed the sole right to use it, but McClellan granted a mixed-blood Choctaw named Peter Folsom the right to carry the civilian traffic. Colonel Arbuckle sided with Nicks and Rogers, claiming that the fort was under military control, and that he had put Nicks and Rogers in charge of all the facilities. The department of war supported Arbuckle's claim to authority, and McClellan moved his agency eighteen miles west to Pebble Springs.

Military forces returned to Fort Smith in 1831 in order to control the expanding whiskey trade with the Indians and to assist in the continuing removal of the eastern tribes. Rev. Cephas Washburn, leader of the Dwight Mission, complained in February 1830 that five Indians had died of overindulgence in alcohol within the previous ten days. He had become so exasperated that he bought up liquor and poured it out. Noting that the barrels were being brought up the Arkansas River, he suggested that Fort Smith be supplied with a military force that could search boats and seize the contraband booze. In April 1831, Capt. John B. Clark from Fort Gibson inspected Fort Smith and found it in worse shape than he had anticipated. Windows, doors, and floors were gone, some foundation logs were missing, and others were rotten. "Houses were sinking to the ground, the roofs are falling in on many." Nonetheless, within two weeks Lt. Gabriel Rains and a detachment of the Seventh Infantry occupied the installation.

Rains and his successor, Capt. John Stuart, devoted much energy to the suppression of the whiskey trade, which was a complicated and thankless task. A federal grand jury convened in Little Rock in 1832 and found that six businesses were selling whiskey within a few feet of the Choctaw Line at Fort Smith. Witnesses claimed that it was not hard for Native Americans to buy as many as six barrels of the product. Indeed, "drunken Indians" had set fire to "public buildings" at or near the fort on three separate occasions. Despite the obvious problem, however, the grand jury claimed that there was nothing it could do. Federal law allowed the president of the United States to take steps to halt the selling of liquor to Indians on Indian land, but it prescribed no role for grand juries. There was a territorial law that forbade selling liquor to Indians within Arkansas, but this jury felt that it should be enforced by grand juries within the county where the transaction occurred.

Captain Stuart blamed the alcohol problem on the white citizens who lived near the fort. He distinguished two groups—"adventurers from different Parts of the world" and "such as have been all their Lives moving along in Advance of Civilization and good order"—both of whom were willing to make money any way they could. He had tried to prosecute those who had sold liquor to the Indians under the territorial law, but he was frustrated by local officials, who were "elected by the Tag, rag, and bobtail population" and were always anxious to serve public opinion rather than justice. When he tried to discourage Indians from making purchases, the storekeepers threatened to sue the army. Indeed, the Cherokees, at least, were equally litigious, claiming that "it is their right to have whiskey in their country if they Please." They were, claimed the army captain, "almost as clamorous about their cival [sic] rights, and Indian Privileges . . . as the Nullifiers are about the rights of the Sovereign State." Under the law, the soldiers had the right to prevent the Indians from taking whiskey across the border, but that was not easy to do: "And when they get their Kegs filled and well Strapped on their back . . . they break into the thick brush and underwood, and cross the Line wherever it may suit their convenience . . ." Despite these problems, Stuart's command did seize and destroy a significant amount of liquor. Smuggling large quantities of whiskey on the Arkansas River became a more difficult and dangerous process. One result was the growth of Van Buren, Arkansas, as a whiskey depot. Located across the Arkansas River and six miles downstream from Fort Smith, Van Buren was freer of military interference. Whiskey was sold there and then carried overland into Cherokee country.

In May 1834 Fort Smith was again evacuated. The army sent Stuart and his men ten miles west to a place called Swallow Point, where they built a small post called Fort Coffee. The new site was closer to the Choctaw Agency, and Stuart believed it to be a more healthful site. Colonel Arbuckle, who was still commanding at Fort Gibson, favored making Fort Smith a large and permanent military installation, a view supported by Capt. John Rogers, who now owned about 640 acres located next to the old installation. Rogers organized a petition campaign in western Arkansas, getting citizens to insist that the government maintain a fort on the border of the territory. Influenced by this grass-roots activity, the territorial legislature petitioned Congress, arguing that when Fort Gibson had been created, it had been assumed that the territorial border would be located near it—that is, forty miles west of the southwest corner of Missouri. Since that was not where the border was drawn, Fort Gibson was forty miles away from Arkansas, and, it was argued, the territory would be undefended unless Fort Smith were revived.

Captain Stuart was opposed to the rehabilitation of Fort Smith. His experience there had left him with a low opinion of Capt. John Rogers and of the local merchant community in general. He believed Rogers was motivated solely by a desire to improve the value of his land. Stuart pointed out that the Indians were now peaceful and that western Arkansas was not in need of defense. He also believed, on the basis of both personal observation and research into army records, that Fort Smith was an unhealthy place. He cited both civilian and military deaths, noting, for example, that in 1823 about fifty of the two hundred men of the Seventh Infantry had contracted fatal illnesses. He blamed the Poteau River, which often backed up for miles and became covered with a "green or yellow Scum" that gave off "offensive Effluvia." Stuart's assessment was supported by an army surgeon sent to investigate the post, who found its adjacent "immense marshes, lakes, and stagnant waters" and its humid climate all conducive to the production and spread of "miasmic poison." He proclaimed it "intrinsically unhealthy."

Eventually the fate of Fort Smith became entangled with a national plan to develop a roadway and a line of forts from the upper Mississippi River to the Red River. In July 1836, Secretary of War Cass asked Col. Stephen W. Kearny to lead a commission that would do survey work and recommend locations for the forts. After a visit to the Arkansas frontier, Kearny's commission selected the site of Fort Coffee as the best location for a permanent fort. Arkansas responded with newspaper advertisements and a petition in favor of Fort Smith, again apparently the work of Capt. John Rogers. Under the impact of this local pressure, Arkansas Senator Fulton confronted the new Secretary of War Joel Poinsett in late 1837 and pressured him to get another opinion. Army officers wanted a fort located twenty miles or so inside the Indian Territory in order to keep the whiskey vendors away, but Fort Smith became the choice because the people of Arkansas clamored for it. As the final decision was being made, Rogers arrived in Washington and soon sold 306 acres of his land around Fort Smith to the army for fifteen thousand dollars. In July 1838, construction began on a new fort that would have a "stone wall about twelve feet high, and from two to three feet thick," enclosing a rectangle six hundred feet by four hundred feet.

While the fate of Fort Smith was being decided, Indian refugees were traveling the Trail of Tears into Indian Territory just to the west. The Removal Act of 1830 gave legislative sanction to the idea that Indians from east of the Mississippi should give up their land and be relocated west of the Mississippi. Over the next decade, the Five Civilized Tribes—the Creek, Choctaw, Cherokee, Chickasaw, and Seminole—were forced to leave what was left of their homelands and trek to Indian Territory, in what is now Oklahoma. All of these forced migrations crossed Arkansas at some point, and most of them traversed the state. The most favored route was up the Arkansas River, either by steamboat or on land. Some of the Creeks and Chickasaws traveled overland from Memphis to Little Rock before proceeding up the Arkansas River Valley, and some of the Choctaws came up the Ouachita River and crossed south Arkansas to reach land near the Red River. Elements of the Cherokee tribe swung north from their Tennessee homes, crossed the Mississippi in southern Missouri, and headed west before dropping into Arkansas.

The migration of the Choctaws was arranged by the Treaty of Dancing Rabbit Creek, negotiated in September 1830, a few months after the passage of the Removal Act. It was, as historian Ronald N. Satz has said, a "test case of the removal policy." Despite the efforts of the government to make the migration as humane as possible, the Indians suffered greatly. The first group of Choctaws were on the move in the severe winter of 1831, clad only in thin garments and often barefoot. The supply of food and other commodities was hindered by civilian profiteering; at Fort Smith, the whiskey salesmen plied their trade as always.

William F. Pope was in Little Rock in the fall of 1833 when six or seven thousand Choctaws crossed the Arkansas River on their way west. For him, "the presence of this vast body of Indians, with their household goods, cattle and ponies, made a sight never to be forgotten." The citizens of Little Rock had been warned about the possibility of theft, and some items were stolen. For the most part, however, the Indians wanted "to loiter and spy around, and had to be driven almost like sheep." The men wore leather moccasins, leggings, and breechcloths, all of them decorated with beads and porcupine quills. In general, according to Pope, they were "a fine looking body of men." The women rode full-saddle on Indian ponies and carried their small children in blankets.

A little more than four years later, Friedrich Gerstäcker arrived across the river from Little Rock and found a group of Indians encamped at the water's edge. While he watched, they fed their horses and cooked their meals. Some of them also drank liquor and sang in low, sad, whiskey-thickened voices. A "tall" and "powerful" Indian man decorated with "glass beads and silver ornaments" approached the young German and offered to trade his rifle for a refill of his bottle. Gerstäcker gave him the whiskey for free and then found himself dragged to the fire, where he drank, ate venison, and smoked a pipe with the Indian and his family. Later the host "stood up and in his harmonious language related a long history" of which Gerstäcker "did not understand a word."

One wonders what the warrior might have said. The tale was probably confused and foolishly sentimental, the sort of thing that whiskey encourages; on the other hand, perhaps sensitivity and eloquence were stronger than inebriation. Perhaps he expressed the pathos of his situation—camping by a strange river, ready to give up his weapon for his addiction, already gone from the land where he had grown up and where his people had lived, hunted, fought, and died, and traveling west now to a place that the white men did not yet want.

CHAPTER FIVE

Rich, Poor,
and Rambunctious

Between 1800 and 1860, American society underwent profound changes. Western expansion opened new land, and settlers flocked to occupy it; transportation improvements created a national market, and factories rose up to supply it; and a new democratic ethos led to free white male suffrage and a heightened sense of worth on the part of the common man. A sense of unlimited opportunities infused the country, and the pursuit of wealth became a national pastime. As Alexis de Tocqueville observed: "It is strange to see with what feverish ardor the Americans pursue their own welfare; and to watch the vague dread that constantly torments them lest they should not have chosen the shortest path which may lead to it."

According to many accounts, however, these energetic and ebullient Americans did not settle in Arkansas. George Featherstonhaugh, for example, who traveled extensively in Arkansas Territory in 1834 and 1835, penned vivid descriptions of settlers with poor manners and slovenly habits who had moved west to escape eastern justice and who resorted to violence on the slightest provocation. Near the Little Red River, he spent the night with a man named Hornby, whom he described as a "squalid, half-negro looking, piratical ruffian from Louisiana, living in a wretched, filthy cabin, with a wife to match," and a slave woman and her two children. After a dinner consisting of "some bits of filthy pork, and a detestable beverage they were pleased to call coffee, served on a broken dirty table . . . by the light of a nasty little tin lamp," he slept on the floor of the one-room home. Featherstonhaugh found many industrious and prosperous settlers, but the primitive quality of the territory impressed him. In Little Rock, for example, almost all the men carried pistols and bowie knives, and when he called on Governor Pope, the chief executive was out hunting for his wife's lost pigs. The food in the capital city was routinely "little square bits of pork fried in lard, bad coffee, and indifferent bread," and a similar indifference showed itself in housing: "When the winter season comes, the family huddles round the fire with the door open, and generally five or six pains [*sic*] of glass broken in the window, which no one thinks of mending any more than of shutting the door." To explain these circumstances, Featherstonhaugh cited respectable persons of the territory, who argued that Arkansas was in a period of transition from a society of hunters to one of "outlaws"—"criminals, gamblers, speculators, and men of broken families." The hopeful sign was that the existence of government seemed to be moving the territory in the direction of civilization.

Similar points had been made earlier by Henry Rowe Schoolcraft and Thomas Nuttall. Friederich Gerstäcker, a young German who visited Arkansas a few years after Featherstonhaugh, was more positive, but mainly because he came for good hunting and found plenty of it in a state that he described as mostly wilderness. Sanford Faulkner's *Arkansas Traveler*, which described his own experience campaigning in 1840, helped to spread the idea that the typical Arkansan was a squatter too lazy to repair his own roof.

By contrast, these writers had little to say about the agricultural success of Arkansas. A reason for this omission is suggested by Grady McWhiney's book *Cracker Culture,* which analyzes the yeomen of the antebellum South in ways that fit Arkansans very neatly. McWhiney makes the point that northerners—and Englishmen like Featherstonhaugh—were unsympathetic to the lifestyle of the southern lower-class whites, which seemed to them slipshod and lacking in industry. Travelers with these prejudices may have downplayed evidence of agricultural productivity because they disliked the way southerners cared for their homes, fields, and animals and were too busy being critical to take note of positive achievements.

Not all descriptions were so negative. Albert Pike, the Massachusetts-born Arkansas editor and attorney, published an account of the region in the *New England Magazine* even as Featherstonhaugh was still in

Arkansas. Here we have a land of opportunity for the aspiring yeoman: "A poor man comes here [with] nothing but his axe and his rifle. He . . . cuts a few logs, and his neighbors help him raise a hut, with a wooden chimney, daubed with mud. He chops out a hole for the door, and another for a window; splits and hews out some thick slabs, . . . puncheons, for a floor." He works a month for someone else to get a few hogs, then notches their ears and lets them root for themselves. Back on his own, the settler begins "chopping timber, grubbing up cane, and performing the various operations necessary to clearing up land . . . In four or five years that man will raise twenty bales of cotton and a thousand bushels of corn."

Pike's appraisal may exaggerate the positive aspects of Arkansas society as much as others had exaggerated the negative. We have already seen, however, that the agricultural economy of the state compared well with other southern states. Other evidence also suggests that Arkansans were less idiosyncratic than they were presented and more like other Americans.

* * *

One neglected source of information about Arkansas society was the fiction that appeared in the *Spirit of the Times,* a magazine published in New York City by William T. Porter, who had founded it in 1831. The *Spirit* carried news about the popular sport of horse racing and reached a national market of subscription readers. From the beginning, however, Porter filled out his pages with bits and pieces from English magazines and snippets from popular English authors. He also used American correspondents, who provided information about horse races in different parts of this country. As the popularity of horse racing declined after the Panic of 1837 and the ensuing depression, the *Spirit* began to carry other types of indigenous writing, especially fictional humor that achieved its effect through the use of local dialect and the telling of tall tales in a regional setting. Many of these stories were set in the rapidly growing Southwest and particularly in Arkansas and Mississippi. The best known of them is Thomas Bangs Thorpe's "The Big Bear of Arkansas," which also gave its name to a collection of pieces from the *Spirit* that Porter published in 1845.

The central figure of this tale is Jim Doggett, whom the narrator encounters on a steamboat. Calling himself "the Big Bar from Arkansaw," the loud and bragging Doggett quickly wins over the passengers with his good humor, relaxed manner, and his charming tall tales. When it is argued that mosquitoes are large in Arkansas, the Big Bar responds: "If they are large, Arkansaw is large, her varmints ar large, her trees ar large, her rivers ar large, and a small mosquitoe would be of no more use in Arkansaw than preaching in a cane-brake." Later in the evening, Doggett's steamboat companions press him to tell of his most interesting bear hunt, and he responds with the tale of a great male bear that confounded him and his dogs to the point of ruining their reputations as outstanding hunters. During one chase, this bear was hit by a rifle ball in the forehead, but still jumped over a ring of dogs surrounding him and eventually escaped by swimming away. The next day, however, as Doggett was walking outside his home the bear came over a fence toward him—in the hunter's words, "stranger, he loomed up like a black mist . . ." Doggett shot the animal, but took little credit for the kill, claiming "that bar was an unhuntable bar" and had died when his time had come.

For Thomas Bangs Thorpe, Arkansas was as much an abstraction as a reality. Its actual qualities were subordinated to its role as a mythic frontier, a primeval battleground where people and nature met in a struggle partly comic and partly heroic. A painter and newspaper editor who lived much of his life in Louisiana, Thorpe was familiar with the lower Mississippi Valley region, but he seems to have had no special knowledge of Arkansas and little interest in it. Nonetheless, he helped to shape others' perceptions of the area.

Much different is the work of Charles Fenton Mercer Noland, an Arkansan who made a national reputation in the years from 1837 to 1858 by writing humorous tales about his home state. Noland's stories are fictional and comical, but they have realistic settings and deal with issues that concerned Arkansans. Indeed, real people are mixed with the invented ones. In Noland's portrayal, Arkansas society is decidedly more friendly and likable than in the pages of Featherstonhaugh or other commentators. His characters are backwoods men, but they are also southern yeomen and Jacksonian Americans, imbued with the democratic values that Jackson found so useful and Tocqueville found so interesting.

Noland's first letters to the *Spirit of the Times* were signed "N" and contained accounts of horse races. Early in 1837, however, he began to write letters under the name of Pete Whetstone, a fictional alter ego who lived on the Devil's Fork of the Little Red River in Arkansas. Whetstone claimed to have "the best pack of bear dogs, the closest shooting rifle, the fastest swimming horse, and perhaps, the prettiest sisters you ever did see." The Pete Whetstone character, whose contributions would continue to appear for the next two decades, represented a new sophistication in the "Big Bear school" of regional humor.

Whetstone's earliest description of life on the Devil's Fork related how a horse race was arranged between his own Bussing Coon, the champion of the Devil's Fork, and Warping Bars, owned by Dan Looney of the Raccoon Fork of War Eagle Creek. Looney was bragging about his horse outside the "Doggery," a local tavern, when Pete's friend Jim Cole offered a challenge: "Dan, the Bussing Coon can slam the Warping Bars this day three weeks, one quarter of a mile, with little Bill Allen's weight on each; for fifty dollars in cash two hundred in the best sort of truck [livestock, produce, or other barter]." "It is a wedding," said Dan. With the negotiations out of the way, both sides began drinking, Dan and Jim Cole having each treated to "a gallon, and sugar enough to sweeten it." Within twenty minutes Dan had offered another sort of challenge: "I can pick the ticks off of any of you hell fire boys," and Jim had responded by hitting him near the ear. Now "the physic was working," and a melee ensued. Eventually the Devil's Fork boys triumphed, although they came away with plenty of facial cuts as well as "bit noses and fingers."

In his next letter, Pete described a bear hunt that took place the day after the fight at the Doggery. He went off on his horse, taking six dogs with him and meeting two friends with their own canines. The following day, some thirty miles away, the dogs found "a tremendous bear," who knocked two dogs "into the middle of next week" and made two more "hear it thunder." Shot twice, the bear escaped, closely pursued by the remaining dogs, who cornered him again. The hunters arrived just in time to save their animals, who were continuing the attack. Even as it was wounded a third and fatal time, the bear grabbed Pete's dog General Jackson, and to save his pet Pete stabbed the dying bear twice. It finally gave up. Seven dogs had died in the fight, and others were badly wounded. To rest both themselves and their animals, the hunters stayed where they were that night, finding honey in a bee tree, killing some turkeys, and feasting on these supplies along with the ribs of the bear.

These two stories are important because they humanize Arkansas in a way that travelers' accounts do not. The boisterousness of the Jacksonian man emerges as the settlers brag and bet their way into a horse race, after which they drink and fight as many Americans of their time might have done. The violence presented here is neither sinister nor deadly, but rather almost friendly and recreational. Noland, however, did not romanticize life in Arkansas. In a later story, he described a horse race on Cravat Stuffing Creek that led to a fight in which Pete Whetstone's friend Bill Spenser was cut. Pete himself went after the man who did it: "The first lick I made slashed him right across the face, cutting his nose in two." Similarly, Pete Whetstone's bear hunt is a violent test of men and beasts. One can easily imagine that eastern sportsmen who read this story in the *Spirit* envied the Arkansas hunters, who enjoyed such excitement and then made an out-door meal of wild game and honey before sleeping under the stars.

Horse racing and hunting remained important topics in all of the sixty-three letters featuring Pete Whetstone or his friends that Noland wrote over the next two decades. Politics, however, was another important interest of Noland's, and thus it quickly became a major part of Pete Whetstone's life. In order to understand the significance of Noland's perspective, it is useful to look at some political comments by Featherstonhaugh. In describing society in Little Rock in 1834, he wrote about the manners of the people, including the fact that nearly all the adult males carried bowie knives. One of his criticisms involved the intense political interest of the people. Featherstonhaugh pointed out that small towns in England simply did not have newspapers, since the poor could not afford to buy them. Little Rock, however, had three newspapers for its six hundred inhabitants, and they were, according to him, "not read but devoured by everybody." The "sovereign people," as he called them, using an ironic phrase of the time, wanted the excitement of learning that "the political party which has omit-ted to purchase their support is composed of scoundrels and liars, and men who want to get into power for no other purpose but to ruin their coun-try." Featherstonhaugh was correct about the intensity of political interest in Little Rock and probably not far wrong about the venality of the voters. On the other hand, Noland, as we shall see, presents the same reality in a much more appealing light.

In the early summer of 1837, the *Spirit of the Times* began publishing a series of letters that described Pete Whetstone's attempt to win election to the state legislature from Van Buren County. Upon arriving at a log rolling on the middle fork of the Little Red, Pete finds his opponent, lawyer McCampbell, "cutting a wide swarth among the sovereigns." In an impromptu stump speech McCampbell emphasizes that he is a loyal member of the national and state Democratic Party. "I am an unambi-tious man—I never sought office . . . I am a disciple of the [Martin] Van Buren, Amos Kendall, Tom [Thomas Hart] Benton, Buck Woodruff [William Woodruff, editor of the *Arkansas Gazette*] school. I have always been a democrat—one that loves the many, and hates the few . . . I pledge myself to vote as Chester Ashley [Arkansas attorney, land speculator, and Democratic leader] and Buck Woodruff tell me." After touting his own qualifications, McCampbell chides Pete for being uneducated.

Pete's speech, which he describes in the third person, places individual character above party loyalty and practical skills above learning. "Pete is an ambitious man—but his is an honorable ambition. Pete always went for Old Hickory, but he can't swallow Marting Van Buring [*sic*] or Buck Woodruff. Pete is a democrat, according to the old fashion meaning . . . Pete is no orator; but when it comes to killing a bear, or finding a bee tree, he is there. If he goes to the legislature, he will do his best for you. Pete tracks no man." In this textbook rendering of Jacksonian politics, Noland the Whig uses Pete Whetstone to flay the Democrats for their tendency to flatter the voters, their insincere humility, and their shameless party loyalty. Pete, on the other hand, makes up his own mind—voting for Jackson, but refusing to vote for Van Buren. He advertises himself on the basis of his democratic values, his practical skills, and his independent judgment. "Pete tracks no man" is an assertion of individual responsibility in a political culture that seems to have placed party above all other values.

The issue of character came up in another letter, in which Pete claims that McCampbell had been "among the religious women, telling them with a long face that I am a sinner—that I play cards, horse race, and drink whiskey." Meeting that charge head on, the hero of the Devil's Fork allows that "he loves God, fears the devil, and hates snakes." More specifically, "he doesn't play cards, except when the truck is up. He doesn't horse race, except for fun, and when there is a sure chance to win. He doesn't drink liquor, except bald face whiskey [moonshine], just to encourage our own 'stil houses." Then Pete goes on the offensive. He says that he is not two-faced, as McCampbell is, and he does not go to camp meetings in order to hug the girls, as McCampbell does. Finally, Pete, who claims that Martin Van Buren is a Dutchman, assails McCampbell for arguing that the president is Irish.

In another letter, Pete elaborates the Whig argument against the Democrats. McCampbell publishes a circular letter with the aid of the Democratic leadership in Little Rock that is full of meaningless rhetoric and false information. McCampbell says: "I was born of democratic parents—I was brought up democratically—the democratic State of Virginia gave me birth—I moved to the democratic State of Missouri, and now live in the democratic State of Arkansas." Then he calls Pete an aristocrat because he believes in the Bank of the United States. Next, McCampbell makes an ironic claim for economic success under the Democrats: "it took the democracy to learn the people to bank without specie capital." Finally, he closes by taking credit for the economic success of the country. As Noland's readers were well aware, Van Buren's

Specie Circular had caused significant economic dislocation, and the United States was actually sliding into a severe depression. Pete Whetstone has the last word: "Well, now, the lawyer beats hell amazingly. All that are stuff about the banks is lies . . . I saw right in the late paper where most everybody in [New] Orleans was broke."

In Noland's fictional election, Van Buren County went for Whetstone over McCampbell by a vote of eighty to fifty-nine. Pete had some last-minute help from two friends who had carried livestock on a flatboat to New Orleans and sold it for paper money that turned out to be nearly worthless because of the "broken banks." Angry at Van Buren and McCampbell, the two men worked hard for Pete in the last days before the election. As things got back to normal after the election, Pete's sister Sal married Jim Cole, and a horse race was planned between "Hyena" and the "Charmed Bullet." Moreover, Pete's aunt Peggy Sims told him that since the camp meeting six months ago, the neighborhood gals had "out-fattened anything she ever saw," adding that nine months after a camp meeting there were always three times as many babies as normal.

Noland, however, had trouble leaving politics alone. In October 1837, Pete sent a letter to the *Spirit* telling how even lawyer McCampbell was against Van Buren's Sub-Treasury Plan: "If the United States Bank was a monster, the Treasury bank would be a double monster." Moreover, there were two clock peddlers from New Hampshire on the Devil's Fork talking about a new political party called the locofocos. According to these two, "the loco focos were the real friends of the people—that they went in for equal rights—that all men were born equal, and that the word equal meant that every man was entitled to an equal share of property." This was an interesting concept to the locals, until the newcomers suggested that Dan Looney's livestock be equally divided among the group. Looney, in particular, and Pete's friends, in general, proved to be more attached to private property than they knew, and they "beat, bruised, and amalgamated" the clock salesmen "until they looked like the last of an ill-spent life." Summing up, Pete allowed that "loco focoism is knocked into a cocked-hat on the Devil's Fork." Lawyer McCampbell's disaffection from the Democratic Party made Pete "proud as a dog with a bunch of red roses tied to his tail." It also made the lawyer an excellent spokesman for the Whig Party. He complained to Pete about Levi Woodbury, Van Buren's secretary of the treasury, argued that a new Bank of the United States was necessary, and said that William Henry Harrison was the only man who could save the country. McCampbell even seemed to have lost his old respect for the people. After a visit to northern Arkansas, he reported to Pete that half of the people in that area thought that Jackson was still president. While in Little Rock, McCampbell visited the office of William Woodruff. When the editor asked McCampbell why he didn't "tell about General Jackson and the great democratic principles" in his race against Pete Whetstone, the lawyer responded that "that was what used me up." When Woodruff realized that McCampbell had changed sides, he called him a "traitor," but the lawyer threatened to reveal "what happened right in this office once," an allusion to the death of John T. Garrett, who had been shot under mysterious circumstances in the presence of Woodruff and Ashley. Noland here exposes a bit of Arkansas dirty linen to the readers of the *Spirit of the Times.*

Pete took one more crack at the Democrats when he got to the legislature in Little Rock. He noted that "they talk about the honest mechanic, and worthy farmer—the bone and sinew—and all such stuff," but at the same time "they wear the best of broad cloth, fur hats, and the like." Just before Christmas, Pete wrote another letter, and this one contained an account of the famous incident in which Col. John Wilson, speaker of the Arkansas House, attacked and killed J. J. Anthony, a legislator from Randolph County, on the floor of the statehouse. Noland was in the legislature at this time, and Pete's response is a reminder that his creator was a former duelist. "I tell you it was a dreadful slaughtering—the way the big knives were pulled out, and such a slashing—it was awful. But I reckon a man has to pay now for toting a knife, pistol, or other dangerous weapon."

C. F. M. Noland wrote fiction, but it came from a large reservoir of experience that was constantly enriched by his active involvement in Arkansas life. He developed his humor from actual circumstances and events that occurred in the state. Noland liked Arkansas, its people, and their pastimes. His characters hunt, gamble, drink, brawl, and occasionally hurt each other seriously, but they are also farmers and citizens, and they have an admirable spirit of independence. Modern readers wince when Pete Whetstone cuts someone's nose, but many would like to go hunting with him or drink at the Doggery and listen to him talk about politics. The idea that Pete walks in no one's tracks is appealing to us. We cannot reinterpret Arkansas based on events in the fictional life of Pete Whetstone; however, Noland's interpretation of Arkansas as a rough but recognizably American society of the Jacksonian era is as plausible as the idea that the state was distinguished by its thoroughgoing culture of backwoods barbarism.

The adventures of Pete Whetstone provide some important insights into Arkansas society, yet they are hardly comprehensive. Noland was a writer, humorist, and politician, but he was not a sociologist. He shows us the character of Devil's Fork society and provides insights into the nature of politics, but he tells us little about the structure of society. There is a rough equality among Noland's characters, a quality that, in reality, was not so much false as it was unrepresentative of Arkansans as a whole. There were few slaves living along the Little Red River, for example, but in Arkansas as a whole one in every four or five persons was a slave. Moreover, while Noland's characters demonstrate the ethos of Jacksonian equality—the sense of one white man being as good as another—they gloss over the remarkable degree of economic inequality that existed among the "sovereigns."

The nature of inequality and of social structure in general can be understood with some precision by looking at tax records, a form of historical evidence much less charming than the Pete Whetstone stories but nonetheless valuable. Arkansas levied a poll tax on white males twenty-one years old and over, and it assessed taxable property that included acres of land, town lots, slaves from nine to fifty-nine years old, horses and cattle over three years old, and capital invested in merchandise. The value of an individual's taxable property was a rough but meaningful measure of that person's economic position. Large random samples of taxpayers for 1840 and 1860 indicate that the wealthiest 10 percent of taxpayers owned more than 70 percent of taxable wealth in each of those years. In terms of the distribution of wealth, Arkansas was a very unequal society, but this was not unusual with respect to the rest of the South or to the United States as a whole.

Like the rest of the South, Arkansas was an agricultural society, and much of its social structure was defined by the ownership of land and slaves. Its most important social classes were yeomen farmers and planters. The former were Thomas Jefferson's hope for the United States, men who owned their own land and earned from it an economic and political independence. Yeomen might own a few slaves, but they operated farms rather than plantations. The difference between a well-to-do yeoman and a small planter was probably unclear even at the time, but for the purposes of analysis, historians have generally claimed that the ownership of twenty or more slaves put an individual into the planting class. Planters often owned many more slaves and commensurate amounts of land. Many of them also practiced law or invested in commercial activities. In addition to their economic power, the southern planters as a class dominated the social and political life of the region.

An analysis of tax records for 1860 shows some of the economic differences among Arkansas households. At the bottom of the taxpaying hierarchy was a group of about 10 percent who owned no taxable property at all and were only on the list because of the poll tax. Most of these men were probably enumerated as laborers. They may have been quite poor, but that is not clear. A large number, perhaps one-third, lived in someone else's household. Many of them were probably young men still living with their parents on land that they would one day inherit. Other propertyless men may have been professional men or townspeople who owned wealth that was not taxed.

TABLE 1

Taxpayer Groups by Taxable Property, 1860

GROUP	PERCENT	MEDIAN PROPERTY
Propertyless	10	
Yeomen	70	80 acres, 2–3 cattle, 1 horse
Slaveholding Yeomen	17	3 slaves, 240 acres, 6 cattle, 2 horses
Planters	3	30 slaves, 900 acres, 25 cattle, 4 horses, 8 mules

Among Arkansas taxpayers, 70 percent owned taxable property but no slaves. The poorest of them may have been less well off than the propertyless, since they seem to have had their own households and little else. Slightly better off were nonslaveholding taxpayers, who owned a horse and one or two head of cattle, but no land. Probably they were squatting on government land and farming for subsistence. The middle group of nonslaveholders were small farmers, owning about 80 acres of land, two or three head of cattle, and a horse. The top 10 percent of nonslaveholders each had about four hundred acres, five or ten cattle, and several horses. Nearly one in five of these taxpayers also owned a mule. Most of them were farmers, but 14 percent of them owned town lots and were probably included among the artisans, professionals, and businessmen of Arkansas.

About 20 percent of the taxpayers owned slaves, and 3 percent of taxpayers owned enough slaves to qualify as planters. Other than their slaves, however, there was little that distinguished the small slaveholders from the more prosperous of the nonslaveholders. The median slaveholder, for example, owned three taxable slaves, 240 acres of land, six head of cattle, and two horses. This was a yeoman farmer who owned slaves. His lifestyle was probably little different from his nonslaveholding neighbors. Indeed, there was considerable movement of Arkansas farmers into and out of the status of small slaveholder.

Planters, however, were different. The median planter owned 30 taxable slaves, probably closer to 40 actual slaves when young and aged slaves were included. In addition the average planter owned nine hundred acres of land, 25 head of cattle, 4 horses, and 8 mules. This was a status that the nonslaveholder would find difficult to achieve. Above the middle range of planters, an economic gulf opened, separating the commoner from the very well-to-do. Elisha Worthington, the richest planter in Arkansas in 1860, owned twelve thousand acres of land in cotton-rich Chicot County and peopled it with 543 slaves. His taxable property in the country was $472,000. On Sunnyside, which was his home, and three other plantations, he produced 2,950 bales of cotton, 31,500 bushels of corn, 2,200 bushels of sweet potatoes, and 1,000 pounds of butter and quantities of poultry, beeswax, Irish potatoes, vegetables, and fruits. His livestock included 16 horses, 200 mules, 80 oxen, 45 cows, 350 head of cattle, and 340 pigs.

In reality, of course, there were lots of men who were neither yeomen nor planters. The Census of 1850 collected data on the vocation of white males in Arkansas and found that only 71 percent were farmers, a designation that included both yeomen and planters. The second-largest category was laborers, probably agricultural workers for the most part, who made up 14 percent of the total. The remaining 15 percent fell into a variety of occupations. The largest groups of occupations, each forming 1 to 2 percent of the whole, were blacksmiths, carpenters, merchants, and physicians; and there were smaller groups of clergymen, overseers, lawyers, clerks, and millers.

Inventories of estates, taken upon the death of an individual in connection with the probate process, provide more information about the lifestyles associated with varying degrees of wealth. Historian Sewanee Bennett has analyzed thirty-nine inventories taken in Pulaski County during the 1850s. Half of these list household furnishings valued at less than a hundred dollars, a bare minimum. Just over half of these twenty estates list beds, bedding, and bedsteads, and less than half list tables. Other items of furniture are still more scarce. Firearms appear in about half of these households and spinning and weaving equipment in about one-third, which suggests a lifestyle that may have been focused on subsistence. The evidence may be skewed, however, by relatives who removed household furnishings prior to the arrival of the estate executors, an activity that may have been common, judging from the fact that four of these estates belong to men who also owned slaves. In general, however, the personal property of the owner is commensurate with the rude nature of his possessions, and both suggest a low level of material existence.

All but one of the remaining inventories are valued between $100 and $500, and they reveal a much wider range of furniture. Almost all list beds, and tables, washstands, chairs, wardrobes, bureaus, bookcases, mirrors, and stoves are common. Significantly, firearms and spinning wheels are more rare. A final inventory, that of Absalom Fowler, an attorney and politician in Little Rock, was valued at $2,310. Fowler was obviously a man who cared about the furnishings of his home, including the sixteen portraits that he owned. R. S. Galloway, however, was at the other end of the consumption spectrum. He was four times as wealthy as Fowler, possessing thirty-six slaves, yet his household inventory only came to $465.

Material culture, the physical remains of the past, provides another way of knowing about society. Not a lot of tangible things have come down to us from Arkansas Territory or antebellum Arkansas, but recent studies make those artifacts more available and easier to understand. We know, for example, something about the homes of early Arkansans, particularly about those of the ubiquitous yeomen farmers. We also know quite a bit about the domestic architecture of Little Rock, which included a number of grand and stylish residences, and we have artwork, which helps us to visualize the elite citizens of the state as they wanted to be seen.

The earliest and most widespread home type in early Arkansas was the log cabin. Derived from the Germans, this vernacular structure came west from the Middle Atlantic region, traveled through the Appalachian Mountains and Kentucky, and spread all over the upland South. Arkansas cabins were usually built from oak logs and were sixteen to eighteen feet square, the size being limited by the length of a log that could be carried by two men. Rough cabins used round logs notched in a simple saddle form. More elaborate versions were made of logs that were hewn on two sides and attached with a half-dovetail notch that created a tight fit and tended to shed water away from the structure. The roofs were made of split shingles, and pieces of shingle were used to chink the spaces between the logs. A stone chimney was located at one of the gable ends, and the door was always in the center at right angles to the ridge pole. Rude log cabins might have dirt floors, but more often split logs with the rounded side down were used as flooring.

The simple single-pen cabin, comprising four interlocking walls, was a form that allowed for expansion. A double-pen house, for example, was essentially two cabins built side by side. The difficulties of connecting two cabins led to the development of what architectural historians call the dogtrot house, two pens built with a space between them and a common roof. The space created a breezeway that was useful for sleeping in the hot summer months, storing things, or simply enjoying the air. Around these single- or double-cabin homes were normally arrayed a variety of out-buildings, corncribs, smokehouses, and occasionally barns, built in the same log-pen style.

One-room log construction was the temporary solution to housing all over Arkansas, although many families soon enlarged their homes by adding a second pen or sometimes a second story. Most of the structures built in Little Rock in the 1820s were made of round logs. In 1827 there were some sixty structures of all types in the capital city; more than three-quarters of them were of log construction, although usually with more than one room. The remaining structures included six brick buildings and eight frame buildings. Frame buildings used lumber from a sawmill, but the timbers were heavy, they were connected by mortises and tenons, and the joints were reinforced by wooden pegs. The architecture and the construction of these structures were similar to those of the log pen.

Log homes, some dating from the 1830s, are still numerous in the Ozarks in northwestern Arkansas, although most have been altered, and many have been turned into barns. An outstanding, albeit atypical, example of the type is the Jacob Wolf House, built about 1830 near Norfork in what is now Baxter County. This is a dogtrot home that features a second story and porches on each level. While they are identified with the highlands of the South, however, log cabins were also common in the lowlands. Seth Eastman made a pencil sketch in 1848 of a home on the bank of the Mississippi River below Helena that was a fine example of a double-pen hewn-log cabin with a roofed porch on both the front and the back. In front of the main structure is an outbuilding constructed of round logs in a rougher manner. Similarly, the Arkansas Territorial Restoration in Little Rock today displays a dogtrot cabin that was originally located near Scott, Arkansas, among the cotton fields on the western edge of the Delta.

We may envision the settlers of Arkansas—the squatters, farmers, and probably many newly arrived planters—as living for the most part with their families in one- or two-log pens. These families averaged about six persons per household, who would therefore be living in one or two rooms of less than three hundred square feet each. In nice weather, many people probably slept outside, on the porch if one was available, and cooking, too, was done in the open air. In the best of conditions, however, these homes must have been crowded, and particularly so in the winter months when family life would be bounded by the walls of the log pen. Comfort would also depend a great deal upon the scale of construction and the skill employed. The four-room Wolf house is a commodious and comfortable structure compared to the single pen, round-log, dirt-floor, porchless cabin depicted by Edward Payson Washburne in his painting *The Arkansas Traveler*. It is very difficult to know whether the home of the average Arkansas farmer was more like the former or the latter.

In any case, it seems clear that the farmers and planters of Arkansas often lived in structures that were not remarkably different from each other. For example, in 1838 Friederick Gerstäcker worked for a man named Saint on a farm near the L'Anguille River in eastern Arkansas. Saint's home was a dogtrot log house. Gerstäcker said that "it consisted of two ordinary houses, under one roof, with passage between them open to north and south, a nice cool place to eat or sleep in summer months." The roof was covered with "rough four-feet plank." Each room had a clay fireplace, but neither had windows. Additional log houses served as a storehouse for corn, a smokehouse, and a stable. Twenty-two years later, on the eve of the Civil War, Henry Morton Stanley stayed at a plantation owned by Major Ingham in south Arkansas. He described the house as being built "of solid pine logs, roughly squared, . . . neatly chinked without with plaster, and lined within with planed boards, new and unpainted." The dimensions of this structure are not clear, but it did have a "verandah," and Stanley credited it with "an air of domestic comfort." Nonetheless, despite owning twenty-four slaves, Ingham was living in a modified log cabin.

By the antebellum period, however, many Arkansas planters and well-to-do farmers, like upwardly mobile agriculturalists throughout the United States, were living in versions of what architectural historians call the I house. These were two-story structures, one-room deep, with at least four rooms and usually a central hallway. A traditional English home, the I house is named for the vertical appearance it presents from the side. Besides being more commodious than the double-pen log houses, the I house allows for good ventilation and presents an imposing facade. A surviving example is the Sarah Louisa and Hosea Marmaduke Maguire house built in 1850 in Maguiretown in Washington County. The Homsley-Shofner house, built near Tuttle in 1845, was a brick I house with a deep two-story portico featuring dentil molding and Tuscan columns.

The gap between the housing of ordinary people and that of the elite was occasionally still more extreme. For example, in the 1820s while Little Rock was still mostly a collection of log houses, Robert Crittenden built a fine home in the style of Jeffersonian classicism. The single-story structure consisted of four rooms and a large central hallway. Two of the rooms were 22 feet square, and the others were 22 feet by 20 feet. Another room at the rear was 24 feet square. The ceilings were 14 feet high. At the front entrance, a large portico featured a pediment containing a fanlight, and the front door stood within a semicircular opening. Along with its outbuildings, the Crittenden home required 300,000 bricks. It was, according to architectural historians Roy and Witsell, "remarkably fashionable for frontier Little Rock." In later years, fine homes would become more common. Chester Ashley built a brick home on a square block and later expanded it into a two-story structure with a Greek Revival portico and six large columns. Albert Pike also built an imposing Greek Revival home; it took up a full block of Little Rock land and contained eight rooms on two floors.

The I house and the elegant homes of Little Rock suggest the maturation of the Arkansas economy in the antebellum years and the unequal nature of material success. Similar evidence of the growing significance of elite society is provided by the oil portraits that well-to-do Arkansans commissioned in order to immortalize themselves and their families. A number of artists were represented in the Arkansas portraiture of this period, but the most prolific was Henry Byrd, who worked in the state between 1840 and 1860. Byrd was born in Ireland in 1805, but he migrated to New York City at an early age and learned to paint there with other family members, who were also painters. About 1841, and with a wife and two children, Byrd moved to New Orleans. From there, he traveled in search of commissions. In 1842 he settled in Batesville and began to paint the local gentry. Despite declaring bankruptcy, he seems to have been kept busy.

The William Byers Family, done sometime before 1845, features Mrs Byers sitting in a chair while her three children attend her. All of the figures are dressed in fashionable outfits, and Mrs. Byers' long hair is done in stylish ringlets. Her chair is a well-turned velvet-covered rocker, and

C. F. M. Noland, creator of Pete Whetstone; painting ca. 1845–50 by Henry Byrd.

Courtesy of the Arkansas Territorial Restoration.

Mrs. Roswell Beebe; painting ca. 1845 by Henry Byrd.

Courtesy of the Arkansas Territorial Restoration.

the overall impression of bourgeois comfort is strengthen by a tall silver vase in the foreground. Appropriately more plain is Byrd's portrait of C. F. M. Noland, shown in a black coat and tie with a white shirt and rounded collar. Long-faced but thoughtful and handsome, Noland looks like the country gentleman that he was; there is nothing here resembling the rustic Pete Whetstone. Similarly, Mrs. Roswell Beebe, the wife of a wealthy Little Rock entrepreneur, looks as if she would be equally comfortable in New Orleans or perhaps even in New York. During the late 1840s, Byrd moved to south Arkansas, eventually settling in El Dorado, but he continued to paint the elite of the state. Peter Hanger of Little Rock had a portrait done that shows him as a confident and prosperous businessman. Byrd also painted Hanger's two wives and his daughter Margaret.

Portraits, log cabins, tax lists, fiction, and travelers' accounts provide a diverse and sometimes conflicting view of Arkansas society. Nonetheless, there are some elements of order. Arkansans, however crude, were much like other Americans in their interests and behavior, in their material culture, in the unequal manner in which their wealth was distributed, and in the way that the wealthy chose to document their success.

CHAPTER SIX

Religion and Family

In 1825 Jared Martin of Little Rock received a letter from his brother Andrew, who was apparently a clergyman, expressing delight that Jared had expressed "contrition" about things that had occurred between them. Andrew also hoped that Jared was not permanently affected by "the early period of your life which gave rise to your becoming acquainted with the fashionable circles of this vain and licentious world." Seven years later, Andrew was happy to receive a letter from Jared that dwelt on "the all important subject of religion." Jared and his wife had lost a "dear relation," and Andrew gave solace by pointing out that "your loss is nothing more than her eternal and everlasting gain" and that she would be "with God, and there enjoy the full fruition of his presence." John Martin, Jared's brother in Missouri, lamented that "I cannot possess religion myself," but he also took pleasure in hearing about Jared's developing piety and acknowledged its significance: "Genuine religion I have always viewed as mans highest calling on this Earth." Jared also received letters from a third brother, Allen, who was surveying in the wilderness of Arkansas. Happy to report his continuing good health, Allen ascribed that circumstance variously to "our great benefactor," "the blessing of our heavenly father," and "the supreme dispenser of our dayly happiness." The Martin brothers are a good example of a family that attended to the spiritual lives of its members, but their religious concerns were shared by many other Arkansans.

Among them were the Butlers. In March 1857, Lewis Butler, who was away at school, wrote to his sister Emma at the family home in Tulip, a thriving little village in southern Arkansas: "Sunday here is the dullest day of all others . . . Now at Tulip, Sunday is always the most welcome day of all others. There we always have preaching the most welcome to go to, and at night down at home, to sit and talk with you all or to sing a song or two, what is more pleasant!"

This same association of religious warmth and domestic happiness was made by George, another brother of Emma's, who wrote a year later from Randolph-Macon College. "How valuable do I find religion far away from home at college. When my soul without it might be oppressed with gloom and melancholy, with it I am made to feel happy trusting in Jesus . . . How I would like to be at Tulip, Home, tonight for it is Friday night and I reckon the church is lit up." Emma, Lewis, and George Butler were not typical Arkansans—their family was more prosperous and better educated than most—yet the attention they gave to religion and the way they found it supported by their home and family were common feelings throughout Arkansas and the South.

Much of this religiosity can be traced back to the influence of the Great Revival of 1800 to 1805, which made evangelical Christianity a common culture among whites and blacks in the South and gave the region a new reputation for piety. During the colonial period, the Church of England had maintained reasonably effective establishments in Maryland, Virginia, and South Carolina, but its claims to regional hegemony were shattered by the large-scale migrations of Germans, Scots-Irish Presbyterians, and New Light Baptists into the backcountry of the South during the eighteenth century. During the American Revolution, the influence of the dissenters was strong enough to disestablish the state churches, but it was another quarter of a century before denominationalism—the free competition of churches that emerged after the separation of church and state—would lead to a new religious order.

The Second Great Awakening is the name given to the spread of evangelical religion throughout the United States in the early years of the nineteenth century. In the South, it began with the Great Revival, a series of frontier revivals that originated in Kentucky in the late 1790s and developed the camp meeting as its most effective means of conversion. Staffed by Methodist, Baptist, and Presbyterian clergymen who took turns preaching to an encamped audience during a period of two or three days, the camp meetings generated a powerful response from backwoods southerners, which included shouting, fainting, tree climbing, and the jerks, a paroxysm of shaking that indicated an intense emotional reaction. From Kentucky the revivals spread west and east until the entire South came under the influence of this new evangelicalism. Calvinism was not completely discarded, but southern Christians came to believe that the practice of personal discipline, combined with powerful preaching, would usually bring about the conversion of even those who had been the most hopeless of sinners. As Donald G. Mathews has written, the paradox of man's free will and God's omnipotence "became resolved in the favor of the commonsense belief in man's ability to repent and commit himself to Christ."

As southern evangelicalism became a dominant and permanent phenomenon in the region, it was particularly significant for women, who represented about 65 percent of church members. Women were also very involved in family religion and the devotions that were associated with it. According to the mores of the time, the ideal Christian family would pray together three times a day, read Scriptures in the morning and the evening, and discuss the state of everyone's soul. While these activities were important in strengthening the faith of adults, their more important goal was to insure that children were raised in a Christian manner. By and large women were responsible for family religion, which became an important aspect of "domesticity," the conception of woman's role in the home. Southern men did not give up the idea that women were a subordinate gender, but they did believe that females were naturally more religious than males.

* * *

While the Great Revival was altering southern religion, however, the few white settlers in Arkansas remained largely Catholic, even though there were apparently no priests stationed on the Arkansas River for two decades after the Louisiana Purchase. A Father Chaudorat arrived at Arkansas Post on his own in the spring of 1820 and stayed about a year, but the inhabitants disliked him. Several other priests passed through Arkansas to gather information for Father Joseph Rosati of St. Louis, who became a coadjutor for the bishop of New Orleans in 1823 and was named the first bishop of the diocese of St. Louis in 1826. In both of these positions, his pastoral responsibility included Arkansas. Not until 1831, however, was Rosati able to obtain funds to send two priests to Arkansas on a permanent basis, and they lasted little more than a year. Small wonder, then, that when Father Ennemond Dupuy arrived at Arkansas Post in

1832, he found an unchurched population: "It is useless to speak to them of abstinence, fasting or confession, or of the duty to marry before a priest." Dupuy labored on the Arkansas River for four years, until he was relieved by Father Peter Donnelly, an Irishman who proved to be more popular, and who worked at building a school at New Gascony, a few miles below Pine Bluff. Five nuns from the Sisters of Loretto in Kentucky worked at the school for a time, but by 1845 it was abandoned along with Catholic schools in Little Rock and in Pine Bluff. In 1843, a Little Rock diocese was created with Bishop Andrew Byrne in charge.

It was the Methodists who brought southern evangelicalism into Arkansas. William Stevenson of Belleville, Missouri, a "local preacher" without any formal training or ordination, traveled down the Southwest Trail in 1814, bringing religious services for the first time to the newly arrived settlers: "Prayer in families and the gospel preached was a new thing." Stevenson's description of his experiences indicates the difficulty of bringing religion to the frontier, but also why the Methodists were so good at it. "Sometimes we camped in the wilderness, by a running stream, the water and range for our horses good; and sometime we found room in the friendly man's cabin, shared with him in the fruits of his chase, belled our houses, turned them out in a large pasture of the wilderness, had prayers with the family, laid ourselves down on a bear or deer skin, slept soundly and arose happy. At some places we found good beds and better fare; but all was well, for God was with us."

At a settlement on the Ouachita River, Stevenson found a man named McMahon, a Baptist from Kentucky who was "greatly backslidden" and very unhappy about the state of his soul. According to Stevenson, McMahon "appeared not rightly to understand the gift that had come upon all men into justification of life." His misery was relieved by the idea that "Christ died for all." Later, during prayers, he wept with joy, and so did his wife and children. At a nearby settlement, Stevenson met a widow named Dickson, whom he called "an old mother in Israel." She was "delighted to hear that God was mindful of the country in sending the gospel to them." Stevenson appears to have had a good deal of success. As he put it, "we got up small societies [congregations] on the rivers and large creeks where the people had found good land."

Stevenson's goal was to create a Methodist circuit that would run from the Current River in northeast Arkansas to Pecan Point in southwest Arkansas, roughly following the Southwest Trail, which was the avenue of immigration. While he was in Arkansas in 1815, the Tennessee

Conference of the Methodist Church did create a Spring River Circuit that covered the settlements in the northeast. The first minister of that circuit was Eli Lindsey, a young man then in his teens. Lindsey was somewhat less orthodox in his teaching than Stevenson had been and rougher in his ways. He visited log rollings, house raisings, and frolics and was happy to have the young people dance before he preached to them. In the vicinity of the present site of Batesville, he once interrupted his preaching when the sound of barking dogs indicated that a bear was near. His male listeners picked up their guns, mounted their horses, and pursued the animal. When they returned with a dead bear, Lindsey gave thanks "for men who knew how to shoot and women who knew how to pray."

In 1816, all of Arkansas north of the Arkansas River was included in the newly created Missouri Conference of the Methodist Church. That same year, the conference sent William Stevenson to preside over a Hot Springs circuit, apparently unconcerned that it was south of the Arkansas River. The Hot Springs circuit seems to have covered the settlements between the Ouachita River and the Red River, where Stevenson had organized a number of small congregations. He himself settled in Mound Prairie, located on the Red River, well south and west of Hot Springs, and that area became an early center of Methodism. The Mount Moriah meeting house built there was probably the first Methodist church building in Arkansas. Mound Prairie and Pecan Point became circuits in 1818, and an Arkansas circuit was created at the same time to serve the settlements along the Arkansas River.

The growth of Methodism is illustrated by events that took place in the year 1831. Washington County was growing rapidly at that time, and a Methodist congregation was organized at Fayetteville. Little Rock, which was often the scene of sermons by members of various denominations, organized a Methodist congregation, which met in the log cabin that the Presbyterians used for worship. At the end of the year, Arkansas Methodism received a boost with the arrival of eight ministers from the Tennessee Conference. They gathered at Memphis, but were unwilling to cross the Mississippi River there and enter the swampland of eastern Arkansas. Instead, they bought a boat and floated to Helena, sleeping out along the way. One man remained in Helena; the rest set out for various locations: Pine Bluff, Mound Prairie, Little Rock, the Creek Nation, and the Cherokee Nation.

Methodists also participated in camp meetings, often along with ministers from other denominations. The earliest of these evangelical events appears to have been held about 1821 at a location near Cadron. Methodists continued to hold meetings at this site, but they also participated in camp meetings held at Crystal Hill on the north side of the Arkansas River just upstream from Little Rock. These camp meetings were probably organized by Rev. John Carnahan, of the Cumberland Presbyterian Church. At one such event in May 1825 a meeting at that site featured a number of Methodist and Baptists, including some "from Kentucky and Tennessee."

Camp meetings continued throughout the antebellum period. Methodist minister Andrew Hunter held meetings near Benton in central Arkansas that were highly successful. One admirer described these events this way: "I have seen the time when hundreds of people came in ox wagons, horse and mule wagons, and many walked for miles to come to Camp Meeting . . . When the horn blowed everyone left their tents and came to the shed and stayed until the service was over. The preachers preached a convincing gospel of Jesus Christ and I have seen mourners pour into the altar in groups of fifty at a time. Old Dr. Hunter's favorite sermon was on the Prodigal Son. When he reached the climax and called for mourners they filled the aisles."

Baptists also entered Arkansas early, and they grew rapidly in numbers and built many churches. George Gill was probably the first Baptist minister in the territory, settling on the White River in 1814. A large number of Baptists were part of the migration that came down the Southwest Trail. David Orr, a minister from Kentucky, entered northeast Arkansas in 1828, where he found a positive reception for his ministry: "Sinners were awakened and mourners were brought to a knowledge of their sins forgiven." Over the next few years, he founded nine churches and was a principal organizer of the Spring River Baptist Association. Silas Toncray, another Baptist minister, founded a church in Little Rock in 1824. Maj. Isaac Watkins, an immigrant from Kentucky who opened a tavern and a mill in Little Rock, assisted Toncray and acted as a clerk in the church.

Baptists in Arkansas Territory were plagued with the divisions that beset the church in general. Hard Shell or Primitive Baptists were hostile to most church organizations and were strong believers in predestination. Other members of the denomination were influenced by the Landmark movement within the church, which advanced a strict orthodoxy and refused to accept the validity of "alien immersions," that is, baptisms done outside the church. Many Baptists were also opposed to missionary work, including the activities of the American Baptist Home Mission Society, which was organized in 1832 and sent a number of missionaries to Arkansas.

Arkansas Baptist membership increased only slowly at first. By 1840 there were thirty-seven churches organized into four associations: Little Rock, Spring River, St. Francis, and Saline. Growth was more rapid in the 1840s, however, stimulating the creation of an Arkansas Baptist State Convention in 1848, which itself led to a new and vigorous missionary effort.

Presbyterianism first came to Arkansas in the breakaway version named for the Cumberland Presbytery in Kentucky, where it originated in 1810. Cumberland Presbyterians wanted more autonomy to ordain ministers who lacked the educational requirements that the parent body required. In keeping with the nature of southern evangelicalism, they believed that the preaching ability of a clergyman was more important than his scholarship. They also disagreed with the "fatality" of predestination as it was presented in the Westminster Confession. Again, this position seems to have been influenced by the camp meeting emphasis on freedom of the will.

In January 1811, four families of Cumberland Presbyterians floated down the Ohio River and then the Mississippi River. Next they made their way up the Arkansas River, finally settling at Crystal Hill, on the north side of the river just above what would become Little Rock. The heads of these families were James and Jacob Pyeatte and James and Samuel Carnahan. John Carnahan, the father of the latter two, was probably with the group as well; the next year he returned to the Cumberland meeting as a candidate for the ministry and was commissioned to form a circuit in Arkansas. Four years later he was back for ordination at what was then the Cumberland Synod. The synod found him weak on the "branches of literature required by the Discipline . . . [but] were well satisfied with his call to the ministry and knowledge of divinity." Impressed by petitions on Carnahan's behalf from people who claimed to have no other minister within five hundred miles, the synod ordained him and sent him back to Arkansas with an admonition to "keep on studying."

Carnahan labored alone until 1823, when more Cumberland Presbyterian ministers began to arrive in Arkansas. During the next decade, churches were organized in the Batesville area, along the Arkansas River, and at Mound Prairie in southwest Arkansas. In 1827 the Carnahan and Pyeatte clans left Crystal Hill and moved to Cane Hill in Washington County, which soon became a center of Cumberland Presbyterian activity.

The orthodox Presbyterian Church developed slowly in Arkansas. James Wilson Moore arrived in Little Rock in 1828 and organized the first congregation in the territory, which has remained in existence since that time as the First Presbyterian Church of Little Rock. Five years later a congregation came into being in Jackson County, but it lasted only a few years. The third Presbyterian minister in Arkansas located in Spring Hill in Hempstead County. A Presbytery of Arkansas was created in 1835 and a Synod of Arkansas in 1852.

Southern religion was fervent, but it was usually more conventional than Christianity in the North, where the Second Great Awakening led to the rise of theologically innovative groups such as the Church of Latter-day Saints and the Seventh Day Adventists. New ideas, however, were introduced into the South by Thomas Campbell, an Irish-born former Presbyterian clergyman, who believed that the Bible was the only source of religious authority, that believers were free to interpret the Word of God as they wished, and that Christians should give up sectarian wrangling and unite in their common adherence to the Bible. The Disciples of Christ, as Campbell's followers became known, were organized in 1811 in Pennsylvania, and their ideas were spread effectively by Campbell's son, Alexander, in part through periodicals published from his home in Bethany, West Virginia. The followers were often known simply as Campbellites. In the early 1830s, they merged with a similar group, known as Christians, who were led by Barton Stone of Kentucky.

As the concept of Protestant ecumenism spread west across the South, a number of Arkansans found it attractive. In 1832 the Little Rock Baptist Church adopted Campbell's perspective, renouncing "creed, rules of decorum, their name and every other appendage of human invention" and resolving to be governed only by "Jesus Christ as their King and Lawgiver" as presented in the Bible. In 1845, the Little Rock Disciples built a brick church to which they added a tower and clock in 1858. Elijah Kelley of Pike County was the first Campbellite to proselytize outside the capital city, but others quickly followed. By 1860 congregations belonging to the Disciples of Christ constituted about 3 percent of those in the state. In 1851, led by Robert Graham, they founded Arkansas College in Fayetteville, the first institution of higher education in the state.

The Protestant Episcopal Church came to Arkansas in 1839 in the person of Missionary Bishop Leonidas Polk, who would later found the University of the South and, still later, die fighting as a Confederate general. Polk visited Helena, Arkansas Post, Little Rock, Washington, and Spring Hill. He concluded that Arkansans were "very destitute of religious privileges." What they had, in his view, were "periodical visits of a Methodist circuit rider, at long intervals, and occasional services of a minister of the Cumberland Presbyterians, infrequently performed." If clergymen could be provided, Polk was optimistic about the future of the Episcopal Church in Arkansas: "The field is large, the harvest white, the labourers few indeed."

Yet the bishop was too optimistic. The Episcopal Church sent a few clergymen, and it continued to appoint energetic missionary bishops, but progress was slow. Episcopal formalism, it would seem, was a difficult sell in an environment nurtured by evangelicalism. The greatest monument of antebellum Episcopalianism seems to have been architectural in nature. Polk had begun the organization of Christ Church in Little Rock, and more official steps were taken in September 1840. Early the following year, Episcopalians began the construction of a church on three lots at Fifth and Scott Streets. In 1842 a brick church with two entrances, two aisles, and pointed arch windows was open for services. Worshipers could read the Apostles' Creed and the Ten Commandments from two walnut reredos on the eastern wall. Costing over forty-two hundred dollars, Christ Church was the grandest religious structure in the state.

The growth of organized religion in Arkansas and something of its nature are illustrated by figures compiled by U.S. Census in 1850 and 1860. Table 2 provides the number of churches by denomination in each of those years and gives the average value of church structures in 1860.

TABLE 2

Arkansas Churches in 1850 and 1860

DENOMINATION	NO. IN 1850	NO. IN 1860	VALUE IN 1860[a]
Baptist	114	281	383
Cumberland Presbyterian	—	71	526
Christians[b]	—	33	383
Episcopal	2	7	1,571
Methodist	168	505	367
Presbyterian	52	65	1,045
Roman Catholic	7	9	2,589
Other	19	37	
Total	362	1008	

[a]Value is measured in 1860 dollars.
[b]Members of the Disciples of Christ.

The Methodists were clearly the largest religious group in antebellum Arkansas, at least in terms of numbers of churches, but the Baptists were a very respectable second. The Presbyterians, including the

Cumberland Presbyterians, were a distant third. Methodist and Baptist and Christian churches appear to have had rather similar structures, which cost, on average, just under four hundred dollars. The Presbyterians and Episcopalians, however, worshiped in finer structures, and their congregations probably included a large segment of the wealthier settlers. Catholic churches may have been the finest of all, although the average figure was raised greatly by St. Andrews Cathedral in Little Rock, a large frame building with a bell tower. There were also more churches per capita in 1860 than in 1850; the population, black and white, doubled during the decade, but the number of churches increased nearly threefold. There were 580 people for each church in 1850 and only 432 in 1860.

Moral reform was an important part of the Second Great Awakening. In the North, reform began with the individual, focusing on those sins that would seem to impede salvation, and then moved on to a concern for the morality of society, giving rise to issues like temperance, penal reform, improvements in the treatment of the insane, and abolitionism. In the South, social reform, in the sense of changing existing institutions, was less significant, in part because slaveholders made it clear that slavery was not a matter for debate. Indeed, after the abolitionists began to attack slavery in the early 1830s, southern society as a whole devoted more attention to defending what existed than to thinking about how things might be improved. Southern evangelicals were also less optimistic than their northern counterparts, who preached with unrestrained enthusiasm about the perfectibility of man. Despite the emphasis on freedom of the will during the Great Revival, Baptists and Presbyterians in the South remained attached to a Calvinist worldview that did not encourage utopian thinking. Southern Methodists were also more tempered in their optimism about the human condition than those in the North.

But some reforms were important. Arkansas evangelicals supported public laws to keep the Sabbath holy and to outlaw both dueling and gambling. They also participated in a variety of Bible and tract societies that were designed to create a more literate religious society. John Buchanan, a Cumberland Presbyterian minister, became an agent for the American Bible Society in 1852. That year he visited ten counties in central and northern Arkansas, "formed or revived auxiliaries, raised funds to some good extent, procured books by purchase or as donations, and . . . [put] them in a course of circulation." Three years later, Buchanan reported that he had worked in twenty-three counties in January and February. He was especially effective in his home county, as the society reported in 1858:

"Washington County Bible Society has completed the supply of its field, every grown person living in its field having been furnished a Bible and every child that could read, with a Testament."

Temperance was a major concern of evangelical reformers. Drunkenness was viewed as a sin by all major denominations, who argued that it subverted the family, weakened the church, and undermined the state. Morality aside, there was good cause for concern. Western farmers turned surplus grain into whiskey, and Americans drank it in prodigious quantities. Between 1800 and 1835, the amount of distilled spirits consumed in the United States amounted to about eight gallons per adult per year. The first temperance society of the South was organized in Virginia in 1826. Five years later a similar organization was founded in Batesville, and shortly after another was organized in Little Rock. Temperance societies were in existence in almost all major Arkansas communities for at least the next decade.

A Fayetteville Temperance Society was organized in 1841; all of its members pledged that they would not drink alcoholic beverages, sell them, serve them to friends, or give them to people in their employ. Anyone who violated the pledge would be expelled from the society. In May A. W. Arrington, a former Methodist minister who had been expelled from the church a decade earlier for sexual irregularities, gave, according to the minutes of the society, "one of the most eloquent and instructive lectures on the subject of temperance ever delivered in the *far west.*" In July, however, the secretary reported that "some unknown *wretch*" had gotten hold of the society's constitution and "obliterated" some one hundred names of members. In January 1843 one of the members confessed that he "had frequently drank Ardent spirits, and sometimes to excess." Two months later, another member charged with a similar offense asked forgiveness but would not promise to give up drinking. Despite organizations and lectures, the temperance movement does not seem to have been effective in Fayetteville—or in Arkansas and in the South generally.

Like other southern evangelicals in general, those in Arkansas accepted the institution of slavery and encouraged the Christianization of the slaves. There were a few exceptions, particularly among the Methodists, whose denomination had once called upon its members to give up owning slaves. Jesse Haile, who was the presiding elder of Arkansas Methodism from 1825 through 1829, was a vehement opponent of slavery. According to Andrew Hunter, Haile "never held a Quarterly Meeting that he did not fire into the peculiar institution . . . The result was that many of the best Methodist families left the church." Hunter referred to the controversy surrounding Haile as a "hail storm." Thomas Tennant, who got in trouble with Haile for marrying a woman who owned slaves, was also an opponent of the institution. He wrote a letter to his friend Delegate Ambrose Sevier, declaring that "slavery is wrong, morally, religiously, politically wrong!"

Methodists in Batesville, in northeastern Arkansas, were particularly concerned about the slavery issue. In 1845, when the national church split over slavery and the Methodist Episcopal Church, South, came into being, the *Arkansas Gazette* claimed to be happy that the northern abolitionists would no longer be able to spread their views in the South. A Batesville correspondent, however, argued that fewer than one in ten Methodists favored the split and that the Methodists of northern Arkansas had not been represented at the meeting. Acrimonious debate took place in the Batesville Church, and a number of those opposed to the breakup left the congregation. One of them claimed he was "branded with being 'abolitionist' and everything else that is mean and dirty," which suggested that his commitment to the antislavery position was limited. Still, he went on to say that he could only see the new church as a "child of slavery."

In the nineteenth century, as women were increasingly confined within a sharply defined domestic sphere, the church was the one institution that offered them an opportunity for significant participation outside the home and for the acknowledgment of themselves as public individuals. Ann Conway, the mother of a territorial delegate and of two Arkansas governors, for example, was a pillar of the Methodist Church in Little Rock. William F. Pope described her role and its significance: "Eloquent in prayer, [she] often led, with trembling lips and simple trusting faith, the public congregation in their devotions."

The frontier demography of Arkansas created special circumstances for women. Young men, some single and some married, were attracted to the "new country" of Arkansas; single women, however, rarely migrated. In 1840, among adults, there were three males for every two women. Arkansas families also contained more children than those in other parts of the United States. The opportunity for subsistence agriculture seems to have encouraged large families to move to the southern frontier and to promote child bearing by resident couples. In 1840, Arkansas women aged sixteen through forty-four were caring for more children than women in any other U.S. state or territory. Twenty years later, Arkansas had fallen to fifth in this category, behind the frontier states of Oregon, Utah, Washington, and Texas.

These facts may become meaningful if we consider the domestic situation of an average women in her thirties living in Arkansas in 1840. Her household would have consisted of five or six children, more than half of them under ten years old. In about half of these households, there would also be an additional adult male, probably a relative. Including her husband and herself, there were eight people in the immediate household. The situation becomes more difficult to imagine when we remember that the average cabin home contained about 324 square feet, although some families may have built double-pen homes, which would have given them a total of 648 square feet. The households of younger women and older women were also somewhat smaller, but the average size was still over six persons.

There is abundant evidence that American women did not confine their activities to the domestic sphere that was assigned to them; rather, they contributed in a variety of ways to the economic welfare of their households. This was particularly true in agricultural areas, where the household was often the unit of production. A group of wills filed in Lawrence County between 1819 and 1836 suggests that husbands in Arkansas trusted their wives to manage the family farm. Rather than give their wives a dower right of one-third and make other provisions for the management of their property, many Lawrence County testators gave their widows full control. John Tyler Jr., for example, gave "the whole of his property after his just debts were paid to his beloved wife Polly Tyler for the use of her family." Others did the same thing, but only until the widow remarried or the children came of age. Obviously, the wives of these men had demonstrated their ability to manage affairs outside the home, probably by assisting their husbands and taking over when they were away. Polly Hillhouse showed what an effective manager she could be after her husband's death: she increased the value of the family farm by two and a half times in a fourteen-year period. At least 2 percent of farms were operated by women, and that figure would have been larger if there had been fewer men for widows to marry.

The property of widows who wished to remarry must have been on the minds of legislators in 1835 when Arkansas Territory passed one of the earliest laws in the United States designed to protect the property of married women. Henceforth, real or personal property owned by a woman before marriage or acquired after marriage by decree, will, or gift could not be taken in payment of her husband's debts incurred before marriage. In 1840 a bill that would have protected a woman's property from being used to pay her husband's debts after marriage was vetoed by Gov.

*Maria Toncray Watkins
Stevenson, an early resident
of Little Rock.*

Courtesy of the Arkansas History
Commission, Little Rock.

Archibald Yell, who saw it as a threat to the family. In 1846, however, a similar measure did become law, with a new provision that allowed a woman to register her property at a courthouse. The wife of Governor Drew, who signed the bill into law, and many other Arkansas women took advantage of the new law.

Despite their busy lives, Arkansas women were also lonely, in part because of the hardships of the frontier. Maria Toncray Watkins, who arrived in Arkansas in 1821, called the new territory "a wilderness of sorrows." She lamented that "the Sound of the Gospel of Jesus is not heard in this village." Three decades later, Cordelia Hambleton wrote back to Kentucky that the country was beautiful, but that she did "not like the wolves[—]they howl so lonely."

Perhaps a more important concern was the fact that the migration west took women away from their families of origin and the close relationships they had with relatives. Maria Toncray Watkins, for example, was heartsick at leaving the children of her sister in Kentucky, who were as "dear to me as my own." Ada Henry of Van Buren remembered receiving a blessing from her bedridden mother when she left for Arkansas about 1841, but she also heard the older woman's "agony of grief" over the parting. When Henry returned to visit, her mother "slept in a silent tomb." Ann Magruder of Batesville wrote to her friend Olivia in 1855, expressing feelings that were common among southern women who had moved west: "It makes one feel very sad at times, when I think of our being separated from all our friends and no prospect of seeing them for a long time if ever again."

Loneliness was sometimes eased by letters and packages sent through the mail. Jane Walker of Fayetteville corresponded regularly with her mother, who lived in Kentucky. In 1833 the older women wrote a charming response to a message from her daughter: "I almost fancied I was sitting at work with you knitting before day, and then enjoyed your sun rise breakfast . . . I was gratified to be made acquainted with Vera and the black cow, and even the dye pot." When Jane had her first baby in 1834, her mother and sisters in Kentucky did their best to bridge the distance and demonstrate their love in a helpful manner: "Aunt Lucy is making him a quilt, his Aunt LE is working him a cap and his Grand Mammy . . . will have him many pretty things."

Ultimately, however, it was new female friendships that made migrating women feel at home in Arkansas. Maria Toncray Watkins met a widowed woman a week after arriving who "appeared to sympathize with me in [having to leave] Dear friends behind." Jane Walker's mother recognized that her daughter needed feminine companionship: "It would be a comfort particularly to you my dear Child when your Husband is so often and so long absent from you to have an affectionate female friend near you." Female friendships were particularly important to Arkansas women in times of sickness, grief, and childbearing. Matilda Fulton's brother wrote apologetically in 1831 that his wife was too ill to come and offer Matilda "a Sister's consolations" after the death of her young son. On another occasion, however, the women's network operated more effectively.

The birth of Matilda's next child the following year illustrates much about women's lives in Arkansas. Married to William Fulton, the territorial secretary of Arkansas, Matilda kept busy around her household. The day before she delivered her baby, she was butchering hogs with a slave in the smokehouse until she became ill. The next night she sent for a friend to stay with her, and the following morning she called for three more friends. That day or the following day, the baby was born. Along with the details, she sent William a report of the result: "He is indeed the sweetest and the most perfect little Creature and the best Child I ever had."

A more personal view of religion and family in antebellum Arkansas is contained in the memoirs of Harriet Bailey Bullock, who was born on her father's plantation, Sylvan Home, not far from the Ouachita River in Dallas County in December 1849. Bullock recalled her life when she was eighty-one years old, and the account may be tinctured both by her age and by the Civil War, which had so changed the circumstances that she remembered. Nonetheless, her memoirs provide some insight into the daily life of a south Arkansas plantation and the role of religion in the family that owned it. The Bullocks had come from North Carolina and settled for some time in Tennessee before moving on to Texas. On the way, however, Charles Bullock, Harriet's father, decided to remain in the Ouachita Valley. Three years later his wife died, leaving two sons and nine girls, of whom Harriet was the next to youngest. Eventually, after courting several women, he married Mary Carter, a missionary in Indian Territory whom he had known in Tennessee.

Charles Bullock built an impressive home for his family. It had "six large rooms, two wide halls, dressing-rooms and closets." The front rooms were constructed of hewn logs with dovetail notches that were chinked with wooden strips and covered with weatherboards. The roof was shingled, the floors were planked, the large windows had small glass panes, and the structure was painted white. Even the slave cabins, as Harriet Bullock remembered them, were well constructed with puncheon floors and windows with wooden shutters.

Charles Bullock owned a large number of slaves and seems to have practiced some degree of paternalism toward them. His children, for example, were required to be courteous to the servants and to call the adults "Aunt" and "Uncle." On the other hand, Charles had sold a female slave in Tennessee and brought her two young sons with him, causing the mother much pain. Harriet's view of all this is ambiguous. She wrote that the overseer was a kind man, but then added that when he was drinking he occasionally "whipped some of the women until the clothes on their backs were clotted with blood." She herself claimed to have played happily with slave children and was strongly attached to Aunt Rose, who was her mammy, Aunt Moriah, or 'Riah as the children knew her, who was the family cook, and Harriet's own nurse, Liza. Aunt Rose was also the plantation doctor, dispensing "turpentine, castor oil, Jerusalem oak or Worm-seed syrup, and sulphur" to black and white alike.

A Presbyterian who usually attended the local Methodist church, Charles Bullock made religion a major force in his household. After his first wife died, he would shut up the house in the evening, singing softly: "Welcome, welcome, dear Redeemer, Welcome to this heart of mine." He regularly held prayers with the family in the morning and the evening, requiring the servants to attend when their duties allowed. When a Presbyterian minister from Little Rock came for a visit, Bullock had all his children baptized. He also helped to organize a Presbyterian congregation in Arkadelphia and built a one-room brick church there. Harriet, who attended the church only once before the outbreak of the Civil War, remembered that men sat on one side, women on the other, and slaves worshiped from a raised platform in the rear. The choir sat in front of the pulpit, and the founding families each had a pew. The pastor of the Arkadelphia church came to Sylvan Home once a month in good weather to preach to the family and their slaves.

Most of the time, the Bullock children went to one of two Methodist churches located near their plantation, where the congregation knelt to pray, rather than standing as parishioners did in the Presbyterian church. A major event in the life of young Harriet was a visit by Dr. Andrew Hunter, a Methodist clergyman, who spent a week or two preaching to slaves in the area while the white people listened from the back rows or from carriages outside. There was an integrated if stratified procession to church: "Farm wagons carried the dinners, the old colored women, and the little children. The other Negroes walked. A buggy and carriage were for Ma and the other white folks . . . Sometimes we children were allowed to walk with our black mammy and her husband." Harriet understood, however, that the slave owners took a condescending attitude toward the religious behavior of their servants: "I fear the white people who sat at the windows enjoyed the talk and the actions of the colored people more than they did the preaching." Hunter himself was not above treating his black listeners as if they were children. When one slave women "screamed and jumped up and down" at his description of heaven, he told her to "stop jumping like a chicken with its head cut off."

The Bullocks also attended camp meetings for white people. After one such event at a Methodist church, a cousin, Martha Bullock, experienced a conversion during the night at Sylvan Home, waking the household with her excitement: "Uncle Charles, I am so happy! I am so happy! I have found my saviour! Sing to me!" Bullock sent for Uncle Billy, a slave exhorter, who came with several other slaves to sing and rejoice with the convert.

Education was another preoccupation of the Bullock family, one that did not involve slaves. Harriet's mother had wanted all of her eleven children to be educated, and one of Harriet's older sisters, Fanny, had been left in school in Tennessee when the family moved to Arkansas. Charles

Bullock and his second wife were equally adamant on that issue. The younger children were taught at home. During the week they studied from Webster's spelling books, McGuffey's readers, Davie's arithmetic, grammar books, and Sir Isaac Watts' *Improvement of the Mind.* On Sundays, they memorized Bible texts and hymns, studied Sunday School lessons, and "read good books." At various times, they also attended day schools near home, one of them taught by Mr. Gilky, a Yankee who played the fiddle, wrote poetry, and painted in oil. The school Harriet attended when she was ten or eleven was a log house with a fireplace and a shuttered window. It was furnished with one writing desk and a series of benches about eight feet long. There was one chair, used by the teacher.

Harriet's old brothers and sisters went to school in Tulip or Arkadelphia, and at least three of them also studied in Tennessee where Fanny had been. Sister Kate was one of these, and she went on to become a professional teacher, a vocational choice that made her father unhappy. As Harriet explained it, "The culture of his children had not been designed for a life in the school-room . . . With most ladies among our associates, accomplishments were for making a good 'match' and a good home."

Aside from the untimely death of her mother, Harriet Bailey Bullock's first eleven years were very happy. She formed a close bond with her stepmother and believed herself to have been surrounded by warm and loving people. She played happily with black and white children; some of the highlights of their play included standing on an elevated board to deliver mock sermons, stealing watermelons, and chasing rabbits, snakes, and baby skunks. Harriet's life was privileged, and in that way it was different from the lives of most Arkansas children. Yet the closeness of her family and the importance of religion in her life were things that were replicated throughout Arkansas.

Chapter Seven

Human and Chattel

Slavery preceded American settlers in Arkansas. The French had brought slaves to Louisiana, and by the 1798 there were 56 of them living among the 393 people enumerated by the Spanish government at Arkansas Post, 14 percent of the total population. The Americans who arrived in the next decade brought relatively few slaves with them, and the 136 slaves living in eastern Arkansas were only 13 percent of population counted by the Census of 1810. Similarly, in the period of rapid growth that followed the War of 1812, the settlers who came into Arkansas down the Southwest Trail were mainly small farmers, who had few if any slaves. In the Census of 1820, the slave population dropped again, from 13 to 11 percent of the total population. During the 1820s, however, Arkansas began to establish its agricultural foundation, and migrating cotton producers settled in the lowlands, bringing their labor force with them. Slaves were 15 percent of the population by 1830, and they made up part of an embryonic plantation society.

The question of whether slavery should exist in Arkansas was most vigorously debated in 1819 by people who had never been there. In February of that year, James Tallmadge of New York shocked the U.S. House of Representatives by moving that slavery be prohibited in the future state of Missouri and that all slaves living there be freed at age twenty-five. A few days later, John W. Taylor from the same state moved that similar provisions apply to the proposed Arkansas Territory. Northern

opposition to the three-fifths clause of the Constitution, granting southerners representation for their slaves, seems to have had more to do with
these motions than opposition to slavery. Both Tallmadge and Taylor did
argue, however, that small farmers should be given the opportunity to
grow tobacco and cotton without having to compete with slave labor.
Felix Walker of North Carolina replied that white farmers would not cultivate "a low and warm country."

Congress was on firmer ground in outlawing slavery in a future territory than in a prospective state, but Arkansas was also south of Missouri,
a distinction that became critical. At one point a motion to free slaves in
Arkansas at age twenty-five passed the House by two votes, but it was
reconsidered the following day, and Speaker Henry Clay broke a tie by
voting against the measure. Taylor later tried a motion that would have
allowed individual slaves to remain in Arkansas Territory for only nine
months. By this time, however, the idea was emerging that the southern
boundary of Missouri, the latitude line of 36 degrees 30 minutes would
be the division between future slave states and free states. The House
finally passed the bill to establish Arkansas Territory without any restric-
tion on slavery, and the Senate followed suit. In effect, Congress accepted
the logic of geography and gave Arkansas to the South.

And the South took it. One out of every four persons living in
Arkansas on the eve of the Civil War was a slave. Slaves produced much
of the wealth of the state, and they were an important form of wealth in
themselves. Their numbers and their significance had grown over time
and were much greater in some parts of the state than in others. In those
respects, slavery was like cotton—and the geography of the slave population in Arkansas was closely correlated with that of cotton production.
Slavery was an institution governed in part by law, in part by public opinion, and in large measure only regulated by the will of the slave owner.
Slavery controlled the lives of slaves, offering few opportunities to the
ambitious, providing horrible penalties to the recalcitrant, and circum-
scribing the activity of all. Even in these circumstances, however, slaves
found ways to exercise some control over their own lives. As individuals,
they had their own lives, at least in part, and collectively they made elements of a culture for themselves.

* * *

The growth of slavery in Arkansas was closely linked to economic
development. In 1820, a year after Arkansas became a territory, agricul-

ture was in its infancy. Not only did slaves make up as little as 11 percent of the population, but also they were not concentrated geographically. Hempstead County on the Red River in the southwest had a population that was 21 percent slave, the highest in the territory. Arkansas County and Phillips County on the Mississippi River had only 14 percent and 12 percent respectively. The highlands counties had fewer slaves; for example, Lawrence County in the north and Clark County in the southwest had 9 percent and 7 percent respectively. In this frontier, subsistence economy, slaves must have labored, probably alongside their masters, in a variety of tasks, such as clearing land, constructing homes and buildings, and tending livestock. Work was more diversified and less regimented than it would be on the cotton plantations that were coming. The institution of slavery was probably also less oppressive than it would become when more slaves would required more organization. Arkansas, for example, did not institute evening slave patrols to keep slaves from traveling about without permission until 1825.

By 1840, things had begun to change. In that year the census recorded that slaves composed 20 percent of the population in Arkansas. Instead of being slightly more than one in ten persons, as they had been in 1820, slaves were one in five. Moreover, a geographical pattern had emerged as the slave population began to be concentrated in the Delta and the Gulf Coastal Plain. At the north end of the Delta, Mississippi County now had a slave population that was 36 percent of its inhabitants; at the south end, the slaves in Chicot County made up 71 percent of the persons living there. Arkansas County now covered a portion of the lower Arkansas River, and its slave population was 39 percent of the total. In the Gulf Plain, Lafayette County, which lay along the Red River, was 75 percent slave, and Hempstead County was 39 percent slave. These high concentrations of slaves were evidence of the commercial agriculture that was developing in areas of Arkansas where a long growing season combined with rich alluvial soil and a location adjacent to water transportation. Not surprisingly, Chicot County and Lafayette County were the two leading producers of cotton in Arkansas.

Between 1840 and 1860, slaves became more numerous, and the geographic pattern of slavery became even more distinctive. The 111,115 slaves in Arkansas in 1860 were 26 percent of the total population; instead of every fifth person, every fourth person in the state was a slave. The slave population had grown to 81 percent in Chicot County, and it was well over 50 percent in Arkansas County, Desha County, and Phillips County.

Eastern Arkansas was now blacker than southern Arkansas, but the slave belt still extended across the southern tier of counties, and slaves were a majority of the population in Union County and Lafayette County. By contrast, in the highlands counties of the Ozark Mountains, slaves constituted about 6 percent of the population. The overall average was about 11 percent in the Ouachita region, where it was increased by higher concentrations of slaves in the counties of the Arkansas River Valley, where rich bottomland and a relatively long growing season allowed cotton to be produced in significant amounts.

Economic development increased the number of slaves in Arkansas and concentrated them in the lowlands, but the structure of slaveholding was relatively stable. One in every five taxpayers owned slaves in 1840, and the ratio was the same in 1860. During the same two decades, most slaveholders in Arkansas owned only one to four slaves. Ownership, however, did become more concentrated. The small slaveholders of one to four slaves made up about 56 percent of slaveholders in 1850, but only 50 percent in 1860. By contrast, owners of twenty slaves or more, who are conventionally referred to as planters, were about 6 percent of all slave owners in 1840, but they increased to 9 percent in 1850 and to 11 percent in 1860. Large planters with more than fifty slaves increased from slightly more than 2 percent in 1840 to 3 percent in 1860. Planters almost always lived in the lowlands, while the small slaveholders lived all over the state.

Before leaving these numbers, it is worth pointing out that while most slaveholdings were small, a near majority of Arkansas slaves lived on plantations. In 1850 the 56 percent of slaveholdings that involved less than five slaves contained only 14 percent of the slave population. By contrast, the plantations that were only 9 percent of all slaveholdings were home to 46 percent of the slaves, 21 percent of them living on the large plantations that included at least fifty slaves. The regimen of the plantation extended to many more lives than its numbers would suggest.

How well slaves were treated has been debated since the 1830s, when abolitionists attacked what they perceived as the exploitation of slaves by their masters. Apologists for slavery argued that the slaves were treated with a degree of paternalism that was unknown in the North, where working people were paid wretchedly and left to starve when they could no longer work. The ideal slaveholder, in this argument, thought of his slaves as inferior to himself but recognized a responsibility to take care of them and acted with benevolence. One may wonder how an individual can manifest fatherly care toward a person he holds in bondage, or be benevolent toward someone he forces to work without pay. On the other hand, it is clear that some slaveholders were more solicitous toward their slaves than others. Moreover, in general slaves were fed and housed well enough so that they reproduced at a level not much below that of the whites. The slave owner who gave his slaves enough food and shelter for subsistence was still financially ahead of the factory owner, however, since the annual cost of maintaining a slave was estimated at one-sixth the cost of hiring free labor.

Slaves were also valuable commodities. The average price of all slaves in Arkansas during the 1820s was $380; in the 1830s it rose to $485; in the difficult economic times of the 1840s, it dropped to $455; but in the 1850s it soared to $627. The average price, however, reflected large differences based on age, gender, vocational skills, and physical characteristics. An appraisal in 1860 of 211 slaves on Bellevue and Yellow Bayou Plantations in Chicot County, part of the estate of Junius W. Craig, provides a sample of the differential. The average price of all slaves was $881. Most valuable were artisans, including a young blacksmith, who was valued at $2,500. Field hands ranged from $1,500 to $1,000, with most valued at about $1,200. Adult women were appraised at about $1,000. Children were about $100 at birth and $500 at five or six years. In general the price of a slave rose rapidly until about the age of twenty-five years. A child of eight was more valuable than an adult at fifty.

The value of a slave may have been as important as his owner's benevolence in ensuring that care be taken for his well-being. On the other hand, slavery put enormous power in the hands of a slave owner, and rationality, whether based on paternalism or profit, was not the only motivating force in determining how masters cared for their slaves. Depression, alcoholism, and more serious mental illnesses often led to a brutality that was inconsistent both with public opinion and with economic self-interest.

Slavery differed with its environment. Slaves who lived on the small farms of Arkansas may well have functioned much like hired hands. For example, Hardy Banks of Magazine Township in Yell County owned four slaves: a man, a woman, and two boys. He was a subsistence farmer who grew corn, peas, beans, and potatoes and raised hogs, a small number of sheep, and cattle. He also cultivated a small amount of cotton from time to time to earn some cash, but relied more heavily on the occasional sale of a horse. He also produced thin strips of oak that he sold as binders for cotton bales. Banks' slaves were involved in all these activities, one benefit of which was that his wife could confine herself to housework and stay out of the field. Banks and his two sons worked side by side with the slaves at what must have been a varied set of activities—felling trees, grubbing out the stumps, butchering the livestock, chopping wood for the winter, and doing the ploughing, planting, cultivating, and harvesting for the various crops. The line between master and slave seems to have been blurred. The two families lived side by side in "dogtrot" log cabins, and the men all hunted together.

There is an idyllic-sounding quality to the Hardy Banks story that requires a note of caution. For one thing the evidence comes entirely from the Banks family, and it may exaggerate the degree of racial harmony. One wonders if the slave family members were as happy with their circumstances as the Bankses appear to have been. But even if Banks' farm was a good place for slaves, it tells us very little about the other small slaveholdings in Arkansas. The slave master had enormous power over his bondspeople, and their work and welfare would vary greatly with his circumstances and disposition. For better or worse, however, slaves on small farms must have had more contact with their master than slaves on a plantation, and their lives were probably more varied and less regimented. These may have been benefits, but there was a trade off: slaves living in small groups on isolated farms were denied the benefits of the slave culture that developed on the plantations.

On most plantations the work of slaves was shaped by the cotton calendar. New land was cleared in January, plowing began in February, planting was done in April and May, the plants were hoed in June, and then they were "laid by" sometime in July. Cotton picking began in September, and the ginning process took place in October. These jobs and other plantation work were done by groups of slaves whose lives were organized for the purpose. Columbus Williams was a slave on a plantation in Mount Holly in Union County. He later remembered the work assignments of his youth, which were clearly part of a larger pattern of labor: "The very first work I did was to nurse babies . . . When I got bigger they carried me to the field—choppin' cotton. Then I went to picking cotton. Next thing—pullin' fodder. Then they took me from that and put me to plowin', clearin' land, splitting' rails." Williams and the other slaves worked from sunrise to dark, coming out of their cabins in the morning at the sound of a horn. The hard work and long days of the plantation slave may have been eased somewhat by the camaraderie of like situation and group effort.

Henry Morton Stanley, a visitor at an Ashley County plantation in 1860, found himself fascinated by the slaves engaged in the cutting, hauling, and burning of logs. While carrying or rolling the logs, groups of slaves competed with one another, "each gang chanted heartily as it toiled." Stanley had been cutting timber for his host, but now he joined the slaves: "As they appeared to enjoy it, I became infected with their spirit and assisted at the log rolling, or lent a hand at the toting, and championed my side against the opposition." Stanley's response to all this suggests his later career as an African explorer: "The atmosphere laden with the scent of burning resin, the roaring fires, the dance of the lively flames, the excitement of the gangs while holding on, with grim resolve and in honour bound, to the bearing-spikes, had a real fascination for me." One suspects that this was more romantic for Stanley than for anyone else, but his account does suggest that groups of slaves could find ways to lighten their work and gain a degree of emotional and sensory fulfillment.

Since the logic of slavery involved the idea that labor would go unrewarded, owners relied heavily on punishment as a way of encouraging slave effort or modifying slave behavior. The most memorable form of punishment was the whipping. Columbus Williams remembered that his former master would whip women as well as men, "strip 'em to their waist and let their rags hang down from their hips and tie them down and lash them until the blood ran all down over their clothes." Lizzie Barnett, another former slave, told an interviewer in the 1930s that she had many times "heard the bull whips a flying, and heard the awful cries of slaves." The effects of these whippings were still vivid for her: "The flesh would be cut in great gaps and the maggots would get in them and they [the victims] would squirm in misery." In 1842, a man named Spencer sued another named Pyeatt for selling him a slave who Pyeatt knew was "unsound, unhealthy, and mentally deranged." In the course of the trial, it was established that Pyeatt had stripped the woman, staked her to the ground, face down and with limbs extended, and whipped her with "a plaited buckskin lash about 15 inches long." After drawing blood from her back, he had salted the open wounds. These details were only incidental to the trial, which was about what Pyeatt had done to Spencer, not what he had done to his slave.

"Whipping was probably the most common punishment meted out against errant slaves," according to *Time on the Cross,* an influential study of American slavery done in 1974 by Robert Fogel and Stanley Engerman. The authors also provide specific evidence on whippings conducted at a Louisiana plantation whose owner, Bennett Barrow, was a firm believer in punishment. Over a two-year period during which he kept records,

Barrow had about 120 working slaves, and he administered 160 whippings to them. About half of the slaves were not whipped at all, and the whipped slaves received 2 to 3 whippings each in the two-year period. Whether this rate of whipping was in any sense standard is hard to know, although Fogel and Engerman emphasize that many masters had reservations about whipping and tried to minimize its use.

Whipping, moreover, was not all there was to slave control. Planters often used small rewards to motivate their slaves and withheld privileges to punish them. John Brown, a Camden planter, set up cotton-picking competitions among his slaves and provided prizes for the winners. He also gave them holidays off and paid slaves who chose to work on those days. To punish recalcitrant slaves, Brown revoked their holidays. James Shepard also gave slaves time off at Christmas, and he provided a holiday beef ration as well. Orville Taylor, the historian of Arkansas slavery, believes that slaves were fed a nourishing diet based on the southern staples of pork and corn: "The year-round staples were meat, cornmeal, and molasses, supplemented at times by products of the gardens, fields, and orchards of the plantation, and by 'store-bought' groceries." Columbus Williams remembered it somewhat differently. The slaves' rations were about three pounds of meat a week for each working person and "a little meal. That is all they'd give 'em." In his experience, slaves cooked their own meals after coming home from the fields. The very young and the superannuated had to be fed out of the workers' rations, although babies got milk, cornbread, and molasses. Lizzie McCloud, another Arkansas slave, remembered a blander diet and a more impersonal mode of serving: "We et out of a trough with a wooden spoon. Mush and milk. Cedar Trough and long-handled cedar spoons. Didn't know what meat was. Never got a taste of eggs."

Unlike the slave cabin sitting side by side with that of the master on Hardy Banks' farm, plantation slaves lived among themselves in the slave quarters, a cluster of cabins. Columbus Williams described his home as "an old log house—one room, one door, one window, one everything . . . They had cracks that let in more air than the windows could. They had plank floors." He claimed that there was no furniture except for a bed, which had two feet on one side and was anchored to the wall on the other side. Slaves wore all sorts of clothing, much of it cast off by white people. Plantation owners tended to clothe their slaves in osnaburg cotton, a very coarse fabric, that was cut and sewn into baggy and shapeless garments.

Arkansas slaves appear to have received such benefits as medicine could offer in the antebellum period. A man named Rogers, for example, leased a slave from a woman named Watkins in 1856, and when the bondsman came down ill, probably with malaria, Rogers hired a Doctor Bailey to treat him. The slave got worse, however, and Rogers informed Watkins, who hired a second doctor. Neither Rogers nor Watkins paid Doctor Bailey, who sued successfully for $31.65, his bill plus interest. Whether Rogers and Watkins were motivated by self-interest at the possible loss of property or by concern at the suffering of a human being, it is clear that they wanted the slave to have medical care. The same seems to have been true generally on the farms and plantations of Arkansas and throughout the South generally, where slaves were given quinine and other medicine, various home remedies, and practical assistance in dealing with cuts, sprains, and other ailments.

According to the Census of 1850, 498 Arkansas slaves had died from disease in the previous year. The deadliest killer was an epidemic of cholera, which accounted for 155 deaths. In second place was malaria, which caused the deaths of 85 slaves. A regular fact of life along the lower Arkansas River and in the lowlands generally, malaria was far more deadly to whites than to blacks. Other important causes of slave mortality included worms, pneumonia, whooping cough, croup, "dropsy," consumption, and scarlet fever. In the same period, 1,197 white people died from the same diseases that killed their slaves. Whites were much less apt to succumb to cholera than were the slaves, but slightly more susceptible to malaria. Slaves were also more apt to die from disease generally than were white people; the slaves made up 20 percent of the population, but they accounted for 29 percent of the deaths from disease.

The higher disease mortality of the slaves was part of a pattern of vital statistics in Arkansas. For the year ending June 1, 1850, slaves died of all causes at a rate of eighteen per thousand, while white Arkansans succumbed at a rate of only thirteen per thousand per year. Similarly, slave births for the same period were twenty-five per thousand, while those of whites were thirty-four per thousand. Thus, the natural increase among slaves was seven per thousand and that of the whites was twenty-one per thousand, three times higher. In other respects, the two populations were closer together. Both were young by modern standards: nearly half of all whites and of all slaves were under fifteen years old, only about 5 percent of either group was over fifty years old. The white population had a small excess of men over women, an imbalance that was particularly significant among adults over thirty years old, where there were more than 130 men for each 100 women. Men were a slight minority in the slave population, an imbalance that began with the youngest children.

To talk about the treatment of slaves, as we have, implies a degree of passivity on the slaves' part. Whether we suggest that slave owners were benevolent or cruel, we are defining them as the active parties, the controllers of the situation. The slaves are the objects of others' action, those to whom things are done. This perspective is not totally wrong, since slavery did place most of the power in the hands of the master, but it is not completely right either. Slaves had some power against their masters. Slaves were capable of violence, for example. They would be punished for it, but that might not help the owner or the overseer who was the victim of their wrath. Slaves were also valuable, both in themselves and in terms of the work they could do. In order to protect slaves' market value or to keep them working with optimum skill and speed, a master was often willing to provide them with special considerations in the form of gifts or privileges. Slaves with valuable skills, blacksmiths, for example, were in a strong position to bargain for improvements in their lifestyle. Joe Sullivant, a Dallas County slave, went hunting with one gun he borrowed from his owner and another that belonged to a man whom Sullivant worked for on the weekends. Overseers also understood that groups of slaves could not be pushed to do more than they felt was reasonable; if they were, equipment began to break and things began to go wrong.

Other than violence, which was almost certainly self-defeating, running away was the most dramatic way slaves resisted slavery. Slaves ran away for a variety of reasons, among them harsh working conditions, previous or pending punishments, and the desire to be closer to their families. In general, the decision to escape was a desperate one, since most slaves appear to have been recaptured, and they were usually punished very severely. On the other hand, some slaves, particularly those in Little Rock, ran away and hid in the woods for days in order to impress upon their owners the seriousness of their complaints. Running away was common enough and upsetting enough to most owners that Arkansas newspapers regularly carried advertisements for missing slaves. Anxious for the return of their property, owners described the slaves in ways that were often at odd with the assumption of African inferiority.

For example, Jerry, who fled in 1830, was described in the *Arkansas Gazette* as "a very likely, cunning and artful fellow." He had experience as a carpenter and was "very handy at most kinds of work required about a plantation." Jerry was apparently also literate, since the advertisement suggested that he had forged a pass and other papers. Peter, who ran off from his home near Hot Springs in 1849, seemed eminently employable: "He is a good house carpenter, plays the fiddle, and speaks Spanish." Spanish was his first language, however, and his English was not good. Peter's owner apparently regretted that he had not been a harsher master: "Any man is at liberty to whip this fellow, as I myself have never done it." Moses, who ran off from William Woodruff's farm in 1844, was not particularly talented, but his description could fit some in the master race. He was about thirty-three years old, five feet six or eight, and weighed two hundred pounds, "very fleshy and heavy built," according to Woodruff, and "fond of liquor." He was "a notorious liar, and quite boisterous when intoxicated." Woodruff believed that Moses might be "still lurking around Little Rock." In general, about 10 percent of runaways were females. Jinny, for example, was a twenty-five-year-old slave who ran off in 1850 and may have hidden for a time in the Little Rock area. She was described as "5 feet 4 inches high, very bold, [and] speaks and laughs loud."

Running away was one way that slaves controlled their own lives. Another way was by adapting Christianity to their own circumstances and using it as a psychological support and a communal bond. American slaves were first exposed to Christianity early in the eighteenth century through the efforts of Anglican missionaries, who emphasized religious instruction as a means of conversion. With the Great Awakening of the 1740s, evangelical preachers found that slaves as well as whites were converted by the emotionalism of the revival. The number of Christian slaves remained small, however, until the early nineteenth century, when the Second Great Awakening evangelized the white people of the South and convinced large numbers of slave owners that providing religion for the slaves was the master's Christian duty. By 1850 the Methodist Church in the South could boast that more than one-quarter of its members were slaves. In Arkansas, where the slave population was much less than in some other states, the 1,769 black Methodists were about 14 percent of the Methodists in the state. Baptist slaves were probably more numerous than were the Methodists, but we have no accurate record of them. Presbyterians and Episcopalians also worked with slaves and had slave members. Still, religious adherence was far from complete. Columbus Williams, a slave from Union County, claimed that on his plantation they "didn't have no church nor nothing. No Sunday-schools, no nothin." Historian Orville Taylor estimates that less than 20 percent of slaves were affiliated with any denomination.

The ambiguous role of Christianity within the institution of slavery is amply illustrated by an Arkansas Supreme Court decision in the case of *Hervy* v. *Armstrong,* given in 1854. Armstrong sued Hervy and others who were part of a slave patrol in Ouachita County that stopped a group of slaves who were out on a Sunday evening. After ascertaining that the blacks did not have proper passes, the patrollers tied each of them up and whipped them ten times. Armstrong believed that the patrol was outside its proper jurisdiction, that the punishment was unwarranted, and that the whip had left his slaves "bruised and hurt . . . as to be unable to perform labor." The court was concerned that the slaves had been coming home from an orderly religious meeting where white persons had been present. It pointed out that "there is an implied license for them to attend religious meetings, when conducted in an orderly manner, on Sunday," a day on which it was unlawful to force them to work. In reaching its decision for the members of the patrol, however, the court noted that damages of the sort asked for would encourage slaves to defy legitimate authority. Summing up, the court added: "The elevation of the white race, and the happiness of the slave, vitally depend upon maintaining the ascendancy of one and the submission of the other." Maintaining control over slaves was a higher good than encouraging their religious progress.

Similarly, it is clear that while plantation Christianity focused on saving the souls of the slaves, it also provided them with values that would benefit the planter. The duty of the servant to obey his master and the commandment against theft were staples of these values, and they were accompanied by moralisms having to do with issues like laziness and drunkenness. Lucretia Alexander, who had been a slave in Chicot County, remembered that white clergymen would preach to whites in the morning in a church and then to slaves in their quarters in the afternoon. The message was "'Serve your masters, Don't steal your master's Turkey . . . chickens . . . hawgs . . . meat. Do whatsomeever your master tells you to do."

But what was given was not always what was received. White Protestantism formed a basis for black Christianity, but the religion of the slaves became something different from the religion of the masters. As Lucretia Alexander explained, slaves would have separate gatherings among themselves: "That would be when they would want a real meetin' with some real preachin.'" Emma Tidwell, another Arkansas slave, remembered that slaves prayed under a washpot lest the sound of the worship carry outside the cabin and be heard by whites. African religion was largely lost from the culture of American slaves, but elements of it survived. Slave conjurers, for example, practiced sorcery and magic that had African roots. The Arkansas slave Clara Walker remembered a slave who had come from Africa and was known as a "witch doctor." "He make a little man out of mud. An' he stick thorns in its back. Sure 'nuff, his master got down with a misery in his back." More important than these isolated survivalisms was the African heritage of music and dance. The same cultural legacy that led the slaves to compose songs and sing them at work and at play, to make music on the fiddle, the banjo, and the hollowed-out drum, and to keep time through the intricate clapping rhythms known as patting Juba also made them enrich religious worship in ways that were often the envy of white people.

Black religion was an often secret subculture of southern Protestantism in which slave preachers taught Christian messages adapted to the interests of the slaves, rather than the whites, and whose forms were developed by its devotees. Freedom was an important theme, one easily extracted from the Old Testament experiences of the Hebrew people in Egypt and incorporated into the music of black Christianity. When slaves sung of being "bound for Canaan," however, they were thinking of a promised land to the North. Spirituals also served a role in the religious education of an illiterate people.

> O Satan is a busy ole man
> and roll rocks in my way
> But Jesus is my bosom friend
> And roll 'em out of my way

Black Christianity often existed side by side with plantation Christianity, and the slaves on many plantations dressed on Sundays to worship with the white masters as well as by themselves. Revival meetings were important events, not only for the preaching and the conversions, but also for social interaction. Christmas came to be an important holiday for slaves, both as a celebration of the birth of the Christ child and also for the respite from work that was often part of the season. Baptisms were important events as well. Weddings were also a cause for celebration. Slaves did jump the broom stick to solemnize the event, but religious ceremonies were important too.

Christianity bound white and black together in the antebellum period as the South developed the deep religious beliefs that would later become fundamentalism and create the Bible Belt. At the same time, religion also became something that bound black people to one another and gave them the psychological strength to carry on in the midst of their special adversity. It must have lightened the cares of many a slave to sing, alone or in the company of singing, clapping, and dancing brothers and sisters:

Nobody knows the trouble I've see
Nobody knows but Jesus
Nobody knows the trouble I had
Glory hallelu.

If religion insulated slaves from some of effects of racism and slavery, so did the family, although the benefits of that institution have not always been clear. Alexis de Tocqueville, the astute French observer of American life in the 1830s, thought that marriage and slavery were simply not compatible: "A man does not marry when he cannot exercise marital authority, when his children must be born . . . destined to the wretchedness of their father; when . . . he can neither know the duties, the privileges, the hopes, nor the cares which belong to the paternal relation." It is not easy to fault this logic, but it was not borne out in reality. Slaves' marriages were not recognized by law, but they took place all the time, and they often resulted in lasting unions. From time to time, owners did separate husbands from wives and parents from children. The slave woman staked out and whipped by Pyeatt was punished for running away in order to be with her children. Slave marriages were also intruded upon by the sexual aggression of owners, some of whom exercised their power by using any black woman that they wished. The extent of interracial sexual intercourse in Arkansas is suggested by the fact that some 60 percent of the free African Americans in the state and more than 10 percent of the slaves were mulattoes. The problems the slave family faced were immense, but the testimony of slaves indicates that it not only gave joy and solace to husbands and wives but provided children with happy memories and positive feelings about themselves.

The legal status of slaves in Arkansas, and in the South in general, was seemingly contradictory. Slaves were property, first and foremost. They were usually defined as chattel property as distinct from real estate, and therefore they were in a category that would include horses and farm implements. "All slaves," stated the Arkansas legal code, "shall be taken and held as personal estate." It also provided that "deeds and instruments of writing for the slave of slaves" could be recorded and treated in the same manner as similar documents related to real estate. While the law recognized slaves as property, however, it also treated them as human beings under certain circumstances. The Arkansas Constitution gave the general assembly the right "to oblige the owner of any slave or slaves to treat them with humanity." It also provided that slaves charged with crimes should have the benefit of trial by jury. This was not something that happened often, but it did happen. Moreover, despite the lack of constitutional support, slaves were also occasionally involved in civil litigation.

Along with all other slave states, Arkansas also provided for manumission, the setting free of individual slaves by their owners. Under Arkansas law a slave could be made free by the will of an owner or by some other written instrument, although they could be seized by creditors if the owner had not discharged his debts. Slaves were manumitted for various reasons, sometimes because the owner disliked the institution of slavery, more often out of a special regard that he or she had for an individual slave. The fact that well over half of the free Negroes in Arkansas were mulattoes suggests that slaves were often freed because they were related to the owner. The will of John Latta of Washington County freed his slaves at his death in 1834 and gave them each twenty-five hundred dollars in gold. Latta was apparently an opponent of slavery. Francis Roycroft of Chicot County, on the other hand, simply felt warmly toward his "old and faithful slave Nancy" when he freed her in his will.

The tension between the slave as property and as a potential free person and the human drama inherent in that situation is illustrated in the incomplete yet fascinating story of the slave Mark, freed by the will of Joseph Kuykendall. Kuykendall was a veteran of the Revolutionary War who had lived and held office in Kentucky prior to emigrating to Arkansas, where he arrived at least by 1819. He took up residence in what became Pulaski County. Upon his death in 1828, at age seventy-six, he freed his four slaves and provided them with land, with the stipulation that they pay eight hundred dollars to Kuykendall's heirs within five years. On May 28, 1828, the *Arkansas Gazette* reported that Mark, one of the emancipated slaves, had shot and killed Benjamin Kuykendall. Mark had fled, but he was captured and interred in the Pulaski County Jail for a month and a half. In the middle of August, he escaped: someone had provided him with a "case knife" to remove his irons and later unlocked the cell door at a time when both the jailer and his wife were gone. In addition, the necessary keys "had been carelessly left in plain sight" in an adjoining room. A reward was offered for the apprehension of the escaped prisoner, who was described as about thirty years old, bearded, over six feet, and about 175 pounds. Mark was "rather light for a negro," and well-dressed for a prisoner in "a tow linen shirt and pantaloons, and a new pair of thin buck-skin mockasins [sic]."

Mark remained at large for several months, but the prospects were not good for a fleeing black man in the antebellum South. He was apprehended in Baton Rouge, but escaped again with a group of runaway slaves. Finally, after more "hairbreadth escapes," he was captured and returned to Pulaski County, where the sheriff "ironed [him] in such a manner as to prevent his escape, or his holding any intercourse with any person on the outside of the jail." His case came before the circuit court at the end of March 1829. After the day-long trail with many witnesses, the jury deliberated all night and finally returned a verdict of manslaughter. The court sentenced the defendant to a three-year confinement and fined him five hundred dollars. Nine months into his prison term, Mark refused to leave when a group of prisoners escaped from the jail. He did, however, give the authorities false information to throw them off the track of the escapees. In June 1830, after serving a little more than one-third of his term, Mark received a pardon from Gov. John Pope.

Mark's case was extraordinary. On several occasions in ensuing years, Arkansans burned slaves to death when it seemed obvious that they had murdered white people. Mark, however, was helped to escape, had his charge reduced by the jury, and was pardoned by the governor. Clearly there are unanswered questions. Was Mark's "light" skin owing to the fact that he was Joseph Kuykendall's son? Was the killing of Benjamin Kuykendall a case of fratricide, a Cain versus Abel struggle between black and white, slave and free? It does seem likely that the jury believed that Mark had acted in self-defense, which suggests Benjamin Kuykendall may have been enraged by his father's will. Even without answers, however, Mark's story illustrates the ambiguity of an institution that treated people as property most of the time—but not always.

Manumission was more directly the issue in *Jackson* v. *Bob*, a case heard by the Arkansas Supreme Court on appeal in 1857. Bob was a slave who had successfully sued his master for his freedom in the Sevier County Court. The basis for his claim was the will of his original master, Elliot Brown of Mason County, Virginia, which had provided that when Bob was twenty-one he would be allowed to work for himself and use the proceeds to buy his freedom. Elliot Brown had died in 1825, and his grandson, George A. Brown, inherited Bob, who was about eleven years old. George took Bob to Arkansas in 1834 and sold him to Robert Hamilton of Sevier County for $600. Hamilton agreed to have Bob appraised six years later, apparently at age twenty-five, and then to allow him to purchase his freedom for that amount. Witnesses believed that Bob was worth

$600 or $700 and that he could have earned $150 per year. Hamilton failed to fulfill his agreement, however, and Bob remained a slave. In 1845 he ran away, but was returned to Hamilton. Shortly after, Hamilton died, and Bob was sold as part of his master's estate, eventually ending up as the property of Isaac N. Jackson. In 1851 he sued Jackson, apparently with the assistance of counsel, bringing an "action of trespass" and asking for his freedom.

The county court freed Bob, apparently convinced by the abundant testimony, including that of George A. Brown, that an agreement had been made with respect to Bob's freedom, that Hamilton had obligated himself to fulfill it, and that he had not followed through. The jury probably knew Bob and believed he had not been treated fairly, seeing him as more of a human being and less of a chattel. The supreme court, however, was concerned about protecting the institution of slavery. The original will of Elliot Brown was not part of the evidence, and the court stated that there was "no competent proof that he was emancipated" by that instrument. Nor did George A. Brown or any other owner actually carry out a legal emancipation. The various statements and documents introduced might have been persuasive "if there were no persons interested in the controversy but the parties to the suit." But such was not the case: "Slavery is a status or condition of the negro race in this State; the community at large are interested in it, and the mode of emancipation for considerations of public policy is regulated by law." Having ruled that emancipation must be done according to the letter of the law, the court also stated that Hamilton had obligated himself to Brown, not to Bob, and that Bob could have no claim on his master, since "Emancipation is an act of grace or benevolence on the part of the master to the slave." The court ruled that if a master agrees to free a slave for some amount of labor or money, the slave may do the work or pay the money, but he cannot compel the master to uphold the bargain "because both the money and the labor of the slave belong to the master and could not constitute legal consideration for the contract."

Not all African Americans in the South were slaves and most whites were not slaveholders; yet, slavery was a racial institution. In the antebellum South, black people were presumed to be slaves, and free blacks had to be prepared to prove their status. White people were presumed to be free. The definition of "white person" could be very critical, and it was particularly important given the sexual activity between masters and slaves. In 1857, the same year that it had strictly construed the law on manumission, the Arkansas Supreme Court also struck down a lower court decision that would have made it easier to be defined as white.

Daniel v. *Guy et al.* came on appeal from the Ashley County Circuit Court, where Abby Guy and her four children had won their freedom from William Daniel in 1855, claiming that they were free people wrongfully held in slavery. Guy had lived as a free person on Bayou Bartholomew, supporting herself by farming. She socialized with white people and had a daughter who attended boarding school. She was apparently treated as if she were white. Daniel claimed, however, that Abby Guy was a slave and that he owned her. James Condra, Daniel's brother-in-law, had owned both Abby and her mother, a slave named Polly, a "tolerably bright mulatto . . . a shade darker than Abby." Daniel had a bill of sale showing that he had purchased Abby from Condra in 1825 when she was thirteen years old. Other testimony indicated that she had been under his control until 1844.

The circuit court judge instructed the jury that the issue of the plaintiff's freedom hung on "whether they belonged to the negro or to the white race." He went on to argue that if they were "less than one-fourth negro" then they were presumed to be free, unless the defendant could show that they had a mother who had been one-fourth Negro and a slave. In order to aid the jury members in making their decision, he allowed them a personal inspection of the plaintiffs and encouraged them to use their own judgment about racial differences. Daniel was unhappy about this emphasis on race. He suggested that the jury be instructed that if Abby's mother was a slave (regardless of her racial mixture), it was prima facie evidence that Abby was a slave and her children were slaves. The judge refused, and the jury found for the plaintiffs.

The supreme court was also unhappy with the judge's instructions. According to law, a slave had to prove his freedom if he were a Negro or a mulatto. But what constituted a mulatto? Sometimes the term meant someone who had at least one-fourth Negro blood, but other times it was less clear. This court finally decided that it usually meant "an intermixture of white and negro blood, without regard to grades." Therefore, if Abby's mother had been a slave, even with only a one-eighth Negro blood, then Abby was a slave. As the court put it, "The theory of fourths . . . is based on a hypothesis not sustained by law." On the basis of faulty instructions, those given and those denied, the court called for a new trial.

One Arkansas slave found himself the subject of international litigation, and his case became the concern of abolitionists in the United States, Canada, and Great Britain. Nelson Hacket was about thirty years old and a valet and butler for Alfred Wallace, a prominent businessman who lived on a farm near Fayetteville, in July 1841 when he ran away to Canada. Wallace was out of town when Hacket left, and the slave took with him a beaver overcoat (presumably for protection against the Canadian winter), a gold watch, a saddle, and his master's fastest horse. These thefts were ultimately his undoing. In the meantime, however, Hacket made his way east across Arkansas, traveling at night and eating little more than berries. A black ferryman fed him and took him over the Mississippi River. Then he headed northeast through a portion of western Kentucky and crossed the Ohio River onto the free soil of Illinois. Now traveling in the daytime and better able to find food, Hacket headed north and crossed the Detroit River into Canada. Six weeks after his flight from Fayetteville, he was settled into a small community some fifty miles from Detroit.

Meanwhile, however, Alfred Wallace was on the trail of his bondsman, assisted by a peace officer from Washington County. After learning where Hacket was, Wallace went to Windsor, Canada, and filed an affidavit claiming that the slave had stolen his property. Then he and his associate captured Hacket, beat him, and lodged him in a Canadian jail. Wallace then went to Michigan and successfully petitioned the state to request the extradition of Hacket as a fugitive criminal. The Canadian government pointed out, however, that Hacket had never been tried for any crime and that Michigan had no jurisdiction over him. Undaunted, Wallace returned to Arkansas, where Gov. Archibald Yell requested that the Canadian government turn over Hacket for trial in Arkansas. In January 1842, Canada returned Nelson Hacket to Arkansas. The resourceful slave escaped in Illinois for a few days on the way home, but he was recaptured and eventually restored to Wallace.

While they could do nothing for Hacket, American abolitionists were deeply concerned about the precedent set by his case. Would criminal extradition become a means by which former owners could recapture the twelve thousand former slaves who had escaped to Canada? The situation seemed more desperate when the text of the Webster-Ashburton Treaty between the United States and Great Britain became public. Article 10 provided that each side give up fugitive criminals wanted in the other country. The American Anti-Slavery Society contacted British abolitionists about the case, and the wheels of benevolence began to turn on behalf of the refugees from slavery who were residing in Canada. Lord Ashburton provided a statement that Article 10 had not been intended to apply to escaped slaves. In the summer of 1843, as the treaty was being debated in the House of Lords, the British ministry made it clear that while the extradition provision was a useful one, all matters concerning former slaves would be dealt with very carefully. Abolitionists would have preferred the elimination of the article entirely, but they became more comfortable the following year, when the British government refused to extradite from the Bahamas some former slaves accused of murder.

Nelson Hacket, Abby Guy, Bob, and Mark were all slaves whom we know something about because their circumstances were out of the ordinary. We know less about the masses of slaves whose work contributed to the development of Arkansas and whose children would become its citizens. Like ordinary people everywhere, their normality made them less visible. The conditions of slavery, particularly the absence of education, add to the problem. Slavery must have lay heavily on them, but it seems clear that servitude also allowed for family life, for religion, and for some measure of accomplishment. Amidst the work, there was some entertainment, there was some happiness despite the sorrow, and some joy mitigated the pain. The interaction with white people was characterized by fear and obedience, but it was also more complex than that. As a young slave girl, Lizzie Barnett was raised around white children. She had fond memories of her white mistress: "Yes Siree, I was miss Fanny's child. Why wouldn't I love her when I sucked titty from her breast when my mammy was working in the fields." Whatever else it was, slavery was not a simple institution.

CHAPTER EIGHT

Looking West

The nature of American expansion changed in the 1830s. In earlier decades, while British Canada and Spanish Florida had excited interest and concern, Native American land within the boundaries of the United States had been the focus of American attention. To justify their conquests, Americans had told themselves that they were the representatives of Christianity, civilization, and agriculture and were entitled to land being held by barbarous, pagan hunters who scarcely used it anyway. As the United States became interested in Texas, Oregon, and Mexico, however, a broadened justification was necessary.

Manifest Destiny, as the new doctrine became called, was supported by a larger racism than that which had allowed the dispossession of the Indians and the enslavement of Africans. During the 1840s, Americans argued that Mexicans were also inferior and that their rights could be ignored in the interest of Anglo-American expansion. On the other hand, the expansionist ambition could go too far. The decision at the end of the Mexican War to accept less than all of Mexico was heavily conditioned by the fact that any larger acquisition of land would mean that large numbers of nonwhite people would become part of the United States. As historian Thomas Hietala has shown, Americans wanted the "wealth, power, and security" that came with the acquisition of Texas, Oregon, and parts of Mexico, but they also wanted to maintain "racial and cultural homogeneity" within their empire.

If racism conditioned the Manifest Destiny, economic considerations were its driving force. The economic problems of the 1830s, and the Panic of 1837 encouraged American leaders to think about new land that would lead to increased agricultural production and new foreign markets for American commodities. Sen. Ambrose Sevier of Arkansas, for example, favored the annexation of Texas because he opposed abolitionism and wished to strengthen the slave South. He also argued that having Texas in the Union could lead to an American monopoly on the production of both cotton and sugar. The *Democratic Review,* a leading journal of imperial ideas, argued that the United States had to ensure American access to land: "Until every acre of the North American continent is occupied by citizens of the United States, the foundation of the future empire will not be laid."

Manifest Destiny also contained an element of mission, the idea that the expansion of a republican empire would benefit the world by spreading democracy. And then, of course, there was God. According to John O'Sullivan, who coined the phrase, the manifest destiny of his country was to "overspread the continent allotted by Providence." The American people, here and in other times, in much the same way as other powerful societies, believed that God was on their side.

The politics of slavery also played an important role in American interest in the Southwest. The American settlers who moved into the northeast province of newly independent Mexico in the 1820s were agents of expansion, consciously or unconsciously. With the achievement of Texas independence in 1836, the question of annexing the newest American republic to the oldest was of major concern to both. In the United States, however, the Texas issue was immediately caught up in the controversy over slavery. Sensitized by the Missouri Compromise and by the abolitionist controversy, northerners opposed the idea of adding an additional slave state to the Union, while southerners favored it for the same reason.

The discovery of gold in California affected Arkansans much as it did other Americans and led many of them to trek west in search of easy wealth. Fort Smith played an important role in the migration of forty-niners, functioning as the starting point of a southern route to California. Arkansans endured many hardships on the trail and in California, but the greatest tragedy among westward movers occurred in 1857, when an Arkansas wagon train was attacked by Mormons at a place in Utah called Mountain Meadows.

* * *

Arkansas's official involvement with Texas began in April 1820, when the territorial legislature established Miller County in the extreme southwest corner of the territory. The county straddled the Red River extending west into what is now southeastern Oklahoma and south into the Sulphur River basin of present-day Texas. That Arkansas Territory claimed the portion south of the Red River is difficult to explain, since the Adams-Onis Treaty, negotiated a year earlier, had given that area to Spain. The new boundary between the United States and Spain ran up the Sabine River to the point where it crossed the thirty-second degree of latitude, then due north to the Red River, and finally west along the Red River. The line north from the Sabine River to the Red River passes through Texarkana today and marks a portion of the boundary between Louisiana and Texas and between that of Arkansas and Texas, but it was not surveyed until 1841. The territorial legislature may have believed that Miller County lay east of that line and that the area south of the Red River was still a part of the United States. In any case, the county's situation became still more tenuous in 1825, when the Choctaw Treaty lopped off the greater portion of Miller County north of the Red River and included it in Indian Territory.

Meanwhile, Mexico had become independent and claimed the Red River boundary. Visible evidence of this claim came in July 1830, when Benjamin R. Milam wrote to Gov. John Pope and professed to have a grant from the Mexican government for land in Miller County; he also declared that he was authorized to receive colonists under the laws of Mexico. Milam was informing Pope because the settlers there had been subject to the jurisdiction of Arkansas. Pope then wrote the U.S. government, and Secretary of State Martin Van Buren discussed the issue with the Mexican ambassador. Both governments agreed to avoid aggressive action until the boundary line was surveyed. Milam's activity ceased. In 1836, however, the situation changed again when the Republic of Texas took over the Mexican claim to Miller County below the Red River.

Arkansans had an ambiguous attitude toward Texas. In June 1822, an editorial in the *Arkansas Gazette* stated that "the rage for emigrating to Texas is beginning to subside." But of course it was not. More settlers arrived in the fertile valleys of the Brazos and Colorado Rivers in the 1820s than migrated to Arkansas, and many of the new Texans had once been Arkansans. Arkansans believed that the success of Texas lowered land values in Arkansas, and it probably did. Still, there were many connections between the American territory and the Mexican colony. Stephen Austin had farmed, speculated in land, run for territorial delegate, and held a territorial judgeship in Arkansas before going on to promote his father's colony in Texas. Sam Houston was a friend of Arkansas writer and politician C. F. M. Noland and invited Noland to go to Texas with him in 1832. Arkansans cheered the Texas Revolution, although there is no evidence that any of them went south to aid in the fighting.

The establishment of the Texas Republic sealed the fate of Miller County. Residents of the area sent delegates to the Texas constitutional convention even as they remained nominally under Arkansas authority. Then, in 1837, Texas established a land district that included the land between the Red River and the Sulphur River—all of Miller County and a portion of Lafayette County to the east. Gov. James S. Conway of Arkansas warned the residents of Miller County that they must obey Arkansas laws, but took no other action except to inform U.S. Secretary of State John Forsyth of what was happening. Early in 1838, Conway learned that Texas courts were operating in Miller County and that residents were having their land surveyed by Texas authorities. The sheriff of Miller County resigned his position and became a Texas citizen, the Arkansas circuit court ceased to function, and no Arkansas elections were held there in the fall. Speaking to the legislature in November of that year, Conway stated that the people living in Miller County simply preferred to be governed by Texas. The existing situation became legal in 1841, when a joint U.S.–Texas commission drew the boundary line of the Adams-Onis Treaty from the Sabine River to the Red River. Arkansas retained the land in Lafayette County that was south of the Red River, but east of the new line running through Texarkana. What had been Miller County, lying west of that line and south of the Red River, became officially a part of Texas.

If Arkansans were upset about the loss of territory, it did not dampen their enthusiasm for U.S. annexation of Texas. The *Arkansas Gazette,* now under Whig control, worried about the slavery issue nationally and voiced the old concern that as a state Texas would draw immigration away from Arkansas. The Democrats were enthusiastic, however, and that view seems to have been the general one. Arkansas favored the growth of the United States. It favored the annexation of Texas, the annexation of Oregon, and it supported James K. Polk in his efforts to acquire a large portion of Mexico. Arkansans also demonstrated their patriotism in the Mexican War, but that participation was neither untroubled nor uncomplicated.

In May 1846 Congress gave President Polk the authority to call up

50,000 volunteers to prosecute the war against Mexico, and the secretary of war asked Arkansas to provide one mounted regiment. During the next month, aspiring officers recruited soldiers, and 44 officers and 749 men, organized into ten companies, gathered at Washington, Arkansas, in July and were mustered into the service of the United States. The officers of the companies elected regimental officers. Archibald Yell, a former governor of the state, had not yet resigned his seat in the U.S. House of Representatives, but he had come home and enlisted as a private. He became the colonel of the regiment by being elected over Albert Pike, an attorney and former newspaper editor who was the commander of the Little Rock Guards, a militia artillery unit that had turned itself into a company of mounted volunteers. John S. Roane, a twenty-nine-year-old attorney and politician from a prominent family, was elected lieutenant colonel, and Solon Borland, editor of the *Arkansas Banner,* a Democratic newspaper, was chosen major. The defeated Captain Pike was a Whig, while all the elected officers were Democrats.

Josiah Gregg, a pioneer merchant on the Santa Fe Trail and a perceptive man of sound judgment, traveled with the Arkansas regiment and came to know its leaders. He found Yell a "very clever pleasant, social fellow, but decidedly out of his element . . . in a sphere so different from his forte of political demagogy." Roane was also an enjoyable companion, but "too dull and indolent" to be successful, unless stimulated by "active service or a thirst for glory." Borland was well educated and possessed literary talent, but he had little aptitude for the military. Pike, however, was "the best disciplinarian and drill officer of the corps" and its most promising military figure. On the other hand, he was too "stiff and aristocratic . . . to be popular."

Behind these leaders, the Arkansas regiment of mounted volunteers left Washington on July 18 and made its way first to Shreveport and then to San Antonio, where it arrived on August 28. There it came under the command of Gen. John E. Wool, who was preparing an invasion of the Mexican state of Chihuahua. A month later, Wool's army began to move south, crossing the Rio Grande River on October 15. By the end of the year, it was encamped at Saltillo, a small town about 125 miles southwest of Monterey, a city that Gen. Zachary Taylor had captured in September.

From the beginning, the Arkansas regiment did not get along well with General Wool. He disliked the way Yell had set up the Arkansas camp at San Antonio and ordered the regiment to move to a place the colonel found much inferior. After that, the unit found itself constantly located downstream from other units and forced, therefore, to use dirty water. On one occasion Yell disobeyed orders and put his men in a more desirable location, and Wool placed him under arrest when he refused an order to move. Roane and Borland were also arrested when they would not carry out Wool's order. The arrests were over in a few days, but the hard feelings continued. When the general's orderly visited the Arkansas regiment one night to tell the men to make less noise, the soldiers told him: "Tell Johnny Wool to kiss our [ass]." An Illinois volunteer wrote home that an Arkansas soldier had threatened to shoot Wool to his face. General Wool, for his part, referred to the regiment as "Colonel Yell's Mounted Devils." Only Albert Pike among the Arkansas officers seems to have gotten along with Wool, perhaps because both were members of the Whig Party and both believed in discipline. The general frequently detached Pike and his company and Captain Preston and his company from the Arkansas regiment and used them as a squadron under Pike's command.

Early in 1847, two events raised larger questions about the soldierly qualities of the Arkansas regiment. Major Borland led thirty-four Arkansas volunteers on a reconnaissance mission some fifty miles south of Saltillo to the town of Encarnacion, where he was joined by a similar force of Kentucky volunteers. On the evening of January 22, the combined force spent the night at the village of La Encarnacion, apparently without posting a guard. The next day they awoke to find themselves surrounded by three thousand Mexican cavalry, and they quickly surrendered. General Taylor, who joined Wool at Saltillo in early February and took command of the combined force, wrote that the capture had resulted from "carelessness and want of vigilance and . . . direct disobedience of orders."

The second event happened after an Arkansas volunteer was killed by Mexicans near where the unit was stationed in the town of Agua Nueva, about fifteen miles south of Saltillo. Shortly after the incident, a group of enlisted men from Captain Danley's Company B and Captain Hunter's Company G rode one night to the nearby town of Cantana and killed an undetermined number of civilians who they claimed had been involved in their comrade's murder. The incident was widely reported and condemned back in the United States. An investigation ordered by General Wool concluded that "at least 4 unarmed civilians were murdered" but could not determine the names of the guilty parties. Taylor was extremely angry, and he feared that the incident would jeopardize his relations with the Mexican people. He demanded that the men be found and punished in order to "remove the foul stigma which now rests upon the whole number of being the cowardly assassins of unarmed men." If the perpetrators were not found, he wanted the two companies to be sent back to the Rio Grande "as a mark of disapprobation." Yell apparently took no action, however, and in a few weeks Taylor found that he needed every available soldier in order to deal with a large Mexican army under President Santa Anna, which was approaching rapidly from the south.

The Battle of Buena Vista took place on beautiful and rugged terrain that was very favorable to the Americans. The road between La Encarnacion in the south and Saltillo in the north ran through a broad valley bounded by impassable mountains. Between La Angostura and Buena Vista, the ground on the east was sharply eroded into a series of gullies and canyons, which pushed the road against the mountains to the west and sharply narrowed the field of maneuver. Two months earlier, General Wool had passed through the area and declared that Angostura was the best place in Mexico for a small army to defend itself against a large one. A force attacking from the south would find that the mountains prevented it from moving to the west and the broken ground would make it difficult to attack from the east.

That was essentially the situation that presented itself on July 22, when Santa Anna and about fourteen thousand Mexican soldiers came up against the five thousand Americans commanded by Zachary Taylor. Taylor had fortified the road with artillery and then spread the rest of his units off to the left, with the Arkansas and Kentucky cavalry on the extreme end of that flank. Pike's squadron of two companies was on detached duty and not on the field. The remaining eight Arkansas companies were divided in two with Yell in command of four companies of cavalry and Roane in charge of four dismounted companies. Late in the afternoon, Roane's men saw action as they were ordered to climb the heights on their left and fight off Mexican soldiers, who were attempting to climb around the American position. That fighting continued until darkness. Sometime before that, General Taylor, believing that Santa Anna would not attack immediately, had left with a detachment of troops to check on the defenses at Saltillo, which was open to attack by Mexican cavalry operating in the north.

Short of supplies, however, Santa Anna sent his troops against the Americans in earnest at daybreak on July 23. The Mexicans began by continuing their push against the American left along the mountains. As the pressure became intense, Wool sent artillery pieces under Lieutenant O'Brian and more troops to support the left wing. Then, about 8:00 A.M.

the enemy attacked the artillery guarding the road on the American right and, at the same time, sent a strong force against the center of the American left, which was defended by the Second Illinois Regiment and the Second Indiana Regiment, both volunteer units. Roane's four companies of Arkansas volunteers, numbering perhaps 225 men, were located just behind the 600 or so Indiana troops. As O'Brian shifted his guns to face the Mexicans, who were now in front of him rather than on his left, General Lane ordered the Indiana troops to move forward. Colonel Bowles, the unit commander, confused perhaps by O'Brian's movement, thought that the American line was pulling back and ordered his men to retreat. Under very heavy fire, the Indianians turned and ran. According to Colonel Roane's account of these events, his men had been near the front "under the most galling fire from the Mexican small arms" when the Indiana troops came running among them, separating the men from their officers, and "bearing many off." Roane claimed that many of his troops continued to fight, simply joining the Illinois regiment, which remained on the field. On the other hand, Josiah Gregg thought that the four Arkansas companies were "almost entirely dispersed," and Roane himself stated that he could find no one to rally and simply "mounted [his] horse and joined Colonel Yell."

The mounted Kentucky and Arkansas units were embattled when Roane arrived. Having created a weakness on the American left, Santa Anna was exploiting it by forcing his way around the American flank. According to Col. Humphrey Marshall, who commanded his own Kentucky cavalry and Yell's Arkansans, the American horsemen fell back from a superior force of infantry and cavalry, slowing the enemy with one counterattack, but then having to fall back more. At about this time, General Taylor returned from Saltillo, bringing with him a regiment of Mississippi volunteers under Jefferson Davis and Colonel May's dragoons, to which were now attached Albert Pike's two mounted companies. Pike later reported seeing Yell on the field. The colonel was in high spirits, waving a pistol and declaring that "we are the fellows that checked them down there." He asked Pike to join him, but Pike replied that he was under a different command. Marshall's men continued to fall back until they made a stand a few hundred yards in front of Buena Vista.

There the Americans, numbering some four hundred men, awaited the attack of perhaps twelve hundred Mexican lancers, the cavalry brigade of General Torrejon, which was armed with muskets, swords, and eight-foot lances. When the lancers were about sixty yards away, the Americans fired, and then some apparently charged forward. Colonel Yell was "far in advance of his men," according to Roane, when he was killed. He was wounded in several places and then stabbed in the head by the point of a lance. The Americans split the Mexican assault, creating two swirling melees of Mexican and American horsemen, which were enveloped in dust and smoke. While the mounted men slashed and jabbed at each other, several hundred American soldiers fired at the Mexican soldiers from the sidelines.

The lancers were disorganized to the point that they no longer represented a significant threat, but the American left was still in peril. As a new Mexican cavalry attack formed, Taylor sent Jefferson Davis to stop the Mexicans from getting behind the Americans. Davis's men, armed with caplock rifles rather than flintlocks, broke up a charge that was foolish enough to stop within seventy yards of the Americans. Desperate fighting continued in front of the American position throughout the afternoon. Taylor's forces held their position, however, and eventually Santa Anna ordered his men back to Agua Neuva; all of them were heartsick over pulling back when victory had seemed so near.

The American victory created an aura of good feeling that made official reports less censorious than they might have been. General Taylor stated that the "brilliant success" of the army freed him from "specifying many cases of bad conduct before the enemy." Despite these good intentions, however, he criticized the Second Indiana, which he said was ordered to attack but "could not be rallied." Among the units that he praised was "a portion of the Arkansas regiment" that joined with Marshall's Kentucky cavalry in "meeting and dispersing the column at Buena Vista." He went on to report that during that charge "Col. Yell fell gallantly at the head of his regiment." Taylor also mentioned Lieutenant Colonel Roane and Captain Pike among the officers who had distinguished themselves. There was, however, one negative account of the Arkansas troops among the official reports. Lieutenant Shover, commanding at Saltillo on the day of the main battle, reported a cloud of dust from the direction of Buena Vista, which eventually turned into "a considerable number of mounted volunteers . . . rushing along the road." These fleeing soldiers identified themselves as belonging to the "Arkansas cavalry"; despite the best efforts of the officers at Saltillo to rally them, they continued on their way.

The harshest critic of the Arkansas regiment was Captain Pike. He wrote a lengthy account of the battle on March 8, and it appeared in the *Arkansas Gazette* on April 24. Referring to Roane's command, although confused as to its location, Pike wrote that "the skirmishers fled from the mountains in utter confusion and a great many of them ran to Saltillo, including one captain of the Arkansas regiment." When Yell later ordered his cavalry to retreat, Pike stated that the men, "untaught to maneuvre, and totally undisciplined . . . ran off in great confusion." In his view, "the want of discipline in his Regiment cost [Yell] his life." He died "facing the enemy and trying to rally his men" at Buena Vista, but his "command was routed," the "mass both of Arkansas and Kentucky troops, [were] dispersed, and many fled to Saltillo." The defeat of the Mexican cavalry at Buena Vista, according to Pike, came when Colonel May's cavalry, of which Pike's squadron was a part, came on the field and charged the Mexicans.

While Arkansans were reading Pike's account, however, the captain was changing it. Pike's views on the battle, expressed orally as well as in writing, caused significant resentment within the regiment, and the captain asked for a court of inquiry in order to defuse the situation. In this proceeding, held in Mexico at the end of May, Pike listened to the testimony of other Arkansas officers, and then he wrote out a statement of revisions. He claimed that they did not affect his earlier account in any material way, but in fact the revisions altered his description of what had taken place. He stated that he had learned that a "large part" of the dismounted volunteers who fled from the enemy later returned "to the front in detached parties." Moreover, Marshall and Yell did not lose control of the cavalry as it retreated, but rather most of the men kept together and rallied at Buena Vista. Indeed, Pike now accepted the fact that it was Marshall's force of Arkansas and Kentucky mounted volunteers that broke up the Mexican charge. May's cavalry arrived only after the Mexican force had been split in two and was in disarray. The mounted volunteers were dispersed as well, but they were being carried along by the fight, not fleeing from it. Only about forty of the Arkansas soldiers had fled to Saltillo, and most of them had left before the fight at Buena Vista. The situation had appeared worse, Pike now claimed, because infantry soldiers had fled on the horses of the dismounted men in Yell's regiment, making it appear that the deserters were Arkansans.

Pike's letter, however, did not create immediate harmony. Roane, then the commander of the Arkansas troops, issued a final order in Mexico that praised the officers and men for their service, but did not mention Captain Pike. Roane and other officers argued that Pike had not been a part of the battle—an odd position in light of General Taylor's praise for Pike's role. It was this slight that eventually led Pike to challenge Roane to a duel. The two men met on a sandbar in the Arkansas River, near Fort Smith but within the boundary of the Cherokee Nation. They each fired twice without doing any damage, after which the attending surgeons convinced them to stop. The combatants had dinner together, and the controversy came to a close.

Most of Yell's volunteers had been home for six months when the United States and Mexico ended their hostilities. The Treaty of Guadalupe Hildalgo, which was signed by the negotiators on February 2, 1848, gave the United States a Texas boundary on the Rio Grande River, the Mexican territory of New Mexico, which would eventually become the state of New Mexico and parts of Utah, Nevada, Arizona, and Colorado, and the Mexican territory of Upper California, which would shortly become the state of California. Unknown to the treaty makers was the fact that a week earlier gold had been discovered at a sawmill on the American River belonging to John A. Sutter, who had developed a small agricultural settlement near the present city of Sacramento. News of the discovery of gold in California reached the eastern United States in the summer, and its existence was confirmed by President Polk in his State of the Union address in December 1848. In 1849 the gold rush began as hundreds of thousands of Americans set out for California in hopes of becoming rich.

The news of gold in California generated a great deal of excitement in Arkansas. A large number of the state's citizens quickly made up their minds to become forty-niners, and Arkansas began to promote itself as the gateway to California. Fort Smith had a brand-new federal military installation and could be reached by steamboat up the Arkansas River nine months of the year. More important, it was the eastern terminus of a direct and relatively level trail that led through Indian Territory and on to Santa Fe, from where travelers could make their way to San Diego. With these advantages, the little garrison town on Belle Point saw itself as the logical jumping-off place for easterners headed to California.

The *Little Rock State Democrat* argued for the southern route in a lengthy editorial designed to convince adventurers that they should go west through Arkansas, rather than Missouri. As the newspaper saw it, the journey up the Arkansas River and through Fort Smith was "natural and direct," while that up the Missouri River and through Independence was "circuitous and perilous." The *State Democrat* also claimed that the St. Louis papers were suppressing information about the ease of travel between Fort Smith and Santa Fe. Brig. Gen. Matthew Arbuckle, the commandant of Fort Smith, not only recommended the southern route, but also called Fort Smith "the best point for emigrants . . . to assemble, and make preparations for their journey, as every thing necessary for their transportation and subsistence can be procured as cheap here and with as great facility as at any other point."

The Arkansas congressional delegation was also highly supportive. Citizens of Little Rock and Fort Smith petitioned Congress to build a road from Fort Smith to Santa Fe, and these petitions were presented to the Senate by Sen. W. K. Sebastian and to the House by Rep. Robert W. Johnson. After realizing that a national road was unlikely to be built immediately, Sen. Solon B. Borland, the former captain of Arkansas volunteers during the war with Mexico, convinced the U.S. War Department to provide a detachment of dragoons to accompany the first group leaving Fort Smith as far as Santa Fe and a topographical engineer to survey the route.

Many Arkansans made plans to go to California. As early as September 1848, a large group of Fort Smith residents met to organize and publicize their expedition. One of its leaders was John J. Dillard, who had been one of Archibald Yell's captains at Buena Vista. In January the Little Rock and California Association was created in the capital city. The subscribers to this association agreed to outfit themselves and leave for California in March. James McVicar, who had been Yell's quartermaster sergeant, was one of the organizers of this group. Clarksville also organized a company that was ably led by Redmond Rogers and by A. D. King, whose journal is a major source of information about the Arkansas forty-niners. Small groups also left from Fulton, Izard, Marion, and Hempstead Counties, and from the city of Batesville. A hundred men from Fayetteville were joined by a smaller number of Cherokees. Led by Lewis Evans, former sheriff of Washington County, this expedition headed northwest to Fort Bridger and Salt Lake City, pioneering what became known as the Cherokee Trail. A few Arkansans took steamboats to Panama and crossed the isthmus, and one went all the way around Cape Horn.

Packing for the gold rush was a daunting task. The Fort Smith Company published a circular titled "HO! FOR CALIFORNIA" that included the conventional wisdom on what to bring. Every man was to have a gun, ammunition, and a bowie knife. Livestock, including horses, mules, and oxen, were available in western Arkansas, but easterners were advised to bring their own wagons. Food per person included 100 pounds of bacon, 150 pounds of flour, 20 pounds of coffee, 30 pounds of sugar, and large quantities of salt, pepper, crackers, meal, rice, molasses, dried peaches, beans, tea, spices, saleratus, and vinegar. Each wagon was to carry 2,000 pounds. Fort Smith and Van Buren, six miles down and across the Arkansas River from Fort Smith, competed for the opportunity to outfit travelers. An advertisement in the Fort Smith paper touted "Pans and kettles" that could be used on the trip and then "will do to wash gold." Ready-made clothing was popular among the forty-niners. Flannel shirts, baggy pants, and broad-brimmed hats were the leading items.

Early in 1849, the forty-niners began to arrive. An estimate in Van Buren was that a thousand people had come through by mid-March, a crowd that would have more than doubled the town's population. In Fort Smith the cluster of people from different parts of the country gave rise to concerns about disease. A popular activity in that town was learning to break mules. Another was having one's picture taken with the new daguerreotype camera. By the end of the year, an estimated three thousand people had headed to California over the southern trail. One estimate was that they spent nearly $120,000 on livestock and supplies, dividing the business rather equally between Fort Smith and Van Buren.

The Arkansas companies of gold seekers were well aware of the need for order and discipline on their journey. They drew up regulations, elected officers, and generally adopted a military-like organization. The Fort Smith group included a provision in its regulations that each member change clothes at least once a week and carry three pounds of soap. Departure times were staggered so that livestock would not wipe out the grass along the route. The initial group of the Fort Smith company left the city on April 11. This departure was larger than most, but it illustrates the prevailing ratio of people, livestock, and wagons. There were 479 travelers, seventy-five wagons drawn by five hundred oxen and the same number of horses and mules, and hundreds of saddle and pack horses. This wagon train, which stretched for three miles, would soon prove too unwieldy for the trail, and it broke up into smaller units. Robert Brownlee, a Scottish stonecutter who had worked on public buildings at Little Rock, joined with four other men to form a "mess." Together they bought a wagon and four mules and each man provided himself with a horse. The Little Rock group of which he was part contained some sixty wagons.

West of Fort Smith the trail followed the Canadian River across Indian Territory. The Choctaw Agency was fifteen miles out, thirty-five miles farther on was a tiny place called North Fork Town, and eighty-five miles beyond that was Little River, the last American settlement on the journey. Arkansans were stunned by the difficulty of moving their wagons along little-used track, especially in the wet weather that marked the spring of 1849. John Dillard, no stranger to difficult conditions, wrote his mother that "we have been compelled to take ropes and pull our wagons out of the mud every day, not making more than from four to five miles per day . . . It has rained on us every other day for the past week, and we have been compelled to sleep on wet bedding all the time." Still, the travelers persevered and developed routines that would stay with them until they reached California. They stopped at midday—"nooning" it was called—to rest and eat a light meal. On Sundays and other occasions the groups would stay where they were and allow the people and the livestock a well-deserved rest. Robert Brownlee had a warm memory of the quiet times: "In camp, most of the time was spent in telling yarns, singing and playing the fiddle, and also a flute, clarinet and horn."

Most of the gold seekers were men, but there was a scattering of families among the Arkansas companies. John Conway, brother of Arkansas governors James S. and Elias Conway, was an army doctor who packed his entire family, consisting of a wife and ten children, into an army ambulance and headed for the gold fields. Mary, his seventeen-year-old daughter, rode her own horse. A pretty and personable young woman, she was very popular with the company. Lt. J. H. Simpson, who was the topographical engineer accompanying the Fort Smith party, named a sandstone promontory in western Oklahoma "Rock Mary" in her honor. Mary had a closer relationship with Lt. M. P. Harrison of the dragoons, however, and they had a tearful parting when the army detachment headed south for Santa Fe and the wagons continued on toward Albuquerque. Harrison was killed by Indians in west Texas later in the year, and Mary eventually reached California, married a sea captain, and raised six children.

Santa Fe, originally a Mexican trading center, was now part of the United States and marked the halfway point on the southern route. Most of the companies stopped at Albuquerque or at other communities in the area, since Santa Fe was thought to be too expensive. Prices were high, and the town was dangerous as well. A member of the Fort Smith company visited there and said that "men shoot one another for past time." A Little Rock company man called it the "meanest hole in existence" and claimed that it was necessary to stay mounted to keep his horse from being stolen. Of course, similar things had been said about Little Rock within the previous decade. The letters written by Arkansans about Santa Fe also included numerous references to the fandangos and the senoritas who danced at them. A number of changes also occurred as the travelers prepared for the second half of the journey. Loads were lightened, and many valued items hauled from home were discarded in preparation for the rugged miles to come. Tensions within the companies came into the open. John Dillard resigned as the captain of the Fort Smith company, and the group divided into smaller units. The Little Rock company also split into smaller parts.

From Santa Fe there were two routes to California. One led northwest to Salt Lake City and followed the Old Spanish Trail to Los Angeles. The second, known as Cooke's Wagon Road, had been opened during the Mexican War. It followed the Rio Grande River south to Dona Ana, about thirty-five miles above El Paso, and then went west over Guadalupe Pass and along the Gila River, eventually reaching San Diego. This was the route taken by most of the Arkansas companies.

The journey down the Rio Grande valley was accomplished with relative ease, but finding water became a problem as the wagons moved west. While traveling with a Little Rock group, Alden M. Woodruff, son of Arkansas's first newspaper editor, had heard that there would be no water for thirty-six miles. Luckily, he found a catch hole eighteen miles out, which allowed him to water the stock. Twenty-five miles farther on at Rio Mimbres, there was more water. The following day, they camped near a spring. From then on, water was very scarce. Robert Brownlee left the company for several days to look for gold and found himself without water on the second day. He thought he saw his party some distance off, but it turned out to be a mirage. Eventually he did catch up and was given a cup of water and sand dug from a well, allowing him to ease his thirst and swollen tongue by sucking the liquid through a handkerchief.

The most spectacular point on the trip was Guadalupe Pass, in what is now southeastern Arizona. Just before reaching the pass, the wagons traveled between two lines of mountains, and F. J. Thibault of the Little Rock Company took time to climb one and "view the mere speck of ground occupied by our train, and then let the eye range over the immense waste of plain, and the towering heights that sport with the clouds." The sight gave him a palpable sense of "the Omnipotent power that created and rules this immensity of space." At the pass itself, Alden Woodruff was more prosaic, writing home that the trail was "almost perpendicular for two miles" as it descended into the valley below. It was "the worst place for wagons I ever saw." Teams were unhooked and guided down with ropes. Men dismounted lest they fall over their horses' heads.

After making their way down the pass, the companies enjoyed a relatively easy journey to Tucson, finding cattle and other fresh food at

Mexican villages along the way. The next phase was harder: eighty-five miles across very dry country to the Pima Indian villages on the Gila River. The shortage of water and of grass for the cattle placed a strain on everyone, and a terrible tragedy struck the Clarksville Company. At midday on September 5, George Hickey and Elijah Davis began fighting. Hickey got the worst of it, but then he pulled a knife and stabbed Davis. Mortally wounded, Davis attempted to shoot Hickey but was too weak and died in ten minutes. After burying Davis, the Clarksville company arrested Hickey, chose a sheriff, judge, and jury, wrote out an indictment, took evidence, and held a trial. The jury found Hickey guilty and recommended that he be executed by a firing squad. That decision was ratified by the company in a forty-six to eleven vote. At three o'clock the next day, the sentence was carried out.,

After traveling down the Gila River, the Arkansas forty-niners struck the Colorado River, which required some effort to cross. Then there was ninety miles of hot and dry California desert before they reached the coast. Alden Woodruff arrived in San Diego on October 4. Other Arkansans arrived later in that month. The journey from Arkansas to the gold fields was anticipated to take six months; more often, it took seven and occasionally eight.

While some Arkansans struggled along the southern route, others went to the north. The combined Fayetteville Company and Cherokee Company included 130 people with forty wagons and perhaps four hundred head of livestock. These forty-niners followed the line of the Arkansas River across Indian Territory and then headed north toward the Oregon Trail and Fort Bridger. They crossed the Santa Fe Trail in May and left a carved stone marker at the juncture. At what is now Pueblo, Colorado, part of the group sold their wagons and purchased mules so they could cross the mountains at that point. It was a difficult journey, requiring a month to reach Salt Lake City, and one man and many supplies were lost in the Green River. The remainder of the group, led by Lewis Evans, continued north to the Oregon Trail and followed it into Salt Lake City, where they arrived in August, three weeks after the mule packers.

The Evans Company found good treatment and plenty of food in Salt Lake City. Leaving there, they heading west to the Humboldt River and followed it into what is now southwest Nevada. Then part of the group went north to follow the Lassen Trail into northern California, while the rest, led by Evans, followed the Truckee River route or the Carson River route, both of which led to the south. Evans and his people arrived in

Sacramento early in November, apparently in good shape. Those on the northern route suffered greatly as a result of early snows, and many were rescued from the Sierra Nevadas by government relief parties.

Eventually the Arkansas companies arrived in California. The Reverend W. W. Stevenson, who had been a geologist for the Little Rock company, found Los Angeles a virtual garden of Eden. Writing in November, he pointed out that "grass and oats are now springing up as in May in Arkansas. The orange, lime, palm, and olive are in my sight while writing . . . Wheat produces most abundantly. 50 bushels is regarded as an average crop. Gardening is carried on all the year. One crop is taken up and another planted." Mining, of course, was the focus of the forty-niners. Reports indicated that a placer miner (who worked riverbeds) might earn about twenty dollars a day, but only in the dry season and many miners earned much less. During the wet weather of the winter, the Arkansas men were happy to earn eight dollars per day. Despite the agricultural potential of California, many members of the newly arrived population suffered from scurvy and could afford only potatoes and vinegar to serve as a cure.

In 1850, a large number of Arkansans joined together to drain a half mile of the Tuolumne River in hopes of finding gold at the bottom of the dry channel. They began digging a diversionary canal in January with the idea of damming the river in July or August, when the flow was at its lowest point. Alden Woodruff paid two hundred dollars for a share in this Arkansas Damming Association in expectation that it could pay him five thousand dollars. James McVicar put up "a large trading establishment, eating-house, bakery, and rummery," doing a lively business on credit. In September, disaster struck all the water-diversion operations on the Tuolumne. The water dropped enough to allow the dam building to begin, but then heavy rains upstream sent a torrent of water downriver, ripping out the works under construction. Woodruff wrote an upbeat letter home, saying that he intended to mine the banks of the river, but admitted, "It is rather a sore lick on me, and has nearly broke me." Shares in the association were going for next to nothing. F. J. Thibault, who owned part of another dam washed out in the same flood, was more pessimistic. Noting that many of his associates were now penniless, he was happy to have a few hundred dollars owed to him. When he collected the money, he wrote his wife, he would "start for home."

The tone of disillusion became more general. William Woodruff, now again editing the *Arkansas Gazette,* noted in November 1850 that three of the Arkansas forty-niners were back in Little Rock and "represent most of the emigrants from Ark. as anxious to return home," but lacking the money to do so. Thomas Parcel was engaged in damming the Merced River, but he was apprehensive about the success of the operation. He wrote about the large number of robberies and murders. There were opportunities for merchants, but the odds of success were very low. He warned his friends not to come to California.

Some Arkansans, however, got what they came for. Robert Brownlee started out packing supplies to miners and then opened a store in Agua Fria that led to a happy and prosperous career in California. Limus Armstrong of Johnson County arrived in Little Rock in November 1850 with four thousand dollars, and two residents of Camden brought home five thousand dollars each. Thus, the lure of California lingered on. More immigrants set out in 1850 and in ensuing years.

One group of Arkansans who headed for California in 1857 wound up being killed in southwestern Utah in what became known as the Mountain Meadows Massacre. The wagon train included more than one hundred persons, most from Carroll and Marion Counties in Arkansas, led by a man named Charles Fancher. They were apparently prosperous farmers who had good equipment and livestock and carried considerable property with them. Unfortunately for the Fancher party, these immigrants became the victims of intense religious fanaticism.

Led by Brigham Young, the members of the Church of Latter-day Saints came to the Salt Lake City area beginning in 1847, when it still belonged to Mexico. After the United States acquired the Southwest, the Mormons created a state called Deseret and applied for admission to the Union. Congress instead created the Territory of Utah in 1850, appointing Brigham Young as territorial governor. Tension developed, however, between federal officials in Utah, who attempted to implement national laws on behalf of authorities in Washington, and Young and the Mormons, who were engaged in creating a Zion for the Church of the Latter-day Saints. In 1856 Young instituted a religious revival known as "the reformation," which called the Mormons to achieve greater purity but also encouraged them to remember the bloody persecution that they had endured in Missouri and Illinois and the murder of the prophet Joseph Smith and his brother Hyrum. The following year, President James Buchanan decided to send twenty-five hundred federal troops to Utah in order to put down what he believed was a rebellion by the Mormons against the authority of the United States. Determined to maintain their religion and not become victims again, Young and the Mormons organized into military units and prepared to resist the authority of the U.S. government, enlisting in their aid the Paiute Indians of southern Utah.

The Fancher party apparently arrived in Salt Lake City in early August. Continuing on its way, the group traveled south, following the Los Angeles Trail rather than going north to the Humboldt River route that led to San Francisco. The Fancher party was probably the first group to use the southern route that season. Along the way, they must have found it very difficult to find supplies, since the Mormons had resolved to keep all their food in preparation for war. In the small towns of southern Utah, moreover, the Saints were more intense in their feelings than those in Salt Lake City. Isaac C. Haight's comments at a meeting in Cedar City on September 6 illustrate what seems to have been a general mentality. In recalling their flight from Missouri and the fact that many members had been killed, Haight exclaimed, "We have left the confines of civilization and come far into the Wilderness where we could worship God according to the dictates of our own conscience . . . But the Gentiles will not leave us alone. They have followed us and hounded us . . . Now they are sending an army to exterminate us . . . I have been driven from my home for the last time. I am prepared to feed to the Gentiles the same bread they fed to us."

Haight's threats were directed toward the Fancher party, which was in the area, and which had become the focus of intense resentment. Mormon accounts of what happened next emphasize that the travelers were abusive, taunting the residents about their religion, and the practice of polygamy in particular, and rejoicing in the violence that had driven the Mormons into the West. One emigrant claimed to have the gun that shot Joseph Smith. In addition, members of the Fancher party were accused of killing an Indian and poisoning a well. It is impossible to judge the validity of these reports, but one does wonder why a wagon train facing a perilous journey west would want to antagonize the only people who could help them. Whatever the case, the Mormons became enraged at the Fancher party, and the meeting in Cedar City ended with a decision that it be "done away with."

The Fancher party was camped at Mountain Meadows in the extreme southwestern portion of Utah, about thirty-five miles beyond Cedar City, when it came under attack on the morning of September 7 or 8, 1857, by a large group of Paiute Indians. About seven of the emigrants were killed, but the rest drove off the attackers and circled their wagons. A day or two later three men left the besieged party to seek help in Cedar City. All were killed, including a man named William Aiden, who was known to the Mormons. For reasons that are not clear, the Mormons now began to fear that their participation in the attack would become known and that it was necessary to eliminate anyone who might tell that tale. A detachment of Mormon militia was sent to the scene, and a plan was devised to end the five-day siege. Mormon John D. Lee met with the emigrants and persuaded them to lay down their arms and come out. He said the survivors would be allowed to walk to Cedar City, while the livestock would be left to placate the Indians. Two wagons carrying the sick and wounded and very small children came first. They were followed by the women and the older children. When that group had walked a quarter of a mile, the male emigrants came in single file, each walking alongside an armed Mormon. At a signal, each Mormon killed his man, the Indians fell on the women and children, and the sick and wounded were shot. Seventeen children were the sole survivors of the Mountain Meadows Massacre.

The aftermath of the tragedy was remarkably prosaic. Mormons returned to the scene the next day and buried the bodies. There were, however, reports of wolves eating the carcasses. Jacob Forney, superintendent of Indian Affairs in Utah Territory, visited the site the following April and found a "skull & other bones and hair lying scattered over the ground." Local Mormon leaders had immediate misgivings about the event. An attempt was made to portray it as an Indian attack, but information about the Mormon involvement was soon publicly known. John D. Lee, for example, appeared with Indians carrying loot from the wagon train a week after the event. Meanwhile, President Buchanan pardoned the Mormons for their insubordination to the U.S. government, but appointed a governor from outside the church in place of Brigham Young. A U.S. district judge, John Cradlebaugh, visited Cedar City with a detachment of troops and impaneled a grand jury to investigate the massacre. Mormon leaders in the area went into hiding, however, and the jury refused to return any indictments. The seventeen surviving children were found and returned to Arkansas. The Arkansas legislature attempted to win a federal indemnity for them, but that effort was interrupted by the Civil War. Eventually John D. Lee was tried twice in 1876. The first time he implicated other Mormons and was found innocent. The second time he accepted all the blame himself, was found guilty, and was executed by a firing squad at Mountain Meadows.

Juanita Brooks's 1950 study, *The Mountain Meadows Massacre*, explains much about the Mormons but very little about the emigrants or the Indians. She believes that Brigham Young had no knowledge of the event before it took place, and that may well be the case. Young, however, must bear heavy responsibility for creating the hysteria that led the Saints of Cedar City to do what they did. On the other hand, the Mormons had suffered at the hands of their fellow Americans, and the massacre was certainly a kind of retribution. Perhaps a useful lesson from this grisly and sad episode is the fact that the Fancher party, whatever its own wrongdoings, was a victim of fear and intolerance, some of it manifested by Mormons in Utah in 1857, but some of it by the enemies of the Mormons in Missouri and Illinois a decade earlier.

CHAPTER NINE

Sovereignty and Secession

Statehood gave Arkansas the opportunity to participate in the affairs of the United States and to deal with its own internal matters. In general, it was more successful at the former than the latter. Arkansas elected a number of capable men to Congress, the political factions of the territorial period became part of the national Democratic and Whig parties, and the state probably wielded as much influence as was warranted by its population and wealth. At home, the legislature created two banks in its first session, as we have seen, both of which failed within a few years, leaving Arkansas with a large debt and a damaged reputation. State government accomplished little else in the antebellum period.

Politics, however, was much more lively than government. The Sevier-Conway-Johnson faction, known first as the family and later as the dynasty, dominated the Democratic Party, which controlled the state. The Crittenden faction became the Whig Party and provided energetic opposition, despite its minority status, until 1852, when the Whig Party faded from the national scene. Statewide races often revolved around personalities, but they attracted the participation of 75 percent or more of eligible voters, often 20 percent more than voted for president.

The ideology of the Jacksonian Democratic Party was strongly influenced by republicanism, the political ideal that Americans had strove to implement and protect since the American Revolution. Its central tenet was that individual liberty was constantly threatened by excessive power and that the virtue necessary to sustain liberty was similarly endangered by corruption, both in terms of political manipulation and excessive materialism. Unlike the revolutionary generation, however, Jacksonian Democrats defined liberty in terms of the right of all adult white males to vote and to have their votes given meaning with respect to decision making. When Jackson lost the election of 1824 through what he defined as a "corrupt bargain," he believed that it was not simply he who had been victimized but the electorate as well.

Similarly, Jacksonians believed that the economic liberty of white males—their right to a livelihood and the opportunity to improve it—was under attack by the economic changes of the market revolution, which was spreading commerce and capitalism, disrupting traditional modes of production and exchange, and creating a volatile, money-oriented ethos. Most important, these changes were benefiting some at the expense of others, creating a new privileged class. Little could be done about economic change, but it became a Democratic credo that government should not assist in the aggrandizement of the wealthy at the expense of farmers and working people. The Democratic Party was also distinguished by its racism. On behalf of white men, it supported slavery, opposed abolitionism, stood against the rights of free blacks, and supported the removal of Indians from any land that whites wanted. All of this was done with energy and without apology.

The Whig Party, organized in 1834 and led by Henry Clay of Kentucky, was, in some respects, a mirror image of its rival. Less concerned about republicanism, the Whigs were apt to believe that the extension of suffrage had gone too far. For them, the most important political abuse was the extensive executive power wielded by the president they called King Andrew. They were at home with the market revolution and believed that the national government should do what it could to assist what they saw as economic progress. Strongly influenced by evangelical religion, they spoke up for morality and humanitarianism and were more tolerant of blacks and Indians. As individuals, many Whigs were opposed to slavery, yet the party supported the rights of slaveholders. They were less enthusiastic than the Democrats about expansion and opposed the Mexican War.

During the 1850s, sectional issues became all-consuming, and Arkansas politicians devoted themselves to defending the interests and mores of the South. By the end of the decade, the Democratic Party was without significant opposition in the state, but the dynasty was finally beaten by Thomas Hindman, a dynamic political figure from Helena.

Most Arkansans were loath to secede from the Union, but the fighting at Fort Sumter united the state behind the Confederacy.

* * *

Most Arkansas voters identified with the Democratic Party, although the Whigs had significant support. In the presidential races from 1836 to 1852, the Democratic candidate got an average of 11 percent more votes in Arkansas than he did in the nation. In state races, Democrats often received 60 percent of the vote and occasionally got more. The Whigs won only one statewide office during this period, sending Thomas Newton to Congress to fill an unexpired term when Archibald Yell resigned his seat to stay with the army in Mexico. Against three Democrats and one other Whig, Newton won by twenty-three votes and went to Washington—where he served for twenty-five days. The Whigs, however, made a mark. They usually controlled one of the statewide newspapers and used it to criticize the incumbents, and they filled about 25 percent of the seats in the legislature. Whig party leaders were wealthier in terms of real estate and slaves than were their Democratic counterparts, and their candidates got their highest voting percentages in the slave counties of the south and east. The Democrats, by contrast, were strongest in the small farmer counties of the northwest.

The parties got off to a slow start in the presidential election of 1836, in part because the contest came only a few months after statehood. Territorial elections had been fought on local issues, and neither the Conway-Sevier faction nor that of the late Robert Crittenden had identified itself with a national party. James S. Conway, the Conway-Sevier faction's candidate for governor, and Archibald Yell, its choice for Congress, both avoided the name Democrat and played down their relationship to Martin Van Buren, who was widely seen as soft on the slavery issue. Neither Arkansas party did much more than publish newspaper articles on behalf of the presidential candidates, but Van Buren won 64 percent of the vote against Hugh Lawson White, one of three regional Whig candidates that year.

The Log Cabin campaign in 1840 was much more hotly contested. The Whigs raised a log cabin and a liberty pole in downtown Little Rock. A Whig Convention drew partisans from around the state and featured a parade with about a thousand people. Meetings and parades were also held in other parts of the state, with whiskey and hard cider much in evidence. Against William Henry Harrison, Van Buren's share of the Arkansas vote fell eight points to 56 percent, which was still 7 percent above his national average. In this election and later ones, the presidential electors chosen by the two parties canvassed the state on behalf of their candidates.

Next to the two-party system, the most important institution of Arkansas politics was the dynasty, a faction that had dominated the state since the 1820s. It was founded by Henry W. Conway, who had come to Arkansas in 1820 with his younger brother James S. Conway and his cousins Elias and Wharton Rector, all of whom were deputy-surveyors under the patronage of their uncle, William Rector, surveyor general of Missouri, Illinois, and Arkansas. Conway was elected territorial delegate in 1823 and re-elected twice before being killed in his famous duel with Robert Crittenden. Conway's political capital, enhanced by the circumstances of his death, was inherited by his cousin Ambrose Sevier, who was elected to fill Conway's unexpired term and went on to serve until Arkansas became a state. In 1827 Sevier had strengthened his position by marrying the daughter of Arkansas Superior Judge Benjamin Johnson, who was the brother of Richard Mentor Johnson, the senator from Kentucky and friend of Andrew Jackson, who became vice-president under Van Buren. Aided by William Woodruff, editor of the *Arkansas Gazette,* and Chester Ashley, the wealthy land speculator and attorney, Sevier built an effective political organization that provided federal and state offices for his extended family and friends.

While serving in the U.S. Senate some years after statehood, the outspoken and ingenuous Sevier declared that "when in the ascendancy, he made it a rule to take care of the interests of his political friends." This would have startled no one in Arkansas, where the senator's nepotism prompted one critic to question the value of upcoming statehood: "We would have all our offices, state and federal, saddled upon us by one family . . ." And, indeed, the prediction was not far off the mark. A decade after it occurred, a now disaffected William Woodruff described the first state Democratic convention in Arkansas. "It was a small Secret affair, composed of six or eight individuals, who very modestly appointed themselves . . . all the principal offices of the General and State Governments; and most of them succeeded in obtaining the offices." Moreover, Woodruff went on, every convention since has similarly "been used for the benefit of a family clique."

Ambrose Sevier had no difficulty being selected by the first general assembly to represent Arkansas in the U.S. Senate. He served in that capacity for a dozen years and became Arkansas's most successful national statesmen of the antebellum period. In his first few years, Sevier's most

Ambrose H. Sevier, Arkansas terri-
torial delegate, 1828–36, and U.S.
senator, 1836–48.

Courtesy of the Arkansas History
Commission, Little Rock.

important role was as a member—and later chairman—of the Indian Affairs Committee, which dealt with matters of much concern to Arkansans. A New York newspaper once called Sevier "one of those rough and tumble geniuses," which it believed were only produced in the western states of the United States. On the other hand, a Whig opponent of expansion referred to him as a "bull headed Jackass." If he was rough and crude, however, Sevier was commendably direct. Speaking on behalf of statehood for Florida, he told the senators that "he had no concealment's on this subject and disdained to be beating about the bush."

During the 1840s, Sevier became a leader among Democrats in the Senate, managing committee assignments, shepherding legislation, and dealing effectively with such luminaries as Thomas Hart Benton and John C. Calhoun. He won a place on the Foreign Affairs Committee, and in December 1846 he became its chairman. A strong expansionist, he at first opposed the peace treaty with Mexico but then came to support it. President Polk, who had a high regard for him, appointed the Arkansas senator as a peace commissioner to Mexico, a post he accepted with reluctance, in part because it involved his resignation from the Senate.

Sevier had hoped to be replaced in the Senate by a friend who would step aside and let him be elected again in the fall of 1848. Instead, his resignation opened the way for his political enemies. William Woodruff believed that Sevier had not supported Chester Ashley's successful bid for the Senate, and now he backed Solon Borland to succeed Sevier. A doctor and newspaper editor, Borland had gained much publicity from his role as a soldier and a prisoner of the Mexicans, while Sevier had grown less and less in touch with his friends and constituents in Arkansas. Sevier secured Borland a diplomatic appointment to get him out of the way, but Borland turned it down. Then Gov. Thomas Drew turned a deaf ear to Sevier's friends and appointed Borland to complete Sevier's term. Finally, in November 1848, the closely divided Democrats in the general assembly elected Borland rather than Sevier to a full term. Sevier died on the last day of the year at his plantation near Little Rock.

The dynasty, of course, was made up of more than Ambrose Sevier. James S. Conway, the brother of Henry W. Conway, was the first governor of the state of Arkansas. Conway was a planter and surveyor who had determined the boundaries of the Choctaw Line in 1825, giving Arkansans extra acreage by slanting it to the west. In 1832 Andrew Jackson had made him surveyor general of Arkansas Territory. Conway served only one four-year term as governor of Arkansas, leaving office in ill-health. The youngest of the Conway brothers, Elias N. Conway, was appointed territorial auditor by Governor Fulton in 1835, when he was twenty-three years old. The state legislature elected him to the same position, which he held, except for a few days in 1841, until 1849. Elias was elected governor in 1852 and served two terms, retiring in 1860. From Sevier's death until the Civil War, the leader of the dynasty was his brother-in-law Robert Ward Johnson, the son of Judge Benjamin Johnson and nephew of Richard Mentor Johnson. Robert was elected to Congress in 1846 and served until 1853. He was then elected to the Senate to fill the unexpired term of Solon Borland. Finally, he was elected to a full term the following year.

All the other Democratic leaders of Arkansas during the period between 1836 and 1852 were allied with the dynasty. William S. Fulton was appointed territorial secretary and then governor by Andrew Jackson, but he worked closely with Sevier and his friends. Fulton originally resisted the movement toward statehood, but finally traded his approval in return for election to the U.S. Senate. When he died in 1842, Fulton was succeeded by Chester Ashley, the third member, along with Woodruff and Sevier, of the original family triumvirate. Edward Cross of Hempstead County, a beneficiary of Sevier's patronage, served three terms in Congress, beginning in 1838.

Archibald Yell of Fayetteville was allied with the dynasty, but he was a political force of his own. He had grown up in Tennessee, had served

Robert W. Johnson, U.S.
congressman, 1847–53, and
U.S. senator, 1853–61.
Courtesy of the Arkansas History
Commission, Little Rock.

with Jackson at New Orleans, and was a close friend of the Tennessee politician and later president, James K. Polk. In 1835 Jackson appointed Yell to a federal judgeship in Arkansas, and he took up residence in Fayetteville and traveled a circuit in the northern counties. He became a popular judge, once collaring a dangerous miscreant whom the sheriff was loath to arrest. But Yell also manifested some sympathy for those who stood before him. He hoped to run for governor in 1836, but the dynasty had decided on James S. Conway for that position, and the new state constitution included a four-year residency requirement for the governorship, one year more than Yell had been in the state. Bowing to the inevitable, Yell ran for Congress with the blessing of the Sevier faction and received 72 percent of the vote. After a successful term in Congress, he was elected governor without opposition. In 1844 he ran again for Congress, defeating his business partner, the popular Whig David Walker. Walker was impressed by Yell's campaigning and by his ability to target shoot, drink whiskey, and pray with equal enthusiasm. Yell was unfailingly affable and gracious, and he gave entertaining and cogent speeches. Back in Washington, Yell served only until the outbreak of the Mexican War, when he went off to fight and die at Buena Vista.

The most important issue during the early years of Arkansas state government was the banking disaster wrought by the Real Estate Bank and the State Bank. Created by the first state legislature under Gov. James S. Conway, both institutions were in serious difficulty when Gov. Archibald Yell took over in the fall of 1840. Political partisanship was reduced by the fact that the Whigs and Democrats had created the banks together and participated in their management. On the other hand, Arkansas Whigs were much more positive toward banking and particularly toward the idea of a national bank. They blamed the Panic of 1837 on Jackson's Bank Veto and on Van Buren's Specie Circular. Yell, on the other hand, shared the Democratic Party's economic views, which favored Jackson's Bank veto and reinforced the notion that the Panic of 1837 was caused by banks, paper money, excessive speculation, and wanton materialism. In his inaugural address Yell indicated a desire to put the state of Arkansas on a specie standard. A year later he received the news that the Real Estate Bank had given up $500,000 in bonds backed by the state in return for $121,000 in cash. Meanwhile, the State Bank had also suspended specie payments, and the cashier of the Fayetteville branch had fled the state.

The Real Estate Bank became more politically divisive in April 1842. The central board conveyed all of the bank's assets to fifteen trustees who were to do what they could to pay officials, redeem currency, pay the interest and principal on 1,530 state bonds that were outstanding, and settle with those who owed money to the institution. The board of directors of the Little Rock bank challenged this action, claiming that the directors of the central bank had simply turned over the bank's assets and affairs to themselves. Since the trustees were employees of the bank and most were debtors to it, their critics claimed that there was a significant conflict of interest. The dissidents also claimed that the drastic measure of trusteeship was not necessary because the bank's assets were $2,200,000 and its liabilities were only $500,000. Further, the Little Rock bankers argued that there was no provision in the new situation to protect the stockholders or even inform them of what was being done.

Governor Yell delivered a bitter message to the legislature in the fall of 1842, claiming that the two banks had given reports that were often misleading and deceptive, that both of them were now unsound, and that they should be closed. He referred specifically to the Holford Bonds disaster, to the fiasco at the Fayetteville branch of the State Bank, and to his own estimate that $80,000 to $100,000 had been embezzled from the two institutions. A legislative report also asserted that the Real Estate Bank had overvalued the land on which it granted mortgages, that large stockholders and directors owed $1,100,000 to the institution, and that the directors had authorized $700,000 in notes in November 1839 when the bank had only $112,000 in specie. The report further claimed that the management of the Real Estate Bank was "distinguished by a series of acts in disregard and open violations of its charter" that were solely designed to benefit the managers and stockholders.

Meanwhile, the spreading wave of recrimination was striking hard at Senator Sevier, who was coming up for re-election. Back in 1838, Sevier and Sen. William S. Fulton had been criticized for allowing Richard Mentor Johnson, Sevier's wife's uncle, to purchase $30,000 in State Bank bonds with a mortgage that was never registered and therefore void. Now an Arkansas House committee was investigating that transaction and also other irregularities in the sale of bonds. Sevier had deposited $10,000 from the sale of State Bank bonds in his Little Rock account and kept it there for two years before turning it over with interest. The committee decided that no wrongdoing had occurred, and, with six Whigs dissenting, the house accepted its report. Sevier was re-elected the same day.

Several weeks later, however, a committee investigating the affairs of the Real Estate Bank was more critical of Sevier. He and T. T. Williamson had sold $500,000 worth of bonds to the U.S. secretary of the treasury, investing most of the proceeds in the currency of banks in western and southern states. Sevier had kept $14,300 of the proceeds for himself, mortgaging his stock account in return. Williamson kept $14,094, supposedly to pay the engraver of the bonds. He gave the man a personal note, however, on which he later defaulted, and the engraver was suing the state for payment. Sevier and Williamson had also hired W. W. Corcoran, under-secretary of the U.S. Treasury, to sell the bonds, paying him $5,000 and keeping the same amount for themselves. The legislators also believed that Corcoran had made additional money when he converted the credit into bank notes. In addition, the report indicated that Sevier and Williamson had loaned Real Estate Bank funds to other Arkansans whom they had encountered in Washington. On this evidence, the committee was sharply critical of Sevier and Williamson, claiming that they had "violated the trust placed in them and seriously damaged the interests of the bank and of the state." In an unprecedented attack on the leader of the dynasty, the house adopted the committee report thirty-three to twenty-seven, with one-third of the Democrats and all the Whigs voting to censure Sevier.

Throughout the antebellum period, the state government also wrestled with the question of public education. Less disastrous than the state's approach to banking, the results were hardly successful. Initially, two sources of federal funding for education were available. As it had with earlier territories, Congress had set aside the sixteenth section of each township in

Arkansas for the support of local schools. In addition, in 1827 it had provided two townships for the support of a university, and in 1836 it gave the general assembly of Arkansas the power to administer that land. Governor Conway attempted to impress the legislature with the importance of its educational stewardship: "The creation of institutions of learning upon a scale as liberal as our means will justify must give to your young State an early, respectable, and proud standing among our sister republics." Beginning in 1838, the state began to sell the seminary lands, as they were called, but the ten dollars an acre was too high a price, and the proceeds were small. In 1840 the price was dropped and installment purchases were allowed. Other adjustments were made but with little success. In 1844 the meager proceeds from the seminary lands were added to the common school fund, and in 1846 they were distributed to the counties. There would be no state university until after the Civil War.

Common schools faired somewhat better. In 1843 the general assembly received authority to sell the sixteenth section of each township and use the interest on the proceeds for the benefit of local schools. At the same time, Arkansas passed a law "to establish a system of common schools." Townships were to elect commissioners to sell or lease the sixteenth section, and school trustees were supposed to build schools, hire teachers, and insure that for a least four months each year the students would be taught reading, writing, spelling, grammar, arithmetic, geography, and "good morals." The township was to support indigent students free of charge, but others were to pay subscriptions. An additional act created a board of education for the state.

Impressive on paper, the 1843 law did not bring about the creation of very many schools. Critics argued that it was too cumbersome for the small and scattered population of Arkansas. In 1853 a "common-school commissioner" was given general supervision over the schools in each county. Despite this reform, there was little improvement. Gov. Elias N. Conway in 1854 lamented that, despite the provisions for common schools, "there are very few in operation." The same year, the secretary of state claimed that the problem was "the indifference that pervades the public mind on the subject of education." A meaningful public school system was not achieved in the antebellum period.

In addition to education, the antebellum governors of Arkansas frequently noted the need for internal improvements. A Helena newspaper, the *Southern Shield,* claimed in 1853 that Arkansas was the only state in the union without internal improvements, listing among the absent items plank roads, turnpikes, canals, bridges, and railroads. There was certainly a felt need for these things, since the territorial legislature had petitioned the national government to provide them. On its own, however, Arkansas did little. The Public Roads Act of 1836 did provide a policy for the construction and maintenance of ordinary roads. It divided counties into road districts, provided for overseers, and requisitioned up to twelve days of work a year from adult males. Roads were to be clear and in repair, with "stumps to be cut low" enough for wagons, carriages, and horseback riders. Bridges were to be built, and signs were to provided at crossings. The evidence, however, suggests that these provisions were not carried out.

Arkansas also did little to moderate its reputation for political violence. The outstanding example occurred in the fall of 1836 during the debate over the Real Estate Bank. Rep. J. J. Anthony of Randolph County attempted to amend an act dealing with a bounty on wolves so that the president of the Real Estate Bank would have to sign the certificate for each dead predator. He was apparently making a joke, but Speaker John Wilson, who was the president of the Real Estate Bank, did not laugh. Instead, when Anthony attempted to explain himself, Wilson told him to sit down. When Anthony refused, Wilson advanced toward him, drew a knife, and, as the two men came together, the speaker stabbed and killed the representative. Singularly shocking, the murder was widely publicized, and it earned Arkansas a reputation for extreme political violence. It was not, however, grossly out of character with less well known events.

In 1843 a personal conflict developed between Benjamin Borden, who was publishing the *Arkansas Gazette* as a Whig paper, and Solon Borland, who was the editor of the Democratic paper called the *Arkansas Banner.* Published attacks on each other's newspapers gave way to personal comments, and these led to a fistfight in January 1844. Borden, who was beaten badly, then challenged Borland to a duel, which they fought in Indian Territory. Again Borden lost, this time suffering a bullet wound just above his heart from which he was very lucky to recover.

In 1851 C. C. Danley, then state auditor, got involved in a disagreement with Lambert Whiteley, the public printer, over a printing bill that Danley thought was too high. The financial issue was complicated by the fact that Whiteley was an editor at the *Arkansas Banner,* which favored Sen. Robert Ward Johnson, while C. C. Danley was an opponent of Johnson. In September 1851, a street fight developed between, on one side, Danley and his brother Sheriff Benjamin F. Danley, later joined by another Danley brother and by Solon Borland, who was now a U.S. senator, and, on the other, Whiteley and Lambert Reardon, the senior editor of the *Banner*. Several shots were fired, but most of the damage was done by clubs, and it was not permanent.

Arkansas politicians also took their violent ways to Washington. In the spring of 1849, Congressman Robert Johnson struck and bloodied Rep. Fincklin of Illinois during a debate in the House. During the sectional crisis of 1850, Solon Borland scuffled with Sen. Henry S. Foote of Mississippi on the streets of Washington after Foote numbered Borland among the "servile followers of Calhoun." Borland bloodied Foote's nose, and the latter challenged the former to a duel, but letters were exchanged instead of shots. Two years later, on the floor of the Senate, Borland bloodied another nose, this one belonging to the superintendent of the census.

More significant than its violent ways was the sectional orientation of Arkansas. Despite the existence of small, family farmers in the north and west, Arkansas was a southern state, made so by its geographic setting, by the cotton that grew so readily along the Mississippi Delta and the other river valleys in the south, and by the Missouri Compromise, which left the territory open for slaves and the planters who brought them. There were occasional political differences between the north and west and the south and east, as in the struggle over representation that emerged during the creation of the constitution of 1836. Nonetheless, while the Democrats were stronger in the northwest and the Whigs in the southeast, both parties drew support from all areas of the state, and regional issues were subsumed in widespread identification with the South. This allegiance was strengthened during the 1850s, as Arkansas experienced a heavy migration from states of the lower South that increased the population of the lowlands areas and the percentage of slaves and planters in the state. Not until the eve of secession, and only briefly then, was the state divided along the geographical fault line running from the northeast to the southwest.

During the Missouri crisis of 1820, the question of slavery, largely quiescent since the American Revolution, in Thomas Jefferson's words, "rang out like a fire bell in the night." The compromise settlement allowed Missouri to enter the union as a slave state, Maine as a free state, and used the line of 36 degrees 30 minutes to delineate future slave states from future free states. Relative calm was restored for a decade. Then in 1830 William Lloyd Garrison began to publish the *Liberator,* and abolitionism was born, and with it came the gradual alienation of the South from the Union.

Abolitionism was a live issue in Arkansas. In February 1837 the Whig newspaper the *Times and Advocate* criticized Archibald Yell, the state's congressman, for being soft on slavery. Congress had narrowly failed to condemn abolitionism petitions, and some of the southern members met the next day to consider further action. Yell refused to attend, explaining to his constituents that he feared that there would be a move to create a southern confederacy, and he did not wish to encourage it. The newspaper upbraided him for refusing to act in concert with other slaveholding states. Broader evidence of local feeling came in 1842, when the *Times and Advocate* published a list of suspected abolitionists among the merchants of Cincinnati and suggested that Arkansans cease doing business with them. Not to be outdone, William Woodruff proposed in the *Arkansas Gazette* that "an individual suspected of the taint of abolitionism . . . be banished from the land." A year later, Solon Borland, then editor of the Democratic *Banner,* suggested that Methodist clergy who sided with the abolitionist elements would find "a more Northern latitude" better for their health.

As the question of slavery became more political, Arkansas also developed a sensitivity about free blacks living in the state. In March 1842 the *Arkansas Gazette* claimed that a white man had arrived in Little Rock, was staying with a free black family, and was encouraging slaves to run away from their masters. Later that year the state passed a law prohibiting the immigration of free blacks after March 1, 1843, and requiring that those living in the state prove that they had arrived before that date. In 1844 the law was modified to allow citizens to bring in free blacks for employment purposes. As sectional tensions mounted in the late 1850s, pressure mounted for the expulsion of free blacks, and in February 1859 a measure was passed requiring them to leave by January 1860 or face enslavement.

Hostility between North and South achieved a new intensity in 1846 when the Wilmot Proviso, which would have prohibited slavery in any territory acquired as a result of the Mexican War, was narrowly defeated by the unanimous opposition of the South. The Whig editor of the *Arkansas Gazette* stated that the nonslave states were determined to resist the expansion of the South and that it was a "matter to excite alarm for the safety of the Union." In December 1848 John C. Calhoun wrote "The Address of the Southern Delegates in Congress," calling on the South to unite behind the rights of slaveholders in the territories. The Arkansas delegation signed the document, and Robert Ward Johnson sent three thousand copies to his constituents.

The Compromise of 1850, or, as historian William W. Freehling has called it, the "Armistice of 1850," grew out of the California gold rush and the resulting need to create a government for that part of the territory acquired from Mexico. President Zachary Taylor chose to create two free states out of California and the remaining portion of the territory acquired from Mexico, a proposal abhorrent to the South. Henry Clay's compromise measures would allow California to join the Union as a free state and the remaining territory to be organized without reference to slavery. To smooth the way for these actions, he would end a dispute between Texas and New Mexico by taking the land from Texas and giving the state monetary compensation, abolishing the slave trade in the District of Columbia, and passing a stronger fugitive slave law. While it eventually passed, the compromise was denounced by the dying Calhoun, who argued that the North was acting as a transgressor and needed to make more concessions to the South.

Robert Ward Johnson quickly emerged as the Arkansas spokesman for southern extremism. In his "Address to the People of Arkansas," he argued that the North was so opposed to the South that the continued existence of the nation was now a matter of question. He believed that the equality of the sections had been constitutionally guaranteed and that southern rights must be restored before California could become a state. If not, according to Johnson, "the Union ought and will dissolve."

The state, however, was deeply split. Democratic newspapers supported Johnson, while Whig newspapers editorialized in favor of Clay and the compromise. "Southern meetings" were held in various Arkansas towns in the spring of 1850, just as "Union meetings" met in the summer and fall. Senators Solon Borland and William K. Sebastian joined Johnson in opposing the compromise. In general, however, southern extremism did not find fertile ground. By June, Johnson was claiming not to be a "disunionist," and two months later he decided not to run for re-election. On the other hand, Governor Roane attacked the compromise after its passage and also denounced President Fillmore's threat to use force to compel Texas to accept the boundary settlement. In a message to the legislature in November, the governor said that if the national government attempted to "enforce obedience to her unjust laws, at the point of a bayonet, I would say dissolve the Union."

In the election of 1852, the dynasty nominated Elias N. Conway for governor against opposition from within the Democratic Party. The dissident Democrats ran Bryan Smithson of Fayetteville, who received significant Whig support by advocating internal improvements, particularly railroads. Conway went on record with the claim that the state needed only "a few good dirt roads," but he still received 55 percent of the vote. Solon Borland, who had alienated the dynasty in 1848 by defeating Sevier for the Senate, resigned his seat in March 1853 to become minister plenipotentiary to Central America. Conway appointed Robert Ward Johnson to the unexpired term, and the legislature unanimously elected him to a full term in 1854. As a result of its population growth as measured by the Census of 1850, Arkansas was allotted a second congressional seat, and the legislature created separate districts north and south of the Arkansas River. The Kansas-Nebraska Act, which allowed the territories to choose whether they wanted to be slave or free, was generally supported in Arkansas. Few if any citizens of the state went to Kansas to strengthen the slaveholding forces there, probably because Arkansas was itself still being settled.

The national Whig Party split apart over the slavery issue in 1852, leaving Arkansas Whigs without a home; they were nurtured only by their hostility to the Democrats. The Know-Nothing Party, organized in 1855, opposed Catholics and immigrants and gave hope to many who feared the trend toward disunion over slavery. Albert Pike organized the new party in Arkansas, aided by Absalom Fowler, C. C. Danley, and other prominent former Whigs. The Know-Nothings stirred up a good deal of support in Arkansas and ran James Yell, a nephew of Archibald Yell, for the governorship in 1856. Pike, however, went to the national convention in the spring of that year and repudiated the party because he believed it was soft on slavery. This apostasy gave ammunition to the Democrats, who probably did not need it very much, and Conway was elected governor with 65 percent of the vote. For the rest of the decade, Arkansas was a one-party state, although the former Whigs retained their antipathy to the Democrats.

Thomas C. Hindman Jr. was the dominant personality in Arkansas politics during the latter part of the 1850s. He had moved to Helena from Holly Springs, Mississippi, in 1854. Only about twenty-six years old, he had already graduated from a classics school in New Jersey, fought in the Mexican War, where he rose to the rank of colonel, and afterwards earned a degree in law. Two years later he married Mollie Watkins Biscoe, scion of Henry L. Biscoe, an Arkansas pioneer distinguished both by financial success and political leadership. Ambitious to the point of audacity, Hindman was probably the best public speaker in his adopted state. The *Van Buren Press* described one of his performances in that town: "His delivery is fluent, smooth, and pleasant; a perfect master of the art, he

Thomas C. Hindman,
U.S. congressman, 1859–61.

Courtesy of the Arkansas
History Commission,
Little Rock.

deals out his argument systematically, and with much energy, and with just enough sarcasm, wit and humor to keep his hearers in cheerful attendance for hours . . . We have seldom seen a person who could hold the undivided attention of a large concourse for such a lengthy address."

Hindman wasted little time in staking a claim to power within the Democratic Party. He made a speech at a Fourth of July celebration in 1854, and in November 1855 he hosted a three-day political gathering that featured food, music, and wholesale attacks on the Know-Nothing Party. In March 1856 Hindman launched his own newspaper, the *States Rights Democrat,* in Helena. A few months later, he campaigned for the congressional nomination of the northern district, losing only after 277 ballots. Two years later, supported by the dynasty, Hindman won the nomination and was easily elected to the House of Representatives from the northern district of Arkansas.

Hindman's ambition was not so easily slaked, however. During the summer and fall of 1859, he actively campaigned for the Senate seat that was held by William King Sebastian, who wished to serve another term. Now the dynasty went on the attack against the upstart. At a Democratic caucus in November, party leaders changed the rules to allow a senator to be nominated by a simple majority and provided insurance for the result by allowing a number of former Whigs and Know-Nothings to vote. Hindman was beaten, but like Andrew Jackson in 1824, he believed the will of the people had been frustrated. Two months before, he had opened his own newspaper in Little Rock, the *Old Line Democrat*, and it soon began open warfare with the dynasty's organ, the *True Democrat*. Hindman's paper supported the South and the right of secession; and it told Arkansans that their "state offices are bartered and peddled by a little stock-jobbing set of thick-headed politicians whose only distinction is derived from the fact that they live in Little Rock and belong to the Dynasty."

For six months Hindman continued his assault on dynasty leadership and organized his own supporters. In the election of 1860, his efforts paid off. In April 1860, against opposition, the dynasty attempted to continue with politics as usual by nominating for governor Richard H. Johnson, the younger brother of Robert Ward. At the northern convention, however, Hindman was renominated by acclamation. Moreover, Hindman also convinced Henry Massie Rector, another member of the dynastic family, to run for governor. Albert Rust, the incumbent congressman from the southern district, joined the Hindman forces and publicly attacked the dynasty that had supported him in the past. During the election, Rector called for delaying payments on the state debt for twenty-five years and using the money to support the construction of railroads. This was perhaps the most positive proposal in a campaign that was largely about the rule of the dynasty and was bitter even by Arkansas standards. When it was over, Rector had defeated Johnson, Hindman had won easily, and a Hindman-backed candidate was elected in the southern district.

The dynasty had suffered a major defeat and was out of power for the first time in Arkansas history. It has been suggested that one reason was the massive immigration, which had created a large element of voters who had no loyalty to the state's older leadership. Historian James M. Woods, however, emphasizes the role of Thomas C. Hindman in portraying the dynasty as an oppressive aristocracy. It may also have been that Arkansas voters were tired of a political leadership that had ruined the credit of the state and did so little to improve its educational system and transportation. For whatever reason, Arkansas had changed its leadership at the last moment of its existence as a part of the United States.

While Hindman was making himself the central figure of Arkansas politics, the United States was being torn asunder by the forces of sectionalism. Sen. Stephen A. Douglas's plan to neutralize the issue of slavery with popular sovereignty had led to bloodshed and two opposing territorial governments in Kansas. Even more ominous was the rise of the Republican Party, dedicated to advancing the values, social structure, and economic interests of the North. In 1857 a badly divided U.S. Supreme Court alienated many northerners when it ruled in the Dred Scott case that black persons were not and could not be citizens of the United States and that Congress had no authority to prevent slaveholders from carrying their human property into any federal territory. Senator Douglas debated these and other issues with Republican Abraham Lincoln in the Illinois senatorial campaign of 1858, winning re-election but generating enough interest to turn the eloquent Lincoln into a national figure. Then, in October 1859, John Brown and twenty-two followers seized the federal arsenal at Harpers Ferry, only to be quickly overpowered by U.S. troops. A military failure, Brown was a public relations success. The South thought him a fiend for trying to arm slaves who would then, so it was thought, murder southern women and children. The North thrilled to his audacious deed, however unsuccessful, to his brave demeanor, to the moving speech against slavery he made at his trial, and to his martyr's death on the gallows.

Stephen A. Douglas was the leading candidate for the Democratic presidential nomination in 1860, but he had alienated many southerners when he led the attack in Congress on the pro-slave, undemocratic Lecompton constitution proposed for Kansas. In Arkansas the dynasty opposed Douglas but would have supported him if he had been elected; Hindman, whose disunionist views had long been clear, would have nothing to do with the Illinois senator. When Arkansas Democrats met to elect delegates to the Democratic Convention in April, they voted down a Hindman-backed resolution calling for a walkout unless the national party supported slavery in the territories. Nonetheless, when Douglas refused to support a pro-slave platform at Charleston, six of eight Arkansans violated their instructions and joined other southerners in leaving the convention. Both Hindman and the dynasty worked hard for John C. Breckenridge, the candidate of the southern democracy, and he carried Arkansas with 53 percent of the vote. On the other hand, John C. Bell and the Constitutional Union Party received 37 percent, presumably from old Whigs and Know-Nothings. Stephen Douglas, who campaigned only in northern states, was ably supported in Arkansas by Congressman Albert Rust of El Dorado. He won 10 percent of the Arkansas vote.

Arkansas remained calm after the election of Abraham Lincoln, although Congressman Hindman and Senator Johnson both favored secession. The first sign of intense feelings came after federal troops under Capt. James Totten occupied the Little Rock arsenal in November 1860. The situation became serious in January 1861, when a new telegraph line carried information to Memphis about what was taking place and allowed word to get to Helena. Residents of that city called upon Governor Rector to seize the arsenal and expel the government soldiers. Rector refused, but his adjutant general (and brother-in-law) sent a message suggesting that the governor would welcome spontaneous action on the part of the people. By February there were volunteers in Little Rock ready to fight. Eventually Rector did call on the troops to surrender, and Totten marched his men to St. Louis.

On February 18, the day of Jefferson Davis's inauguration as president of the fledgling Confederacy, Arkansas voted on whether to call a convention to consider secession. The vote was two to one in favor of the convention. Unionist delegates, most of them from the north and west, outnumbered secessionists, who largely came from the south and east. With the exception of C. C. Danley's *Arkansas Gazette*, newspapers in the state were coming to favor disunion. The dynasty's *True Democrat* called upon the convention to take the state out of the Union: "Let us not be the last to join our sister States of the South . . . For God's sake, give us an ordinance of secession." The delegates voted along geographic lines, thirty-nine against to thirty-five for sending a motion for secession to the voters. Fearing, however, that the governor would convene the legislature to vote Arkansas out of the United States, the Arkansas unionists finally approved a referendum to be held in August.

Unionism, moreover, was conditioned on Lincoln's behavior. Unionists supported slavery and had no quarrel with southern society. Essentially they believed secession was not necessary simply because Lincoln had been elected. They believed that he was already withdrawing troops from the forts in South Carolina and Florida. Unionists also recognized that not all northerners were abolitionists. Arkansas's true role, they believed, was to work with other states of the upper South to find a way to improve the situation. Finally, however, they asserted that they would oppose a Federal attempt to force seceded states back into the Union.

Thus it was that the attack on Fort Sumter changed the situation in Arkansas. When Lincoln called for seventy-five thousand troops to deal with South Carolina, Sen. Robert W. Johnson replied: "What! Call upon the southern people to shoot down their neighbors?" Finally, he had most Arkansas voters on his side. Pockets of unconditional unionism remained among the yeomen of the Ozarks, but most Arkansans were ready to join the South. A new convention was called, and on May 6 it voted for secession sixty-five to five. On a second vote, four delegates changed their votes, and the vote was sixty-nine to one. With Isaac Murphy of Madison County in lone opposition, Arkansas left the Union of which it had been part for a little less than twenty-five years.

* * *

Ever remote and always restless, Arkansas had fashioned its own identity in the half century before 1860. It was not that much different from other American states, and much of its uniqueness may be traced to the fact that it was, in many respects, still a western frontier. Still, its economy of cotton and corn, its social structure of planters and yeomen, its religion, and its politics were all derived from the South from whence so many of its citizens had come. So also was slavery, that most defining of institutions. On the eve of the Civil War, some Arkansans were adamant in their support of secession; others were simply loyal to their friends and kin—another testament to their southern heritage.

Suggested Readings

CHAPTER ONE
American Takeover

On American migration in general, see Bernard Bailyn, *The Peopling of British North America: An Introduction* (New York: Alfred A. Knopf, 1989); David Hackett Fischer, *Albion's Seed: Four British Folkways in America* (New York: Oxford University Press, 1989); Carl Bridenbaugh, *Myths and Realities: Societies of the Colonial South* (New York: Atheneum, 1966); Johanna Miller Lewis, *Artisans in the North Carolina Backcountry* (Lexington: University Press of Kentucky, 1995); Malcolm Rohrbaugh, *The Trans-Appalachian Frontier: People, Societies, and Institutions, 1775–1850* (New York: Oxford University Press, 1978); Benjamin Horace Hibbard, *A History of the Public Land Policies* (1924; reprint, Madison: University of Wisconsin Press, 1965); and Thomas D. Clark and John D. W. Guice, *Frontiers in Conflict: The Old Southwest, 1795–1830* (Albuquerque: University of New Mexico Press, 1989).

On national policies with respect to expansion, I have used Andrew R. L. Cayton, *The Frontier Republic: Ideology and Politics in the Ohio Country* (Kent, Ohio: Kent State University Press, 1986); Stanley Elkins and Eric McKitrick, *The Age of Federalism* (New York: Oxford University Press, 1993); Francis Paul Prucha, *The Sword of the Republic: The United States Army on the Frontier, 1783–1846* ([New York]: Macmillan Company, 1969); Forrest McDonald, *Alexander Hamilton: A Biography* (New York: W. W. Norton, 1982); Thomas Jefferson, *Notes on the State of Virginia*, ed. Thomas Perkins Abernethy (New York: Harper and Row, 1964); Drew McCoy, *The Elusive Republic: Political Economy in Jeffersonian America* (New York: W. W. Norton, 1980); Joyce Appleby, *Capitalism and the New Social Order: The Republican Vision of the 1790s* (New York: New York University Press, 1984); and Malcolm J. Rohrbaugh, *The Land Office Business: The Settlement and Administration of American Public Lands, 1789–1837* (New York: Oxford University Press, 1968).

Here, and throughout, I have benefited from Michael B. Dougan's comprehensive and detailed *Arkansas Odyssey: The Saga of Arkansas from Prehistoric Times to the Present* (Little Rock: Rose Publishing, 1993). On the settlement of Arkansas, see Morris S. Arnold, *Colonial Arkansas, 1686–1804: A Social and Cultural History* (Fayetteville: University of Arkansas Press, 1991); S. Charles Bolton, *Territorial Ambition: Land and Society in Arkansas, 1800–1840* (Fayetteville: University of Arkansas Press, 1993); William E. Foley, *The Genesis of Missouri: from Wilderness Outpost to Statehood* (Columbia: University of Missouri Press, 1989); Samuel Brown, *The Western Gazetteer; or, an Emigrant's Directory, Containing a Geographical Description of the Western States and Territories* (Auburn, N.Y.: H. C. Southwick, 1817); Daniel H. Usner Jr., *Indians, Settlers, & Slaves in a Frontier Exchange Economy: The Lower Mississippi Valley Before 1763* (Chapel Hill: University of North Carolina Press, 1992); Henry Rowe Schoolcraft, *Journal of a Tour into the Interior of Missouri and Arkansas* (1821; reprint, Van Buren, Ark.: Argus Printers, 1955); George W. Featherstonhaugh, *Excursion through the Slave States* (New York: Harper and Bros., 1844); Henry Rowe Schoolcraft, *A View of the Lead Mines of Missouri* (1819); George E. Lankford, "'Beyond the Pale': Frontier Folk in the Southern Ozarks," in *The Folk, Identity, Landscapes and Lores,* ed. Robert J. Smith and Jerry Stannard, University of Kansas Publications in Anthropology, no. 17; Thomas Nuttall, *A Journal of Travels into the Arkansas Territory During the Year 1819,* ed. Savoie Lottinville (Norman: University of Oklahoma Press, 1980); Timothy Flint, *A Condensed Geography and History of the Western States or the Mississippi Valley* (1828); R. Baird, *View of the Valley of the Mississippi, or the Emigrant's and Traveller's Guide to the West* (Philadelphia, 1834); and "The Exploration of the Red, the Black, and the Washita Rivers, by William Dunbar," *Documents Relating to the Purchase and Exploration of Louisiana* (Boston and New York, Houghton, Mifflin, 1904). On the sources of immigration, see Robert B. Walz, "Migration into Arkansas, 1834–1880" (Ph.D. diss., University of Texas, 1958).

Useful articles on settlement from the *Arkansas Historical Quarterly* include the following: E. E. Dale, "Arkansas, The Myth and the State," 12 (1953): 8–29; Milford F. Allen, "Thomas Jefferson and the Louisiana Frontier," 20 (1961): 39–64; Ted R. Worley, "Glimpses of an Old Southwestern Town," 8 (1949): 133–59; Ted R. Worley, ed., "Story of an Early Settlement in Central Arkansas," 10 (1951): 117–37; Robert B. Walz, "Migration into Arkansas, 1820–1880: Incentives and Means of Travel" 17 (1958); Robert W. Harrison and Walter M. Kollmorgen, "Land

Reclamation in Arkansas under the Swamp Land Grant of 1850," 6 (1947): 369–418. William Stevenson's account is in Walter N. Vernon, "Beginnings of Methodism in Arkansas," 31 (1972): 357–61; and Ted R. Worley, ed., "Letters from an Early Settler," 11 (1952): 327–29, contains John C. Benedict's comments.

See also John B. Treat to Secretary of War, Nov. 15, 1805, Clarence Carter, ed., *Territorial Papers of the United States,* 26 vols. (Washington: Government Printing Office, 1934–69), vol. 13: 278–81; John C. Luttig Letter from Pork [*sic*] Bayou, Apr. 16, 1815, Special Collections Division, University of Arkansas Libraries, LOC 385; and Gerald T. Hanson and Carl H. Moneyhon, *Historical Atlas of Arkansas* (Norman: University of Oklahoma Press, 1989).

CHAPTER TWO

Government and Opportunity

Useful background for understanding the political culture of the early nineteenth century is provided by Gordon S. Wood, *The Radicalism of the American Revolution* (New York: Random House, 1993), and Robert H. Wiebe, *The Opening of American Society: From the Adoption of the Constitution to the Eve of Disunion* (New York: Random House, 1985). The most important source for territorial politics in Arkansas is Carter, *Territorial Papers,* vols. 19–21. The best account of that subject is in Lonnie J. White, *Politics on the Southwestern Frontier: Arkansas Territory, 1819–1838* (Memphis: Memphis State University Press, 1964). Margaret Ross, *Arkansas Gazette, The Early Years, 1819–1866* (Little Rock: Gazette Foundation, 1969), provides an excellent narrative focusing on her subject. The account of land issues here is drawn from Bolton, *Territorial Ambition.* The government of Arkansas from 1800 to 1819 is skillfully treated in Morris S. Arnold, *Unequal Laws Unto a Savage Race: European Legal Traditions in Arkansas, 1686–1836* (Fayetteville: University of Arkansas Press, 1985). On dueling, see Timothy Flint, *Recollections of the Last Ten Years in the Valley of the Mississippi* (Boston, 1826), 179; Dickson D. Bruce Jr., *Violence and Culture in the Antebellum South* (Austin: University of Texas Press, 1979); Bertram Wyatt-Brown, *Southern Honor: Ethics and Behavior in the Old South* (New York: Oxford University Press, 1983); and Elliot J. Gorn, "'Gouge and Bite, Pull Hair and Scratch': The Social Significance of Fighting in the Southern Backcountry," *American Historical Review* 90

(1985):18–43. See also Friedrich Gerstäcker, *Wild Sports in the Far West,* with an introduction and notes by Edna L. Steeves and Harrison R. Steeves (1854; reprint, Durham, N.C.: Duke University Press, 1968).

CHAPTER THREE

Agricultural Success and Banking Failure

Charles Grier Sellers, *The Market Revolution, Jacksonian America, 1815–1846* (New York, Oxford University Press, 1991), provides an overview of the American economy that has greatly influenced this chapter. The material on the Arkansas economy down to 1840 is largely drawn from Bolton, *Territorial Ambition.* See also Sam Bowers Hilliard, *Hog Meat and Hoecake: Food Supply in the Old South* (Carbondale: Southern Illinois University Press, 1972). For the latter period, see Carl H. Moneyhon, *The Impact of the Civil War and Reconstruction on Arkansas: Persistence in the Midst of Ruin* (Baton Rouge: Louisiana State University Press, 1994), and Elsie M. Lewis, "Economic Conditions in Ante-bellum Arkansas: 1850–1861," *Arkansas Historical Quarterly* 6 (1947): 256–74. See also Thomas A. DeBlack, "A Garden in the Wilderness: The Johnson's and the Making of Lakewood Plantation, 1831–1876," (Ph.D. diss., University of Arkansas, 1995). The statistics on Arkansas taxpayers come from a random sample of 987 taxpayers in 1840, which I have described in *Territorial Ambition,* and a random sample of 1,387 taxpayers for 1860.

On the Real Estate Bank and the State Bank, I have relied heavily on Dewey A. Stokes, "Public Affairs in Arkansas, 1836–1850," (Ph.D. diss., University of Texas, 1966). Interested readers should also consult four articles by Ted R. Worley, "The Arkansas State Bank: Antebellum Period," *Arkansas Historical Quarterly* 23 (1964): 65–73; "Arkansas and the Money Crisis of 1836–1837," *Journal of Southern History* 15 (1949): 178–91; "The Batesville Branch of the State Bank, 1836–39," *Arkansas Historical Quarterly* 6 (1947): 286–99; and "The Control of the Real Estate Bank of the State of Arkansas, 1836–1855," *Mississippi Valley Historical Review* 37 (1950): 403–26.

See also Jeffrey Alan Owens, "The Richest, Driest Swamp in Arkansas: Levee Building in Chicot County prior to 1850," (paper presented at the Arkansas Historical Association, Texarkana, Apr. 1997); and L. Skinner III, *The Autobiography of Henry Merrell: Industrial Missionary to the South* (Athens: University of Georgia Press, 1991). See also Gerstäcker, *Wild Sports;* and Featherstonhaugh, *Excursion.*

CHAPTER FOUR
Indian Frontier

On the Native Americans of Arkansas, see Willard H. Rollins, "Living in a Graveyard: Native Americans in Colonial Arkansas," in *Cultural Encounters in the Early South: Indians and Europeans in Arkansas,* comp. Jeannie Whayne (Fayetteville: University of Arkansas Press, 1995); David Baird, *The Quapaw Indians: History of the Downstream People* (Norman: University of Oklahoma Press, 1980); F. Todd Smith, *The Caddo Indians: Tribes at the Convergence of Empires, 1542–1854* (College Station: Texas A&M University Press, 1995); Nuttall, *Journal of Travels*; Robert Paul Markman, "The Arkansas Cherokees, 1817–1828" (Ph.D. diss., University of Oklahoma, 1972); Gilbert C. Din and Abraham P. Nasatir, *The Imperial Osages: Spanish-Indian Diplomacy in the Mississippi Valley* (Norman: University of Oklahoma Press, 1983); and John Joseph Mathews, *The Osages: Children of the Middle Waters* (Norman: University of Oklahoma Press, 1961).

The story of the southwestern frontier is told in Grant Foreman, *Indians and Pioneers: The Story of the American Southwest Before 1830,* 2d ed. (Norman: University of Oklahoma Press, 1936); Aloysius Plaisance, "The Arkansas Factory, 1805–1810," *Arkansas Historical Quarterly* 11 (1952): 186–90; Cephas Washburn, *Reminiscences of the Indians* (1869; reprint, Van Buren, Ark.: Argus Press, 1955); W. David Baird, "Arkansas's Choctaw Boundary: A Study of Justice Delayed," *Arkansas Historical Quarterly* 28 (1969): 203–22, 219–20; Edwin C. Bearss and A. M. Gibson, *Fort Smith: Little Gibraltar on the Arkansas,* 2d ed. (Norman: University of Oklahoma Press, 1979); Brad Agnew, *Fort Gibson: Terminal on the Trail of Tears* (Norman: University of Oklahoma Press, 1980); Ina Gabler, "Lovely's Purchase and Lovely County," *Arkansas Historical Quarterly* 19 (1960): 31–39.

On Indian removal, see Arthur H. DeRosier Jr., *The Removal of the Choctaw Indians* (New York: Harper and Row, 1972); Francis Paul Prucha, *American Indian Policy in the Formative Years: the Indian Trade and Intercourse Acts, 1780–1834* (Cambridge, Mass.: Harvard University Press, 1962); Grant Foreman, *Indian Removal: The Emigration of the Five Civilized Tribes of* Indians, 2d ed. (Norman: University of Oklahoma Press, 1953); Ronald Satz, *American Indian Policy in the Jacksonian Period* (Lincoln: University of Nebraska Press, 1975); William F. Pope, *Early Days in Arkansas* (1895; reprint, Easley, S.C.: Southern Historical Press, 1978); and Friedrich

Gerstacker, *Wild Sports in the Far West*, introduction and notes by Edna L. Steeves and Harrison R. Steeves (1854; Durham, N.C.; Duke University Press, 1968). See also Carter, *Territorial Papers*, 19: 144, 328, 445.

Chapter Five
Rich, Poor, and Rambunctious

On the image of Arkansas, see the following articles from the *Arkansas Historical Quarterly:* Robert B. Cochran, "'Low Degrading Scoundrels': George W. Featherstonhaugh's Contribution to the Bad Name of Arkansas," 48 (1989): 3–16; C. F. Williams, "The Bear State Image: Arkansas in the Nineteenth Century," 39 (1980): 99–105; William L. Shea, "A Semi-Savage State: The Image of Arkansas in the Civil War," 48 (1989): 309–28; Elmo Howell, "Mark Twain's Arkansas," 29 (1970): 195–208. See also my *Territorial Ambition.* The larger perspective on the image of the frontier is provided in Grady McWhiney, *Cracker Culture: Celtic Ways in the Old South* (Tuscaloosa: University of Alabama Press, 1988). On Albert Pike see the *New England Magazine* (October 1835): 267–70; and Walter Lee Brown, *A Life of Albert Pike* (Fayetteville: University of Arkansas Press, 1997).

The indispensable source on Noland is Leonard Williams, ed., *Cavorting on the Devils Fork, the Pete Whetstone Letters of C. F. M. Noland* (Memphis: Memphis State University Press, 1979). See also Norris W. Yates, *William T. Porter and the Spirit of the Times: A Study of the Big Bear School of Humor* (Baton Rouge: Louisiana State University Press, 1957), and William T. Porter, ed. *The Big Bear of Arkansas, and Other Sketches, Illustrative of Characters and Incidents in the South and Southwest* (Philadelphia, 1845).

My understanding of inequality and social class in Arkansas is based on two large random samples of taxpayers. The first of these involves 987 individuals located on existing tax records for 1840 and the second includes 1,387 taxpayers from the 1860 tax lists. The methodology involved and the results of the 1840 study are discussed in *Territorial Ambition.* See also Swannee Bennett, "Inventory of an Arkansas Household: 1850–1860," *Ozark Historical Review* 9 (1980): 1–10.

My understanding of Arkansas architecture is based on Jean Sizemore, *Ozark Vernacular Houses: A Study of Rural Homeplaces in the Arkansas Ozarks, 1830–1930* (Fayetteville: University of Arkansas Press, 1994), and F. Hampton Roy and Charles Witsell Jr., with Cheryl Griffith Nichols,

How We Lived: Little Rock as an American City (Little Rock: August House, 1984). On art in general and Henry Byrd in particular, see Swannee Bennett and William B. Worthen, *Arkansas Made: A Survey of the Decorative, Mechanical, and Fine Arts Produced in Arkansas, 1819–1870* (Fayetteville: University of Arkansas Press, 1991), vol. 2.

CHAPTER SIX
Religion and Family

On the development of evangelical religion in the South, see John Boles, *The Great Revival, 1787–1805: The Origins of the Southern Evangelical Mind* (Lexington: University Press of Kentucky, 1972); Donald G. Mathews, *Religion in the Old South* (Chicago: University of Chicago Press, 1977); and Anne C. Loveland, *Southern Evangelicals and the Social Order, 1800–1860* (Baton Rouge: Louisiana State University Press, 1980); Elizabeth Paisley Butler and Ethel C. Simpson, ed., *Tulip Evermore: Emma Butler and William Paisley, Their Lives in Letters, 1857–1887* (Fayetteville: University of Arkansas Press, 1985); and the Martin Family Papers, University of Arkansas at Little Rock, Archives and Special Collections.

There is no book-length survey of antebellum religion in Arkansas, but a number of denomination studies are helpful. I used James M. Woods, "'To the Suburb of Hell': Catholic Missionaries in Arkansas, 1803–1843," *Arkansas Historical Quarterly* 48 (1989): 218–42; Rev. James A. Anderson, *Centennial History of Arkansas Methodism . . . a History of the Methodist Episcopal Church, South, in the State of Arkansas, 1815–1935* (Benton, Ark.: L. B. White Printing Co., 1935); Nancy Britten, *The First 100 Years of the First Methodist Church in Batesville, Arkansas, 1836–1936* (Little Rock: August House, 1968); Thomas H. Campbell, *Cumberland Presbyterians (1812–1984): A People of Faith* (Memphis: Arkansas Synod of Cumberland Presbyterian Church, 1985); Glenn E. Hinson, *A History of Baptists in Arkansas, 1818–1978* (Little Rock: Arkansas State Convention, 1979); *The History of Presbyterianism in Arkansas, 1828–1902* (Little Rock: Press of the Arkansas Democrat Co., 1902); Lester G. McAllister, *Arkansas Disciples: A History of the Christian Church in Arkansas* (n.p., 1984); and Margaret S. White, *White Already to Harvest: The Episcopal Church in Arkansas, 1838–1971* (Sewanee, Tenn.: Episcopal Diocese of Arkansas at the University Press of Sewanee, 1957).

On women, I used Bolton, *Territorial Ambition*; Margaret Jones

Bolsterli, ed., *A Remembrance of Eden: Harriet Bailey Bullock Daniel's Memories of a Frontier Plantation in Arkansas, 1849–1872* (Fayetteville: University of Arkansas Press, 1993); Conevery A. Bolton, "'A Sister's Consolations': Women, Health, and Community in Early Arkansas, 1810–1860," *Arkansas Historical Quarterly* 50 (1991): 271–91; and Michael B. Dougan, "The Arkansas Married Woman's Property Law," *Arkansas Historical Quarterly* 46 (1987): 3–27. Also very useful was Nancy Long, "'This Wilderness of Sorrow,' White Women in Frontier Arkansas," (paper presented at the Southern Association of Women Historians meeting, Houston, Tex., 1995).

CHAPTER SEVEN
Human and Chattel

For American slavery in general, I have relied heavily on John Blassingame, *The Slave Community: Plantation Life in the Antebellum South* (New York: Oxford University Press, 1979). See also Robert William Fogel and Stanley L. Engerman, *Time on the Cross: The Economics of American Negro Slavery* (Boston: Little, Brown, 1974); Eugene D. Genovese, *Roll Jordan Roll: The World the Slaves Made* (New York: Vintage, 1976); Herbert George Gutman, *The Black Family in Slavery and Freedom* (New York: Pantheon, 1976); Albert J. Raboteau, *Slave Religion: The "Invisible Institution" in the Antebellum South* (New York: Oxford University Press, 1978); and Kenneth M. Stampp, *The Peculiar Institution: Slavery in the Ante-Bellum South* (New York: Vintage, 1956). A more recent volume of significance to Arkansas is Randolph Campbell, *An Empire for Slavery: The Peculiar Institution in Texas, 1821–1825* (Baton Rouge: Louisiana State University Press, 1989).

Orville W. Taylor, *Negro Slavery in Arkansas* (Durham: Duke University Press, 1958) is still the basic study of its subject, although it is now somewhat dated. A well-researched, modern survey is provided by Moneyhon in *The Impact of the Civil War and Reconstruction*, chap. 3. There are also a number of valuable articles in the *Arkansas Historical Quarterly*: Paul D. Lack, "An Urban Slave Community: Little Rock, 1831–1862," 41 (1982): 258–87; John S. Otto, "Slavery in the Mountains: Yell County, Arkansas, 1840–1860," 39 (1980): 35–52; Robert S. Shafer, "White Persons Held to Racial Slavery in Antebellum Arkansas," 44 (1985): 134–55; Orville W. Taylor, "Baptists and Slavery: Relationships and

Attitudes," 38 (1979): 199–226; Robert B. Walz, "Arkansas Slaveholdings and Slaveholders in 1850," 12 (1953): 38–74; Roman J. Zorn, "Arkansas Fugitive Slave Incident and Its International Repercussions," 16 (1957): 139–44; William VanDeburg, "The Slave Drivers of Arkansas: A New View from the Narratives," 25 (1976): 231–45; and John Solomon Otto and Ben Wayne Banks, "The Banks Family of Yell County, Arkansas: A 'Plain Folk' Family of the Highlands South," 41 (1982): 146–67.

Narratives of Arkansas slaves interviewed by the Federal Writers Project are collected in George P. Rawick, ed., *The American Slave: A Composite Autobiography* (Westport, Conn.: Greenwood Press, 1972), and its supplements. Also useful is Linda J. Lovell, "African American Narratives from Arkansas: A Study from the 1936–1938 Federal Writers Project 'A Folk History of Slavery in the United States'" (Ph.D. diss., University of Arkansas, 1991).

My discussion of the debate over slavery in Arkansas Territory is drawn from Moore, "Arkansas Territory, 1819–1836," (Ph.D. diss., University of North Carolina at Chapel Hill, 1963). The constitution of 1836 and antebellum laws dealing with slavery are contained in E. H. English, *A Digest of the Statutes of Arkansas* (Little Rock, 1848). Citations for the Supreme Court cases discussed are as follows: *Daniel* v. *Guy* (19 Ark 121), *Jackson* v. *Bob* (18 Ark 399), *Pyeatt* v. *Spencer* (4 Ark 563), *Hervey* v. *Armstrong* (15 Ark 162), and *Watkins* v. *Bailey* (21 Ark 274). The Stanley quotation is from C. Fred Williams, S. Charles Bolton, Carl Moneyhon, and Leroy T. Williams, eds., *A Documentary History of Arkansas* (Fayetteville: University of Arkansas Press, 1984).

CHAPTER EIGHT
Looking West

Two excellent studies on Manifest Destiny are Thomas R. Hietala, *Manifest Design: Anxious Aggrandizement in Late Jacksonian America* (Ithaca, N.Y.: Cornell University Press, 1985), and David M. Pletcher, *The Diplomacy of Annexation: Texas, Oregon, and the Mexican War* (Columbia: University of Missouri Press, 1973). On Miller County, see John Hugh Reynolds, "The Western Boundary of Arkansas," *Publications of the Arkansas Historical Association* 2 (1908): 211–36; Russell P. Baker, "Old Miller County Arkansas," *Arkansas Historical Quarterly* 42 (1983): 344–48; and Stokes, "Public Affairs in Arkansas." On the Mexican War, see Robert W.

Johannsen, *To the Halls of the Montezumas: The Mexican War in the American Imagination* (New York: Oxford University Press, 1985), and James M. McCaffrey, *Army of Manifest Destiny: The American Soldier in the Mexican War* (New York: New York University Press, 1992). On Arkansans' participation, see Walter Lee Brown, "The Mexican War Experiences of Albert Pike and the 'Mounted Devils' of Arkansas," *Arkansas Historical Quarterly* 12 (1953): 301–15; Brown, *A Life of Albert Pike;* and William W. Hughes, *Archibald Yell* (Fayetteville: University of Arkansas Press, 1988). A good account of the battle of Buena Vista is in Justin Harvey Smith, *The War with Mexico* (1919; reprint, Gloucester, Mass.: P. Smith, 1963). The official reports are contained in 30th Cong., 1st Sess. (1847–48), Senate Executive Reports, no. 1, vol. 1, serial 503. See also Josiah Gregg, *Diary and Letters of Josiah Gregg: Southwestern Enterprises, 1840–1847,* vol. 2, ed. Maurice Garland Fulton (Norman: University of Oklahoma Press, 1941).

Rodman W. Paul, *California Gold: The Beginning of Mining in the Far West* (Lincoln: University of Nebraska Press, 1965), provides a good introduction to its subject. For the participation of Arkansans in the gold rush, I relied heavily on Priscilla McArthur, *Arkansas in the Gold Rush* (Little Rock: August House, 1986); I also used Patricia Etter, ed., *An American Odyssey: The Autobiography of Robert Brownlee* (Fayetteville: University of Arkansas Press, 1986). Juanita Brooks, *The Mountain Meadows Massacre* (Stanford: Stanford University Press, 1950), is the standard study of its subject. More information on the Arkansas aspects is contained in Ray W. Irwin, "The Mountain Meadows Massacre," *Arkansas Historical Quarterly* 9 (1950): 1–31.

CHAPTER NINE
Sovereignty and Secession

My sense of national politics has been heavily influenced by Harry L. Watson, *Liberty and Power: The Politics of Jacksonian America* (New York: Noonday Press, 1990), and William W. Freehling, *The Road to Disunion: Secessionists at Bay, 1776–1854* (New York: Oxford University Press, 1990).

The best account of politics in the early state of Arkansas is in Stokes, "Public Affairs in Arkansas." See Stokes also on education, but also see Stephen B. Weeks's *History of Public Education in Arkansas,* from the U.S.

Bureau of Education, Bulletin 27 (Washington, D.C.: GPO, 1912) and Bulletin 11 (Washington, D.C.: GPO, 1922). On sectionalism and secession, I have followed James M. Woods, *Rebellion and Realignment: Arkansas's Road to Secession* (Fayetteville: University of Arkansas Press, 1987). Margaret Ross, *Arkansas Gazette,* is invaluable for both periods. A very useful analysis is provided by Brian Walton, "The Second American Party System in Arkansas, 1836–1838," *Arkansas Historical Quarterly* 28 (1969): 120–55. Other important articles from the *Arkansas Historical Quarterly* include the following: Brian G. Walton, "Arkansas Politics during the Compromise Crisis, 1848–1852," 36 (1977): 307–37; Harold T. Smith, "The Know-Nothings in Arkansas," 34 (1975): 291–303; Elsie M. Lewis, "Robert Ward Johnson: Militant Spokesman of the Old South-West," 13 (1954): 16–30; Cal Ledbetter Jr., "The Constitution of 1836: A New Perspective," 41 (1982): 215–52; Gene W. Boyette, "Quantitative Differences between the Arkansas Whig and Democratic Parties, 1836–1850," 34 (1975): 214–26; Walter L. Brown, "Rowing Against the Stream: The Course of Albert Pike from National Whig to Secessionist," 39 (1980): 230–46. See also Granville D. Davis, "Arkansas and the Blood of Kansas," *Journal of Southern History* 16 (1950): 431–56. A Useful reference is Timothy P. Donovan, Willard B. Gatewood Jr., and Jeannie M. Whayne, eds., *The Governors of Arkansas: Essays in Political Biography* (Fayetteville: University of Arkansas Press, 1995).

Index